Neil Somerville

What the Year of the Snake holds in store for you

Your Chinese Horoscope 2013

This 2012 edition is published for Barnes & Noble, Inc. by
HarperCollins*Publishers*

ISBN: 978-1-4351-4518-4

Manufactured in Great Britain by Clays Ltd, St Ives plc.

2 4 6 8 10 9 7 5 3 1

Cover illustration © Sally Taylor

CONTENTS

———◆———

ABOUT THE AUTHOR
Neil Somerville is one of the leading writers in the West on Chinese horoscopes. He has been interested in Eastern forms of divination for many years and believes that much can be learned from the ancient wisdom of the East. His annual book on Chinese horoscopes has built up an international following and he is also the author of *What's your Chinese Love Sign?* (Thorsons, 2000), *Chinese Success Signs* (Thorsons, 2001) and *The Answers* (Element, 2004).

Neil Somerville was born in the year of the Water Snake. His wife was born under the sign of the Monkey, his son is an Ox and daughter a Horse.

ACKNOWLEDGEMENTS

In writing *Your Chinese Horoscope 2013* I am grateful for the assistance and invaluable support that those around me have given.

I would also like to acknowledge Theodora Lau's *The Handbook of Chinese Horoscopes* (Harper & Row, 1979; Arrow, 1981), which was particularly useful to me in my research.

In addition to Ms Lau's work, I commend the following books to those who wish to find out more about Chinese horoscopes: Kristyna Arcarti, *Chinese Horoscopes for Beginners* (Headway, 1995); Catherine Aubier, *Chinese Zodiac Signs* (Arrow, 1984), series of 12 books; E. A. Crawford and Teresa Kennedy, *Chinese Elemental Astrology* (Piatkus Books, 1992); Paula Delsol, *Chinese Horoscopes* (Pan, 1973); Barry Fantoni, *Barry Fantoni's Chinese Horoscopes* (Warner, 1994); Bridget Giles and the Diagram Group, *Chinese Astrology* (HarperCollins*Publishers*, 1996); Kwok Man-Ho, *Complete Chinese Horoscopes* (Sunburst Books, 1995); Lori Reid, *The Complete Book of Chinese Horoscopes* (Element Books, 1997); Paul Rigby and Harvey Bean, *Chinese Astrologics* (Publications Division, South China Morning Post Ltd, 1981); Ruth Q. Sun, *The Asian Animal Zodiac* (Charles E. Tuttle Company, Inc., 1996); Derek Walters, *Ming Shu* (Pagoda Books, 1987) and

The Chinese Astrology Workbook (The Aquarian Press, 1988); Suzanne White, *The New Astrology* (Pan, 1987), *The New Chinese Astrology* (Pan, 1994) and *Chinese Astrology Plain and Simple* (Eden Grove Editions, 1998).

———◆◆◆———

As we march through life
we each have our hopes, our ambitions and our dreams.

Sometimes fate and circumstance will assist us,
sometimes we will struggle and despair,
but march we must.

For it is those who keep going,
and who keep their aspirations alive,
who stand the greatest chance of securing what they want.

March determinedly,
and your determination will, in some way, be rewarded.

Neil Somerville

———◆◆◆———

INTRODUCTION

The origins of Chinese horoscopes have been lost in the mists of time. It is known, however, that oriental astrologers practised their art many thousands of years ago and even today Chinese astrology continues to fascinate and intrigue.

In Chinese astrology there are 12 signs named after 12 different animals. No one quite knows how the signs acquired their names, but there is one legend that offers an explanation. According to this legend, one Chinese New Year the Buddha invited all the animals in his kingdom to come before him. Unfortunately, for reasons best known to the animals, only 12 turned up. The first to arrive was the Rat, followed by the Ox, Tiger, Rabbit, Dragon, Snake, Horse, Goat, Monkey, Rooster, Dog and finally Pig. In gratitude, the Buddha decided to name a year after each of the animals and that those born during that year would inherit some of the personality of that animal. Therefore those born in the year of the Ox would be hardworking, resolute and stubborn, just like the Ox, while those born in the year of the Dog would be loyal and faithful, just like the Dog. While it is not possible that everyone born in a particular year can have all the characteristics of the sign, it is incredible what similarities do occur, and this is partly where the fascination of Chinese horoscopes lies.

In addition to the 12 signs of the Chinese zodiac there are five elements and these have a strengthening or moderating influence upon the signs. Details about the effects of the elements are given in each of the chapters on the signs.

To find out which sign you were born under, refer to the tables on the following pages. As the Chinese year is based on the lunar year and does not start until late January or early February, it is particularly important for anyone born in those two months to check carefully the dates of the Chinese year in which they were born.

Also included, in the appendix, are two charts showing the compatibility between the signs for personal and business relationships and details about the signs ruling the different hours of the day. From this it is possible to locate your ascendant and, as in Western astrology, this has a significant influence on your personality.

In writing this book I have taken the unusual step of combining the intriguing nature of Chinese horoscopes with the Western desire to know what the future holds, and have based my interpretations upon various factors relating to each of the signs. Over the years in which *Your Chinese Horoscope* has been published I have been pleased that so many have found the sections on the forthcoming year of interest and hope that the horoscope has been constructive and useful. Remember, though, that at all times you are master of your own destiny.

I sincerely hope that *Your Chinese Horoscope 2013* will prove interesting and helpful for the year ahead.

THE CHINESE YEARS

Rat	18 February	1912	to	5 February	1913
Ox	6 February	1913	to	25 January	1914
Tiger	26 January	1914	to	13 February	1915
Rabbit	14 February	1915	to	2 February	1916
Dragon	3 February	1916	to	22 January	1917
Snake	23 January	1917	to	10 February	1918
Horse	11 February	1918	to	31 January	1919
Goat	1 February	1919	to	19 February	1920
Monkey	20 February	1920	to	7 February	1921
Rooster	8 February	1921	to	27 January	1922
Dog	28 January	1922	to	15 February	1923
Pig	16 February	1923	to	4 February	1924
Rat	5 February	1924	to	23 January	1925
Ox	24 January	1925	to	12 February	1926
Tiger	13 February	1926	to	1 February	1927
Rabbit	2 February	1927	to	22 January	1928
Dragon	23 January	1928	to	9 February	1929
Snake	10 February	1929	to	29 January	1930
Horse	30 January	1930	to	16 February	1931
Goat	17 February	1931	to	5 February	1932
Monkey	6 February	1932	to	25 January	1933
Rooster	26 January	1933	to	13 February	1934
Dog	14 February	1934	to	3 February	1935
Pig	4 February	1935	to	23 January	1936

Rat	24 January	1936	to	10 February	1937
Ox	11 February	1937	to	30 January	1938
Tiger	31 January	1938	to	18 February	1939
Rabbit	19 February	1939	to	7 February	1940
Dragon	8 February	1940	to	26 January	1941
Snake	27 January	1941	to	14 February	1942
Horse	15 February	1942	to	4 February	1943
Goat	5 February	1943	to	24 January	1944
Monkey	25 January	1944	to	12 February	1945
Rooster	13 February	1945	to	1 February	1946
Dog	2 February	1946	to	21 January	1947
Pig	22 January	1947	to	9 February	1948
Rat	10 February	1948	to	28 January	1949
Ox	29 January	1949	to	16 February	1950
Tiger	17 February	1950	to	5 February	1951
Rabbit	6 February	1951	to	26 January	1952
Dragon	27 January	1952	to	13 February	1953
Snake	14 February	1953	to	2 February	1954
Horse	3 February	1954	to	23 January	1955
Goat	24 January	1955	to	11 February	1956
Monkey	12 February	1956	to	30 January	1957
Rooster	31 January	1957	to	17 February	1958
Dog	18 February	1958	to	7 February	1959
Pig	8 February	1959	to	27 January	1960
Rat	28 January	1960	to	14 February	1961
Ox	15 February	1961	to	4 February	1962
Tiger	5 February	1962	to	24 January	1963
Rabbit	25 January	1963	to	12 February	1964
Dragon	13 February	1964	to	1 February	1965
Snake	2 February	1965	to	20 January	1966
Horse	21 January	1966	to	8 February	1967

Goat	9 February	1967	to	29 January	1968
Monkey	30 January	1968	to	16 February	1969
Rooster	17 February	1969	to	5 February	1970
Dog	6 February	1970	to	26 January	1971
Pig	27 January	1971	to	14 February	1972
Rat	15 February	1972	to	2 February	1973
Ox	3 February	1973	to	22 January	1974
Tiger	23 January	1974	to	10 February	1975
Rabbit	11 February	1975	to	30 January	1976
Dragon	31 January	1976	to	17 February	1977
Snake	18 February	1977	to	6 February	1978
Horse	7 February	1978	to	27 January	1979
Goat	28 January	1979	to	15 February	1980
Monkey	16 February	1980	to	4 February	1981
Rooster	5 February	1981	to	24 January	1982
Dog	25 January	1982	to	12 February	1983
Pig	13 February	1983	to	1 February	1984
Rat	2 February	1984	to	19 February	1985
Ox	20 February	1985	to	8 February	1986
Tiger	9 February	1986	to	28 January	1987
Rabbit	29 January	1987	to	16 February	1988
Dragon	17 February	1988	to	5 February	1989
Snake	6 February	1989	to	26 January	1990
Horse	27 January	1990	to	14 February	1991
Goat	15 February	1991	to	3 February	1992
Monkey	4 February	1992	to	22 January	1993
Rooster	23 January	1993	to	9 February	1994
Dog	10 February	1994	to	30 January	1995
Pig	31 January	1995	to	18 February	1996
Rat	19 February	1996	to	6 February	1997
Ox	7 February	1997	to	27 January	1998

Tiger	28 January	1998	to	15 February	1999
Rabbit	16 February	1999	to	4 February	2000
Dragon	5 February	2000	to	23 January	2001
Snake	24 January	2001	to	11 February	2002
Horse	12 February	2002	to	31 January	2003
Goat	1 February	2003	to	21 January	2004
Monkey	22 January	2004	to	8 February	2005
Rooster	9 February	2005	to	28 January	2006
Dog	29 January	2006	to	17 February	2007
Pig	18 February	2007	to	6 February	2008
Rat	7 February	2008	to	25 January	2009
Ox	26 January	2009	to	13 February	2010
Tiger	14 February	2010	to	2 February	2011
Rabbit	3 February	2011	to	22 January	2012
Dragon	23 January	2012	to	9 February	2013
Snake	10 February	2013	to	30 January	2014

NOTE

The names of the signs in the Chinese zodiac occasionally differ, although the characteristics of the signs remain the same. In some books the Ox is referred to as the Buffalo or Bull, the Rabbit as the Hare or Cat, the Goat as the Sheep and the Pig as the Boar.

For the sake of convenience, the male gender is used throughout this book. Unless otherwise stated, the characteristics of the signs apply to both sexes.

WELCOME TO THE
YEAR OF THE SNAKE

Silent and still,
The snake may lie coiled and motionless
   for a very long time.
But when it is ready, *it strikes*.

Patient, dangerous and ever alert, the snake has power that it would be folly to underestimate. And the same is true for the Year of the Snake. This is a time of powerful undercurrents and far-reaching effects.

Snake years are times of dramatic events which can alter the course of history. The Russian Revolution which swept away the Tsarist tradition in 1917, the dismantling of the Berlin Wall and collapse of many regimes in Eastern Europe in 1989 and, in the last Snake year, the attack on the New York Trade Center and Pentagon all had profound consequences. In 2013 it is again likely that powerful forces will emerge and some who are repressed will rise up against authority. These changes can be dramatic as well as affect the stability of certain regions.

World leaders and international organizations will need to be vigilant this year. However, amid the tensions, there will also be landmark agreements which can usher in positive change. It was a Snake year when Presidents Bush and Gorbachev held their first summit and announced the ending of the Cold War and also when Nelson Mandela met President Botha, a meeting which led to the ending of white rule in South Africa. This Snake year will again witness historic developments.

A further feature of Snake years is that they are times of intrigue, when rumours are rife. Prominent figures could find themselves under scrutiny and with damaging allegations to face up to. Shady dealings, corruption and espionage may discredit certain countries, industries and organizations, and the year is likely to be marked by several scandals.

However, while the Snake year will see powerful forces at work, it will also be a time of major progress. Although financial markets will remain volatile and be swift to react to rumour and speculation, the year will see a slow but definite economic upturn in many regions. Many governments will also take active measures to stimulate growth and reduce unemployment levels.

Snake years favour innovation and 2013 is likely to see some defining moments with the release of major products. It was in the last Snake year that Apple launched their iconic iPod and other Snake years have seen the invention of the CD and high-definition television. There has also been notable progress in the world of medicine in Snake years, including the discovery of DNA and, in the last Snake year, the first surgical implantation of an AbioCor artificial heart into a patient and Dr Kenneth Matsumura's invention of the artificial liver. Further breakthroughs will occur this year and impact on the treatment of certain conditions. International agencies will also be active this year in providing relief and medicine to undeveloped and troubled regions. There will be considerable emphasis on humanitarian and environmental issues.

The arts and culture thrive in Snake years, and in this one, major events and exhibitions will make various art forms more accessible. On stage and screen, audiences will be delighted by a variety of productions, some of them thought-provoking and profound. There is a reflective quality to the Snake year. The world of fashion is also likely to see notable styles emerge, with the emphasis on the sophisticated and discreet rather than the garish or flamboyant. For the fashion conscious, this can be an exciting year, with new trends (including hairstyles) attracting widespread comment.

The British royal family will also be very much in the news this year, with events that will bring both joy and concern.

More ominously, the extreme weather patterns seen in recent years are set to continue. The previous Snake year witnessed Tropical Storm Allison, which caused $5.5 billion in damage, making it the costliest tropical storm in American history. While it is hoped that the ravages of nature will not be as severe or damaging this year, the omens are, sadly, not good.

This Snake year will, though, see some great human achievements, and whether on land or sea, in the air, in space or indeed in sporting arenas, many records will be broken and feats be inspiring. Interestingly, it was in a Snake year that Sir Edmund Hillary conquered Mount Everest.

For the individual, the Snake year offers considerable potential. It favours learning and personal growth, and whether by reading or studying more, taking up a new skill or setting themselves a personal objective, many people will be persuaded to improve themselves in some way. This is a year for action, and many people will be satisfied by the actions they take.

As is always the way, some signs will fare better in the Snake year than others, but for all there will be opportunities to do something personally constructive. As the Chinese proverb reminds us, 'If you have foresight, you are blessed, but if you have insight, you are a thousand times blessed.' This is an excellent year to gain new insights, reconnect with the real you and give yourself time to add to your knowledge and capabilities. Use your time well so you may do well.

I wish you good fortune for the year ahead.

YOUR CHINESE
HOROSCOPE 2013

18 FEBRUARY 1912 ～ 5 FEBRUARY 1913   *Water Rat*

5 FEBRUARY 1924 ～ 23 JANUARY 1925   *Wood Rat*

24 JANUARY 1936 ～ 10 FEBRUARY 1937   *Fire Rat*

10 FEBRUARY 1948 ～ 28 JANUARY 1949   *Earth Rat*

28 JANUARY 1960 ～ 14 FEBRUARY 1961   *Metal Rat*

15 FEBRUARY 1972 ～ 2 FEBRUARY 1973   *Water Rat*

2 FEBRUARY 1984 ～ 19 FEBRUARY 1985   *Wood Rat*

19 FEBRUARY 1996 ～ 6 FEBRUARY 1997   *Fire Rat*

7 FEBRUARY 2008 ～ 25 JANUARY 2009   *Earth Rat*

THE
RAT

THE PERSONALITY OF THE RAT

To see,
and to see what others do not see.
That is true vision.

The Rat is born under the sign of charm. He is intelligent, popular and loves attending parties and large social gatherings. He is able to establish friendships with remarkable ease and people generally feel relaxed in his company. He is a very social creature and is genuinely interested in the welfare and activities of others. He has a good understanding of human nature and his advice and opinions are often sought.

The Rat is a hard and diligent worker. He is also very imaginative and is never short of ideas. However, he does sometimes lack the confidence to promote his ideas and this can often prevent him from securing the recognition he deserves.

The Rat is very observant and many Rats have made excellent writers and journalists. The Rat also excels at personnel and PR work and any job that brings him into contact with people and the media. His skills are particularly appreciated in times of crisis, for the Rat has an incredibly strong sense of self-preservation. When it comes to finding a way out of an awkward situation, he is certain to be the one who comes up with a solution.

The Rat loves to be where there is a lot of action, but should he ever find himself in a very bureaucratic or restrictive environment he can become a stickler for discipline and routine. He is also something of an opportunist and is constantly on the lookout for ways in which he can improve his wealth and lifestyle. He rarely lets an opportunity go by and can become involved in so many plans and schemes that he sometimes squanders his energies and achieves very little as a result. He is also rather gullible and can be taken in by those less scrupulous than himself.

Another characteristic of the Rat is his attitude towards money. He is very thrifty and to some he may appear a little mean. The reason for this is purely that he likes to keep his money within his family. He can be most generous to his partner, his children and close friends and relatives. He can also be generous to himself, for he often finds it impossible to deprive himself of any luxury or object he fancies. He is very acquisitive and can be a notorious hoarder. He also hates waste and is rarely prepared to throw anything away. He can be rather greedy and will rarely refuse an invitation to a free meal or a complimentary ticket to a lavish function.

The Rat is a good conversationalist, although he can occasionally be a little indiscreet. He can be highly critical of others – for an honest and unbiased opinion, the Rat is a superb critic – and will sometimes use confidential information to his own advantage. However, as he has such a bright and irresistible nature, most people are prepared to forgive him his slight indiscretions.

Throughout his long and eventful life the Rat will make many friends and will find that he is especially well suited to those born under his own sign and those of the Ox, Dragon and Monkey. He can also get on well with those born under the signs of the Tiger, Snake, Rooster, Dog and Pig, but the rather sensitive Rabbit and Goat will find him a little too critical and blunt for their liking. The Horse and Rat will also find it difficult to get on with each other – the Rat craves security and will find the Horse's changeable moods and rather independent nature a little unsettling.

The Rat is very family orientated and will do anything to please his nearest and dearest. He is exceptionally loyal to his parents and can himself be a very caring and loving parent. He will take an interest in all his children's activities and see that they want for nothing. He usually has a large family.

The female Rat has a kindly, outgoing nature and involves herself in a multitude of different activities. She has a wide circle of friends, enjoys entertaining and is an attentive hostess. She is also conscientious about the upkeep of her home and has good taste in home furnishings. She is most supportive to the other members of her family and, due to her resourceful, friendly and persevering nature, can do well in practically any career she chooses.

Although the Rat is essentially outgoing, he is also a very private individual. He tends to keep his feelings to himself and while he is not averse to learning what other people are doing, he resents anyone prying too closely into his own affairs. He also does not like solitude and if he is alone for any length of time he can easily get depressed.

The Rat is undoubtedly very talented, but he does sometimes fail to capitalize on his many abilities. He has a tendency to become involved in too many schemes and chase after too many opportunities at once. If he can slow down and concentrate on one thing at a time, he can become very successful. If not, success and wealth can elude him. But, with his tremendous ability to charm, he will rarely, if ever, be without friends.

THE FIVE DIFFERENT TYPES OF RAT

In addition to the 12 signs of the Chinese zodiac there are five elements and these have a strengthening or moderating influence on the signs. The effects of the five elements on the Rat are described below, together with the years in which they were exercising their influence. Therefore Rats born in 1960 are Metal Rats, Rats born in 1912 and 1972 are Water Rats, and so on.

Metal Rat: 1960

This Rat has excellent taste and certainly knows how to appreciate the finer things in life. His home is comfortable and nicely decorated and he likes to entertain and mix in fashionable circles. He has considerable financial acumen and invests his money well. On the surface he appears cheerful and confident, but deep down he can be troubled by worries that are quite often of his own making. He is exceptionally loyal to his family and friends.

Water Rat: 1912, 1972

The Water Rat is intelligent and very astute. He is a deep thinker and can express his thoughts clearly and persuasively. He is always eager to learn and is talented in many different areas. He is usually very popular, but his fear of loneliness can sometimes lead him into mixing with the wrong sort of company. He is a particularly skilful writer, but can get sidetracked very easily and should try to concentrate on just one thing at a time.

Wood Rat: 1924, 1984

The Wood Rat has a friendly, outgoing personality and is popular with his colleagues and friends. He has a quick, agile brain and likes to turn his hand to anything he thinks may be useful. His one fear is insecurity, but given his intelligence and capabilities, this fear is usually unfounded. He has a good sense of humour, enjoys travel and, due to his highly imaginative nature, can be a gifted writer or artist.

Fire Rat: 1936, 1996

The Fire Rat is rarely still and seems to have a never-ending supply of energy and enthusiasm. He loves being involved in some form of action, be it travel, following up new ideas or campaigning for a cause in which he fervently believes. He is an original thinker and hates being bound by petty restrictions or the dictates of others. He can be forthright in his views but can sometimes get carried away in the excitement of the moment and commit himself to various undertakings without thinking through all the implications. Yet he has a resilient nature and with the right support can go far in life.

Earth Rat: 1948, 2008

This Rat is astute and very level-headed. He rarely takes unnecessary chances and while he is constantly trying to improve his financial status, he is prepared to proceed slowly and leave nothing to chance. He is probably not as adventurous as the other types of Rat and prefers to remain in familiar territory rather than rush headlong into something he knows little about. He is talented, conscientious and caring towards his loved ones, but at the same time can be self-conscious and worry a little too much about the image he is trying to project.

PROSPECTS FOR THE RAT IN 2013

Born under the sign of charm, the Rat has some great personal qualities, including determination and the ability to relate well to others. And in the remaining months of the Year of the Dragon (23 January 2012–9 February 2013), he will be able to make his qualities count. Dragon years hold interesting prospects for the Rat and offer him the chance to accomplish a great deal.

At work it would be worth him keeping alert for opportunities as well as considering other ways in which he could use or extend his skills. Some lateral thinking could reward him well and the closing months of the Dragon year could see encouraging developments.

The Rat's endeavours could also bring him some additional good fortune, possibly the realization of a cherished hope, a surprise gift or a financial bonus. There may be several pleasant surprises on the way at this time.

November and December could also see a flurry of social activity, and for the unattached, affairs of the heart could feature strongly. With so much happening, the Rat does, however, need to think ahead and liaise closely with others. It is also important that he lets his views be known. Without care, there is a risk that some may take advantage of his good nature and in some instances he may need to stand his ground.

Generally, however, the Dragon year is an encouraging one for the Rat. He does need to keep aware of all that is happening around him and act on his ideas, but some important possibilities can open up for him both personally and professionally.

The Year of the Snake starts on 10 February and will be a variable one for the Rat. Progress will be more difficult and the Rat will need to be careful. He is resourceful and can learn a lot from the challenges of the year, as well as enjoy some personal achievements of which he can be truly proud, but he will need to accept that Snake years proceed at a measured pace and results will take some while to filter through.

In work matters, this can be a constructive year. Rats who have recently taken on a new position or who do so during the year should take the time to establish themselves and learn about the various aspects of their responsibilities. This includes taking advantage of any training opportunities as well as being an active member of any team. With involvement and commitment, many Rats are set to impress this year and do their longer-term prospects a lot of good.

For those seeking a position or wanting to advance their career elsewhere, the year can, though, be slow-moving. There could be a lack of suitable opportunities and the Rat could make many applications with little result. While this may be frustrating, one of the hallmarks of the Rat's character is that he *is* a survivor and eventually his persistence will prevail. Also, Snake years can take interesting turns. Although some types of work may be difficult to obtain, by widening the scope of what he is prepared to consider and looking at different industries and, if relevant, retraining opportunities, the Rat could find new possibilities opening up for him. Overall, though, this is a year which favours carefully considered actions rather than haste. April could see some interesting developments, but generally the second half of the year offers more scope than the first, with mid-September to early December a more positive time. For all Rats, modest progress is possible, but the key gains of the Snake year will be the knowledge and skills they acquire.

Although the Rat generally keeps active, he should aim to give some consideration to his well-being this year. With his sometimes demanding lifestyle, he does need to allow time for rest and exercise as well as make sure his diet is nutritious. If at any time he feels under par, he should seek medical guidance.

Another area which requires care this year is finance. The Rat will need to watch his spending and be wary of risk. Without care, he could incur a loss or find his outgoings are more than anticipated. Throughout the year he should keep control of his budget and make provision for larger outgoings and more expensive plans. Also, if entering into an agreement at any time, he should check the terms and implications. This is no year to make assumptions or take unnecessary risks.

The Snake year does, though, favour personal development, and by using his spare time well, whether by furthering an interest or starting something new, the Rat can find his positive actions rewarding him well.

With his outgoing and curious nature, the Rat knows a great many people and can look forward to some enjoyable social occasions over the year. March, May, August and December could be particularly active months. For the unattached, romance could figure strongly, although the path of true love may not always run smoothly. Throughout the year the Rat will need to be his attentive self and remain aware of the feelings of others. Here again, Snake years require the Rat to tread carefully.

The Rat's home life is special to him and during the year he will value the support and advice of those around him. When he is under pressure or making what could be an important decision, he will find the insights of his loved ones can not only reassure him but also guide him. However, to benefit fully, he does need to be open and communicate well with those close to him. The same is true for home projects and purchases: good discussion will not only make some decisions easier, but also help understanding and rapport. Domestically, this is a year favouring a joint approach and good planning. Setting time aside for shared interests, special occasions or a short break away will also do everyone good. The closing months of the year could see some additional travel opportunities and family occasions that the Rat will greatly enjoy.

Overall, the Snake year will be a mixed one for the Rat and he will need to be patient and careful. However, he is resourceful and by making the best of his situation and remaining aware of what is going on around him, he can still make headway and, importantly, add to his skills, knowledge and strengths. Used well, this can be an instructive year, with the Rat's patience and commitment being rewarded, even though results may sometimes be slow in coming through.

The Metal Rat

The Metal Rat has many fine qualities, including the ability to relate to others and empathize, but his sense of awareness is also important. He takes in a great deal and is adept at picking up nuances, and this talent will prove especially useful in the Snake year. This may not be an easy time for the Metal Rat, but it is one of interesting possibility.

One of its most favourably aspected areas is personal development, and by doing something positive, whether that involves learning new skills that could help his work situation, developing his personal interests or taking up recreational pursuits that could help his general well-being, the Metal Rat can take considerable satisfaction from what he does.

He will also find his actions can bring him into contact with others, and over the year can widen his social circle and build up good contacts. His ability to forge good connections can serve him well again this year. For socializing, March, May, August and December could be busy months. Metal Rats who find romance this year do need to remain attentive, however, and take time to get to know their partner rather than proceed too hastily.

Domestically, the Metal Rat can look forward to some interesting times this year. Important decisions will need to be taken and some will have long-term implications. These could concern his or his partner's work situation, the choices facing his children, expenditure on the home or, for a few Metal Rats, a possible move. Ample time needs to be allowed to discuss options and consider costs, implications and the best way forward. While there may be anxious moments, the Metal Rat's judgement will prove useful. Important benefits can follow on and many of the decisions and efforts of the year will prove well worthwhile. In addition, many Metal Rats will take particular delight in the achievements of a younger relation, and the support the Metal Rat is able to give will be valued.

Although his home life will frequently be busy, the Metal Rat should also make sure quality time with his loved ones does not suffer. Shared interests and, if possible, a holiday or short break will be especially appreciated.

At work, the Metal Rat may see important possibilities arising over the year. Metal Rats who are well established where they are could find themselves taking on new responsibilities which will allow them to make greater use of their expertise. In some cases, this could entail considerable adjustments to routine, but the headway made in 2013 may not only be substantial but also satisfying *and* well deserved.

For Metal Rats who are seeking to make a change, as well as those seeking work, the Snake year will be challenging. Obtaining a new position will not be easy, but, to their credit, Metal Rats are tenacious. Effort and patience *will* be required in 2013, but the year will not be without its opportunities. Late March, April and September to early December could see some important work developments.

The Metal Rat will, though, need to be careful in financial matters. With some expensive home plans likely, plus his other commitments, he will need to manage his outgoings well. Also, if entering into any agreement, he should check the terms and, if necessary, seek appropriate advice. This is no year for risk or acting hastily.

Another area which the Metal Rat should give some consideration to is his lifestyle. With his often busy schedule, it is important he builds in time for recreation as well as watches the quality of his diet. If he feels under par at any time during the year, he should seek advice.

Overall, the Year of the Snake will ask a lot of the Metal Rat. The progress he makes will often be the result of considerable time and effort, and in addition the year can bring some important but not always easy decisions. However, by thinking carefully about his situation and the choices before him, the Metal Rat can ultimately benefit. He should take full advantage of any opportunities for personal development, and by furthering his personal interests or adding to his professional capabilities and knowledge, he can derive a lot of satisfaction from what he does as well as prepare for future possibilities. A valuable and potentially rewarding year.

TIP FOR THE YEAR

Be prepared to put in the time and effort. Also, keep alert for possibilities. Although this may not always be an easy year, your efforts and awareness can ultimately reward you well.

The Water Rat

One of the key features of the Snake year is that it rewards long-term planning, and by giving careful thought to his future hopes, the Water Rat can make it a significant time. This may not be a year for speedy results, but slowly and surely many Water Rats *will* be able to make important headway.

The Water Rat's thoughts could concern almost any area of his life, including the way he would like his career to develop, a particular skill or interest he would like to make more of, his accommodation (possibly including relocating) and/or some personal aspirations. No matter what he may be hoping to achieve, by giving thought to what he wants, making enquiries and taking those all-important first steps, he can set important wheels in motion. This is a year for planning, not delay.

Throughout the year, it is important that the Water Rat discusses his thoughts with others, especially in his home life, where he will be particularly grateful for the support of family members. When considering future plans, he can receive much useful help and encouragement from those around him and should not be reticent in asking for advice or assistance. During the year there will be also be some situations that require careful planning. These could include arranging a family gathering, helping a family member to move or starting ambitious domestic plans. Again, good communication and co-operation will be essential. In many Water Rat households, there could also be family news to celebrate and chances to travel late in the year.

As a result of his interests and activities, the Water Rat knows a great many people, and once again will enjoy meeting his friends and some of the social occasions he goes to. March, May, August and December could be especially fine and interesting months socially. However, when he is with others, the Water Rat will need to be his attentive self. Without care, an indiscreet comment could cause difficulty. Here again the Snake year requires the Water Rat to be watchful, alert and aware.

For Water Rats who are alone and maybe hoping for new friendships and romance, the Snake year can bring interesting developments. By making the most of their chances to go out, these Water Rats will have good opportunities to meet others. However, where affairs of the heart are concerned, it would be helpful to allow time to get to know each other rather than rush into any commitment.

The Snake year particularly encourages learning and personal development, and during it the Water Rat should aim to make more of his personal interests or consider taking up something new. Not only can his interests sometimes be an outlet for his ideas and creative talents, but they can also help him relax. He would also benefit by giving some consideration to the amount of regular exercise he gets and to the quality of his diet. If he feels either is lacking, it would be worth seeking advice on the best way to improve.

At work, this is a year for dedicated effort. Water Rats who are well established where they are could face greater demands and challenging situations. However, while the pressures may sometimes be great, by focusing on what needs to be done and using their skills and judgement wisely, not only will they have the chance to impress but also prove they have the abilities necessary for promotion. Success this year will be well deserved and hard won.

Water Rats who decide to move on from where they are or are seeking work will find the job-seeking process requires considerable effort. Openings may be limited and competition considerable. However, by being willing to consider a wide range of possibilities and, in some cases, retraining, many Water Rats will secure what can be an important opportunity. Late March, April and mid-September to early December could see encouraging developments, but throughout the Snake year the Water Rat should act determinedly *and* remain persistent.

In money matters, again this is a year requiring care. With some large home and family expenses likely, plus his other commitments, the Water Rat should manage his budget carefully and keep a close watch on his outgoings. This is a time for good financial management.

In general the Snake year can be an exacting one for the Water Rat. Considerable effort will be needed to make headway and results will not always come quickly. However, what the Water Rat can plan – and achieve – behind the scenes can be significant. Working towards longer-term objectives or gaining knowledge and skills that can be useful later on can bear significant fruit. The long-term benefits of the Snake year can be considerable and it can leave a powerful legacy for the Water Rat to build on.

TIP FOR THE YEAR
Avoid haste. Consider your plans carefully and use any chances to further your knowledge and skills. Investing in yourself can lead to important opportunities opening up for future success.

The Wood Rat

This can be a quietly satisfying year for the Wood Rat. Although it may lack the dynamic activity of some, by setting about his activities in a keen, determined way, he can not only improve himself but also sow important seeds for the future. Indeed, a lot that the Wood Rat does this year can be of far-reaching significance. However, he will need to be patient and thorough, as this is no time for risk or rush.

This is particularly the case at work. In recent years many Wood Rats will have impressed others with their dedication and skills, and this year those who have been with the same employer for some time will often have a chance to take on greater responsibilities and learn about other aspects of their work. However, in setting about their duties, they could face additional pressures. Snake years do not always make life easy for the Wood Rat, but the effort he puts in and skills he demonstrates can help both his present position and future prospects. It *is* worth making the effort.

For Wood Rats who feel there is limited scope where they are and decide to move on, as well as those seeking work, there can be important developments in store. Obtaining a position will require great effort and these Wood Rats should consider widening their search. By doing so, however, many could secure a position that is very different from what they have done before but is a good base to build on. Those who do take on a new position this year should make the most of any training they may be offered and embrace the chance to learn. What they accomplish now can open up further possibilities in the future. April and mid-September to early December could see some particularly encouraging developments.

Although many Wood Rats will enjoy a modest increase in earnings over the year, money matters do require care. With personal, accommodation and sometimes transport expenses likely to be considerable, the Wood Rat will need to budget carefully. Economies may be needed in order to go ahead with certain plans, or even meet commitments, and the keyword in 2013 is *discipline*. The Wood Rat should also be thorough in all financial matters and check the terms and obligations of any new agreement he enters into. The Snake year rewards careful attention.

Over the year, the Wood Rat should also give some thought to his well-being. With sometimes long and demanding days, he does need to allow time for rest and relaxation and also make sure his diet is balanced and sufficient. If lacking regular exercise, he should try to schedule some into his week. Without care, he could find himself under par this year, and if anything concerns him at any time, or he decides to start a new exercise regime, he should seek medical advice.

In addition to learning new skills in his work, he can, however derive considerable satisfaction from his personal interests. Whether enjoying the pleasure and company these can bring or setting himself a new project, he can get much personal benefit from what he does over the year. And with his often busy lifestyle, it is important that he allows himself time for recreation.

This also applies to his social life. In view of his pressures and commitments, the Wood Rat may decide to cut back on his socializing this year. However, he should still keep in regular contact with friends and if he receives invitations to events that appeal to him, he should try to go. March, May, August and December will see the most social activity.

For the unattached Wood Rat, there could be significant romance this year, but if it is to endure, time is needed. Rushing things or building up high expectations early on could lead to heartbreak. Wood Rats, take note and allow any blossoming romance to evolve in its own way and time.

Domestically, this can be a busy year. Some Wood Rats will start a family, some will have ambitious accommodation plans and some will have other key objectives they are keen to realize. A lot is set to happen and the Wood Rat will need to remain attentive and aware. Also, developments in the Snake year can sometimes take a curious course, with plans needing to be revised or new possibilities arising. To benefit, the Wood Rat will need to show some flexibility, but over the year he can find important hopes being realized and bringing him considerable happiness. As with so much in 2013, this may not happen quickly, though, but need to be worked towards.

Throughout the year the Wood Rat will do much to assist others and many will be grateful for his advice. In his home life, once again he will play a full and valued part.

Overall, 2013 will be a demanding year, but while the going may sometimes be tough, the Wood Rat will have the chance to learn new skills, demonstrate personal qualities and prepare the way for subsequent advances. The Snake year will be both constructive and instructive, and while its pressures may sometimes be great, it will also contain some special moments, including the realization of certain personal hopes. Despite the effort required, the Wood Rat can find it a personally satisfying and illuminating year.

TIP FOR THE YEAR
Be thorough and proceed carefully and steadily. Also, allow time for yourself as well as to spend with others. Keep your lifestyle in balance so you can appreciate what you do and those around you all the more.

The Fire Rat
There is a Chinese proverb that the Fire Rat would do well to bear in mind this year: 'Diligence leads to riches.' By setting about his activities in a careful and diligent way, he will find what he can accomplish this year can be of considerable future value.

In his education the Fire Rat should make the most of the opportunities available to him. Even though he may feel uneasy about certain aspects of his education and may find particular subjects challenging, this is still a golden opportunity to learn, acquire skills and discover more about his capabilities. These chances are not ones to waste.

To get the most from his studying, the Fire Rat should be disciplined and allow sufficient time for reading and exam preparation. If he works steadily throughout the year, his overall progress will be that much better. Also, as the year develops, he could get the chance to study certain topics in greater depth or start new courses which can have long-term significance.

Throughout the year, he should be open and communicative, and if he has problems or uncertainties, speak to those who are able to help. Similarly, if he would like to find out more about some courses or work choices, he should ask. This is no time to keep his concerns to himself or miss out on the assistance that is available.

In addition to more academic pursuits, the Fire Rat can derive much pleasure from his recreational interests over the year. By allowing time for these and, if applicable, making the most of the facilities and instruction available, he will enjoy developing his strengths, ideas and skills. Fire Rats who enjoy activities such as sport, music or dance can also enjoy a great sense of camaraderie that adds to the fun.

For any Fire Rats who are feeling alone or unfulfilled, the Snake year can again offer opportunity. However, to benefit, these Fire Rats will need to be active in bringing about the improvement they desire. Looking at what is available in their locality and setting themselves personal objectives will be of benefit. By doing something definite, many Fire Rats will be able to bring meaning and sparkle back into their lives this year as well as improve their outlook.

A factor that the Fire Rat will need to remember, however, is that this year can be a slow-moving one and results will need to be worked for. This is no time to expect swift developments or rush activities. The most rewarding results will come from steady effort. During the year the Fire Rat will also need to be mindful of the views of others. Ignoring the views or feelings of relatives and close friends in particular can lead to some difficult moments. Throughout the year the Fire Rat does need to pay heed to those around him.

This need for awareness also applies to financial matters. If there are particular items the Fire Rat is thinking of acquiring, particularly if they involve considerable outlay, it would be worth him seeking advice on what best meets his requirements. Money matters require careful consideration this year and this is no time for risk, haste or impulse buys.

Fire Rats who decide to leave education and seek work over the year may find it challenging. The pressures and changes may be considerable, but by rising to the challenge, these Fire Rats can not only obtain valuable working skills but also learn more about their capabilities. The Snake year can be an instructive one.

During the year, although the Fire Rat will often be immersed in his own activities, he should also involve himself in his home life. Any help he is able to give may be of more value than he may realize. This is a year favouring participation and openness, and should any differences of opinion arise, these should be talked through and, where possible, a compromise reached. Many Fire Rats will find their home life rewarding and loved ones supportive, but this does require involvement, consideration and a certain flexibility on their part.

Overall, the Year of the Snake is one of great possibility for the Fire Rat, but to benefit he does need to make the most of his situation. He also needs to be patient and have faith in himself and his abilities. By applying himself steadily and seizing his opportunities, he can learn a great deal, and his diligence will help to give him the skills and knowledge he can build on later.

TIP FOR THE YEAR

Be active, willing and committed. Follow up opportunities and ideas and, if necessary, ask for more information. You have a great future ahead of you and the lessons learned now can stand you in excellent stead.

The Earth Rat

Unlike some years, which see events hurtling along at a fast pace, this year favours steady and careful planning. It is the type of year the Earth Rat prefers. Rather than feel buffeted by external forces, he will be able to plan ahead and conduct his activities in the way he wants. 'Slow and steady wins the race', as the Chinese proverb states, and slow and steady will, for the Earth Rat, deliver some worthwhile results this year.

As the Snake year starts, the Earth Rat would do well to give careful thought to what he would like to see happen over the next 12 months. By talking his ideas over with his loved ones, he may find some important and sometimes exciting plans taking shape. Also, as the year proceeds, many Earth Rats may benefit from a slice of luck. Throughout the year, it would reward the Earth Rat to keep alert and aware.

For those in work, this can be an important year. Some may retire or decide to cut back on their working commitments and may have certain ideas and plans they are now keen to implement. Those who do retire should keep alert for opportunities becoming available. Whether these involve activity clubs and groups in their area, courses or, for some, the chance to become more involved in their community, they will find that this is a year to be open to possibility and act on those that appeal to them. By doing so, these Earth Rats can derive a great deal of personal satisfaction from the projects they start. This also applies to Earth Rats who may not have worked for some time and would welcome the chance to do something different. The Year of the Snake favours involvement and participation, and by exploring what is available, the Earth Rat can find some interesting openings arising.

Throughout the year he will also be helped by those around him. If he discusses his ideas with others, he will not only be encouraged and advised, but could also find some plans taking on a momentum of their own. Similarly, if he has concerns or is considering taking up certain activities, he should contact those able to offer expert advice. This is no time to be reticent or hold back. If the Earth Rat needs to know something, *he should ask*.

One area which requires close attention this year is finance. For Earth Rats who retire, there could be pension arrangements and other benefits to finalize, and these should be dealt with thoroughly and, if need be, with professional assistance. Also, if conducting a large transaction or involved in a major purchase, the Earth Rat should check the details and implications and keep the paperwork safe. Financial matters require careful consideration this year.

The Earth Rat would also do well to give some consideration to his well-being, including his diet and general level of exercise. To keep on good form he does need to pay some attention to his fitness and, if he feels it helpful, obtain medical advice on lifestyle improvements he could make. Also, if he has any concerns during the year, he should get these checked out.

Many Earth Rats will decide to travel this year and will again enjoy planning their trips. By finding out about their destination in advance, these Earth Rats will not only enjoy the build-up to their journey all the more but also derive more pleasure from it while away. In addition to any holidays or breaks, the Earth Rat should also take up any invitations to visit family and friends as well as any last-minute travel opportunities that appeal to him.

With his alert and friendly nature, the Earth Rat enjoys good relations with many people and over the year will very much appreciate meeting up with his friends and attending social events. For those who retire, there could be some additional social activity to mark the event and possibly some surprises to look forward to. In addition, activities the Earth Rat may already be involved in or may start during the year can lead to making new friends. Late February, March, May, August and December are likely to see the most social activity. However, while the Earth Rat will enjoy many social occasions, he should remain his attentive self and take into account the feelings of those around him. A *faux pas* or misconstrued remark could lead to some awkward moments. Earth Rats, take note, and in your relations with others, as with so much this year, do be aware.

In the Earth Rat's home life, this is a year that favours combined effort. Sharing activities, pooling talents and helping one another can lead to a lot happening *and* being appreciated. Good discussion and planning can also give the year structure, with activities and events to work towards. In addition many Earth Rats will take particular pleasure in following the progress of younger relations, and for those who are grandparents or become grandparents this year, any additional assistance and support they are able to give could be especially welcome. Over the year, the Earth Rat's home life will mean a great deal to him, but here again, with the prevailing aspects, he does need to take into account the feelings of those around him. Snake years do call for care and awareness, but overall, home life can be satisfying, with many plans slowly but surely being realized.

Although the pace this year may be slower than of late, a lot can still happen for the Earth Rat. This is very much a time for deciding on plans and then setting them in motion. In addition, some interesting opportunities may arise. Whether advancing his plans, developing his interests or pursuing his opportunities, if the Earth Rat remains active and aware, he can make 2013 a satisfying and personally rewarding year.

Do consult others and draw on the advice and assistance available to you. Much is possible this year, and the better your support, the more you can achieve.

FAMOUS RATS

Ben Affleck, Ursula Andress, Louis Armstrong, Lauren Bacall, Dame Shirley Bassey, Kathy Bates, Irving Berlin, Kenneth Branagh, Marlon Brando, Charlotte Brontë, Jackson Browne, George H. W. Bush, Glen Campbell, Jimmy Carter, Jeremy Clarkson, Aaron Copland, Cameron Diaz, David Duchovny, Jean Dujardin, Noël Edmonds, T. S. Eliot, Eminem, Colin Firth, Clark Gable, Liam Gallagher, Al Gore, Hugh Grant, Lewis Hamilton, Thomas Hardy, Prince Harry, Haydn, Charlton Heston, Buddy Holly, Mick Hucknall, Henrik Ibsen, Jeremy Irons, Samuel L. Jackson, LeBron James, Jean-Michel Jarre, Scarlett Johansson, Gene Kelly, Avril Lavigne, Jude Law, Gary Lineker, Lord Andrew Lloyd Webber, Ian McEwan, Katie Melua, Claude Monet, Olly Murs, Richard Nixon, Ozzy Osbourne, Sean Penn, Katy Perry, Sir Terry Pratchett, Ian Rankin, Lou Rawls, Burt Reynolds, Jonathan Ross, Rossini, William Shakespeare, Donna Summer, James Taylor, Leo Tolstoy, Henri Toulouse-Lautrec, Spencer Tracy, the Prince of Wales, George Washington, the Duke of York, Emile Zola.

6 FEBRUARY 1913 ～ 25 JANUARY 1914   *Water Ox*

24 JANUARY 1925 ～ 12 FEBRUARY 1926   *Wood Ox*

11 FEBRUARY 1937 ～ 30 JANUARY 1938   *Fire Ox*

29 JANUARY 1949 ～ 16 FEBRUARY 1950   *Earth Ox*

15 FEBRUARY 1961 ～ 4 FEBRUARY 1962   *Metal Ox*

3 FEBRUARY 1973 ～ 22 JANUARY 1974   *Water Ox*

20 FEBRUARY 1985 ～ 8 FEBRUARY 1986   *Wood Ox*

7 FEBRUARY 1997 ～ 27 JANUARY 1998   *Fire Ox*

26 JANUARY 2009 ～ 13 FEBRUARY 2010   *Earth Ox*

THE
OX

THE PERSONALITY OF THE OX

The more considered the way,
the more considerable the journey.

The Ox is born under the signs of equilibrium and tenacity. He is a hard and conscientious worker and sets about everything he does in a resolute, methodical and determined manner. He has considerable leadership qualities and is often admired for his tough and uncompromising nature. He knows what he wants to achieve in life and, as far as possible, will not be deflected from his ultimate objective.

The Ox takes his responsibilities and duties very seriously. He is decisive and quick to take advantage of any opportunity that comes his way. He is also sincere and places a great deal of trust in his friends and colleagues. He is, nevertheless, something of a loner. He is a quiet and private individual and often keeps his thoughts to himself. He also cherishes his independence and prefers to set about things in his own way rather than be bound by the dictates of others or influenced by outside pressures.

The Ox tends to have a calm and tranquil nature, but if something angers him or he feels that someone has let him down, he can have a fearsome temper. He can also be stubborn and obstinate and this can lead him into conflict with others. Usually he will succeed in getting his own way, but should things go against him he is a poor loser and will take any defeat or setback extremely badly.

The Ox is often a deep thinker and rather studious. He is not particularly renowned for his sense of humour and does not take kindly to new gimmicks or anything too innovative. He is too solid and traditional for that and prefers to stick to the more conventional norm.

His home is very important to him and in some respects he treats it as a private sanctuary. His family tends to be closely knit and the Ox will make sure that each member does their fair share around the house. He tends to be a hoarder, but he is always well organized and neat. He also places great importance on punctuality and there is nothing that infuriates him more than to be kept waiting, particularly if it is due to someone's inefficiency. The Ox can be a hard taskmaster!

Once settled in a job or house the Ox will quite happily remain there for many years. He does not like change and he is also not particularly keen on travel. He does, however, enjoy gardening and other outdoor pursuits and he will often spend much of his spare time out of doors. He is usually an excellent gardener and whenever possible will make sure he has a large area of ground to maintain. He usually prefers to live in the country than the town.

Due to his dedicated and dependable nature the Ox will usually do well in his chosen career, providing he is given enough freedom to act on his own initiative. He invariably does well in politics, agriculture and careers that need specialized training. He is also very gifted artistically and many Oxen have enjoyed considerable success as musicians or composers.

The Ox is not as outgoing as some and it often takes him a long time to establish friendships and feel relaxed in another person's company. His courtships are likely to be long, but once he is settled he will remain devoted and loyal to his partner. He is particularly well suited to those born under the signs of the Rat, Rabbit, Snake and Rooster. He can also establish a good relationship with the Monkey, Dog, Pig and another Ox, but he will find that he has little in common with the whimsical and sensitive Goat. He will also find it difficult to get on with the Horse, Dragon and Tiger – the Ox prefers a quiet and peaceful existence and those born under these three signs tend to be a little too lively and impulsive for his liking.

The female Ox has a kind and caring nature and her home and family are very much her pride and joy. She always tries to do her best for her partner and can be a most conscientious and loving parent. She is an excellent organizer and a very determined person who will often succeed in getting what she wants in life. She usually has a deep interest in the arts and is often a talented artist or musician.

The Ox is a very down-to-earth character. He is sincere, loyal and unpretentious. He can, however, be rather reserved and to some he may appear distant and aloof. He has a quiet nature, but underneath he is very strong-willed and ambitious. He has the courage of his convictions and is often prepared to stand up for what he believes to be right, regardless of the consequences. He inspires confidence and trust and throughout his life he will rarely be short of people who are ready to support him.

THE FIVE DIFFERENT TYPES OF OX

In addition to the 12 signs of the Chinese zodiac there are five elements and these have a strengthening or moderating influence on the signs. The effects of the five elements on the Ox are described below, together with the years in which they were exercising their influence. Therefore Oxen born in 1961 are Metal Oxen, Oxen born in 1913 and 1973 are Water Oxen, and so on.

Metal Ox: 1961
This Ox is confident and very strong-willed. He can be blunt and forthright in his views and is not afraid of speaking his mind. He sets about his objectives with a dogged determination, but he can become so involved in his various activities that he can be oblivious to the thoughts and feelings of those around him, and this can sometimes be to his detriment. He is honest and dependable and will never promise more than he can deliver. He has a good appreciation of the arts and usually has a small circle of very good and loyal friends.

Water Ox: 1913, 1973
This Ox has a sharp and penetrating mind. He is a good organizer and sets about his work in a methodical manner. He is not as narrow-minded as some of the other types of Ox and is more willing to involve others in his plans and aspirations. He usually has very high moral standards and

is often attracted to careers in public service. He is a good judge of character and has such a friendly and persuasive manner that he usually experiences little difficulty in securing his objectives. He is popular and has an excellent way with children.

Wood Ox: 1925, 1985

The Wood Ox conducts himself with an air of dignity and authority and will often take a leading role in any enterprise in which he becomes involved. He is very self-confident and is direct in his dealings with others. He does, however, have a quick temper and has no hesitation in speaking his mind. He has tremendous drive and willpower and an extremely good memory. He is particularly loyal and devoted to the members of his family and has a most caring nature.

Fire Ox: 1937, 1997

The Fire Ox has a powerful and assertive personality and is a hard and conscientious worker. He holds strong views and has very little patience when things do not go his way. He can also get carried away in the excitement of the moment and does not always take into account the views of those around him. He nevertheless has many leadership qualities and will often reach positions of power, eminence and wealth. He usually has a small group of loyal and close friends and is very devoted to his family.

Earth Ox: 1949, 2009

This Ox sets about everything he does in a sensible and level-headed manner. He is ambitious but also realistic in his aims and is often prepared to work long hours to secure his objectives. He is shrewd in financial and business matters and is a very good judge of character. He has a quiet nature and is greatly admired for his sincerity and integrity. He is also very loyal to his family and friends and his views are often sought.

PROSPECTS FOR THE OX IN 2013

The Year of the Dragon (23 January 2012–9 February 2013) will have been a variable one for the Ox and the closing months will be busy but not without opportunity.

One of the many features of the Dragon year is that a lot happens very quickly and in the remaining months of it the Ox needs to keep his wits about him and be flexible in approach. To be too obtuse or vent his feelings too forcibly could cause problems and undermine some of what he is hoping to do. He needs to tread carefully.

At work many Oxen could face additional pressures. While demanding, these will often give the Ox greater chance to use his judgement and demonstrate his skills, and considerably enhance his reputation in the process. Oxen who are seeking work should remember that Dragon years favour initiative. If they are quick at following up suitable vacancies, quite a few of them could secure a position, even if only a temporary one, before the year's end.

With many expenses likely in the closing months of the year, the Ox should try to make early provision for these as well as be disciplined in everyday spending.

He can, though, derive much pleasure from his home and social life at this time, and will not only benefit from spending time with family and friends but also from their advice and encouragement. September, December and early January could be particularly active times, and for the unattached, affairs of the heart could add some excitement to the closing months of the Dragon year.

The Year of the Snake begins on 10 February and the Ox will not only feel more comfortable with its more measured pace but can also look forward to making good headway. Snake years suit the Ox's personality and in this one his prospects are bright.

For Oxen who may start the year nursing disappointment or regret, this is a time to look firmly ahead rather than feel fettered by what has gone before. These Oxen should regard 2013 as the start of a new chapter, one offering scope *and* possibility.

The Ox's work situation in particular can present some excellent opportunities. In view of their recent endeavours, many Oxen will be well placed to be considered for a greater role. When opportunities arise, these Oxen should put themselves forward. Also, while the Ox is usually diligent and focused on his duties, he should also make a point of working closely with colleagues and taking the time to build up contacts. His efforts and dependable manner will impress many. Snake years reward effort and application.

For Oxen who feel unfulfilled in their present position as well as those seeking work, again the Snake year can open up important opportunities. By giving careful thought to what they would like to do and investigating possibilities, these Oxen can see some interesting chances arising. To benefit, they need to be active in their quest, but persistence and tenacity *will* prevail. The positions some obtain will mark a considerable change in their duties and involve a steep learning curve, but a key feature of the Snake year is that it is a time of possibility. February, April, June and November could see particularly encouraging developments.

Snake years also favour learning and if any Ox feels an additional skill or qualification could help his prospects, he should consider setting time aside to acquire this. Whether enrolling on a course, studying online or doing some reading and research by himself, he will find furthering his knowledge and skills can not only be satisfying but also an often valuable investment in himself. For Oxen with specific aspirations, this would be an excellent year to work towards these.

This emphasis on personal development also applies to the Ox's own interests. Whether he prefers creative pursuits, practical projects or something more outward bound, he can derive much satisfaction from setting himself projects and using his ideas and skills.

Progress at work can help financially and some Oxen will have the chance to supplement their income through a hobby or interest. Hard work and enterprise will be well rewarded this year. However, the Ox should manage his money well, making allowance for his commitments and, if possible, reducing any borrowings. If he is able, he should take advantage of any tax incentives to save or contribute to a pension policy. His prudence and discipline will reward him in future years.

The Ox's social life is also pleasingly aspected. Although it can be some time before he feels properly at ease with another person, he will find he gels quickly with some people he meets through his interests or work situation and they will soon become part of his trusted social circle. For the unattached, romantic prospects are encouraging and quite a few Oxen will marry or settle down this year. For socializing, March, June to early August and October can be special months.

One cautionary word does need to be sounded, however: the Ox does tend to immerse himself in his various activities and he needs to be careful that this does not cause him to be inattentive or preoccupied when in company. Also, if tired, he should ensure he does not to take out his irritations on others. No year is free of difficult moments and at such times the Ox does need to exercise care and be mindful.

The Ox's home life will be busy over the year, and with so much activity, it is important there is good co-operation. If the Ox has particular ideas about home improvements, purchases, a possible holiday or special occasions, he will find that mentioning these early on will often give them a better chance of happening. In addition, with the encouraging aspects surrounding the Ox this year, there may be personal successes to share.

Overall, the Year of the Snake offers great possibility for the Ox. He sets about his activities with considerable resolve and this year he will see a lot open up for him. In addition, he will benefit from the support, goodwill and encouragement offered by others. In 2013 he will have a lot in his favour and his purposeful actions will help make this an often special year.

The Metal Ox

The Metal Ox has a determined nature. He is a doer and is also highly perceptive, and in the Snake year his abilities can reward him well.

To help get the most from the year, he should give some serious thought to what he would like to see happen over the next 12 months. Having some ideas in mind will not only give him something purposeful to strive for but can also help motivate and inspire him.

Work prospects are particularly encouraging. Metal Oxen who are well established in a particular profession will now have an excellent chance to take their career to a new level, either through a promotion, perhaps one the Metal Ox has been working towards for some time, or through being offered greater responsibilities or a different role. For many Metal Oxen, this will be a year of progress and their commitment will be recognized and rewarded.

The aspects are also encouraging for those who would welcome more major change as well as those seeking a position. Although the job-seeking process will be difficult, by keeping alert, making enquiries and considering different ways in which they could use their skills, these Metal Oxen could see some interesting possibilities opening up. To strengthen their application, they should find out more about the position they are applying for and emphasize their experience. Their initiative and tenacity can often lead to a new opportunity. February, April, June and November could see particularly good possibilities, but chances could arise at almost any time this year.

An important aspect of the year will be the way the Metal Ox is encouraged to make greater use of certain skills. He should take full advantage of any training offered as well as keep informed about developments in his industry. Such knowledge can not only be useful now but also as he looks to progress or considers other possibilities.

The progress the Metal Ox makes at work can help financially and he may also receive funds from another source. Nevertheless, he should manage his situation well, budgeting for commitments and making provision for future plans. He could find it helpful to review his position and if he is able to reduce borrowings, move funds to a more suitable account or take advantage of tax incentives to save or supplement his pension policy, he should consider this. With care, and advice where necessary, he can improve his financial situation as well as benefit from more major plans and purchases.

With his personal interests, again he should make the most of the encouraging aspects of the year. By allowing time to enjoy and develop his interests or setting himself purposeful new pursuits, he will be pleased with what he gets to do and the benefits that follow on. For Metal Oxen who enjoy more expressive activities in particular, this is a good time to explore new ideas and take their skills further. Metal Oxen who have let their interests lapse should consider starting something new over the year. They will enjoy the possibilities that this can open up.

The Metal Ox's activities can also lead to meeting new people, and although he may sometimes be guarded in manner (a typical Ox trait), he should still make the most of such opportunities. By getting to know others and, in his work situation or with certain key interests, raising his profile and networking, he can do himself a lot of good. This is no year to keep himself to himself or be too independent in approach.

For Metal Oxen who would welcome new friends or romance, the Snake year again offers bright prospects, although these Metal Oxen will need to take the initiative and go out more. Positive action on their part can help make this an interesting and improved year. Late February, March, June to early August and October could see the most social activity and, for some, romantic opportunities.

The Metal Ox's domestic life will also be busy, and with possible alterations to his work routine, some adjustments may be needed. At times of change, the implications do need to be talked through, and here the Ox should be open and forthcoming. Also, this is an excellent year for proceeding with ideas for the home, and good planning and co-operation will help. Domestically, this can be an active year marked with personal and family success and satisfying home undertakings.

Overall, this is a year favouring action and commitment, but it does require the Metal Ox to make decisions and then act. He should also liaise with others rather than attempt too much single-handed. With co-operation and support, he can make even more of this good, interesting and personally successful year.

TIP FOR THE YEAR

Act. With initiative and effort, you can accomplish a great deal this year. Also, be mindful of others and consult them. This year has great potential for you – use it well.

The Water Ox

This year not only marks the start of a new decade in the Water Ox's life but also offers growth, choice and some notable personal success.

One of the many factors in the Water Ox's favour this year will be the way he is able to build on his experience. Whether in his work, interests or ideas, his background and diligence can serve him well. This is very much a time for moving ahead and, for some, drawing a line under recent disappointments and concentrating on the present and near future.

Work prospects are particularly encouraging and many Water Oxen will be well placed to put in for a greater role. Not only will they feel they feel the time is ripe for advancement, but some will also be helped by developments around them, possibly through new positions being created or more senior personnel moving on. However they come about, there will be opportunities for the Water Ox to benefit.

For Water Oxen desiring more major change or seeking work, again the Snake year can be one of interesting possibility. New companies or industries may be developing in the area where the Water Ox lives or he may see a vacancy that very much appeals to him. By putting himself forward and showing initiative, he may well be successful in his quest. Also, he should not let any rejection weaken his resolve. Persistence *will* pay off. February, April, June and November could see important developments, but opportunities could arise at almost any time.

Progress at work will also help financially and many Water Oxen may enjoy a rise in income over the year. Some could also benefit from a bonus or gift. Generally, the Snake year can mark an improvement in the Water Ox's situation. However, to benefit, he will need to remain disciplined and take his time when considering larger purchases and plans.

The element of Water helps make the Water Ox a good communicator and throughout the year family, friends and colleagues will often seek out his views. While he will be glad to assist, he should also avail himself of the help that others can give. This includes getting feedback on ideas, asking for support at busy times and, in work matters, seeking information or expert opinion. The Water Ox may like to do a lot by himself, but he will be helped by readily involving others in his decisions and activities.

He will also have a good opportunity to get to know others over the year. As his work situation changes, he will have the chance to meet new colleagues, and his interests and friends can also introduce him to new people. He will enjoy a particularly good rapport with some of those he meets this year and important new friendships can be made. For the unattached, romantic prospects are also excellent, with some Water Oxen meeting their future partner. March, June to early August, late September and October could see the most social activity.

For Water Oxen who are starting the year dispirited and alone, the Snake year can mark the start of a general improvement in their situation. To help, they should consider what positive changes they could make, including perhaps starting a new hobby, enrolling on a course or joining an activity group. By doing something definite, they can help bring something new and purposeful into their lives. The Snake year is one of possibility.

Although the Water Ox generally keeps himself active, he should also pay attention to his well-being over the year and make sure he has a healthy diet and takes appropriate exercise. To be neglectful of this could leave him lethargic and prone to minor ailments. Water Oxen, take note.

In his home life, the Water Ox can look forward to some special times. Not only will those close to him be keen to mark his fortieth birthday, but there could be several other occasions to celebrate. In addition there may well be chances to enjoy a holiday and trips out with loved ones, and the Snake year may contain quite a few high points and surprises. However, while a lot will go well, it is important that there is good co-operation and that plans (as well as any problems) are talked through. This is not a year for the Water Ox to keep his thoughts to himself, but one favouring openness and sharing.

Overall, the Snake year holds considerable possibility for the Water Ox, and by taking action, he can make important headway. His relations with others will be positive and he will be encouraged by the support and affection shown him. The Water Ox is ambitious and keen to make the most of himself, and as he enters his fortieth year, his actions, determination and considerable personal skills can help get this new decade in his life off to a successful start.

Take action. Purpose and determination can lead to a lot opening up for you. To make the most of yourself and the year's encouraging trends, have faith in yourself and what you know in your heart you can do.

The Wood Ox

The Wood Ox will have seen a lot happen in recent years. There will have been successes and some memorable times, but there will have been disappointments too. The previous Dragon year in particular could have been demanding. However, as the Snake year begins, the Wood Ox can look forward to a shift in fortunes. This is a progressive year and with a willingness to put himself forward, he can realize some of the hopes that he has been nurturing for some time.

Almost as soon as the Snake year begins, if not shortly before, the Wood Ox will sense that this is a time when his actions can make a difference and, feeling more determined, he will quickly put his strengths to good use.

One area in which he will be keen to see change will be his work situation. Wood Oxen who have been in the same position for some time will now feel ready to take on new challenges. Whether with their existing employer or elsewhere, if they consider ways in which they can build on their experience, their background can make them particularly strong and often successful candidates when suitable vacancies arise.

For Wood Oxen seeking work or feeling disillusioned with what they are currently doing, again the Snake year can have important developments in store. Although the job-seeking process can be hard and there will be disappointments along the way, by having self-belief and emphasizing their skills and willingness to learn, many will be given a position with exciting potential. What is started in the Snake year can often be significant. February, April, June and November could see some good opportunities.

The Wood Ox can also help his situation by making the most of any training that is available. Wood Oxen who take on a new role in particular will find that adding to their skills and learning more about their industry will not only help with their present duties but could also indicate possible ways forward. The Wood Ox should also work closely with his colleagues and be an active member of any team. His conscientious nature can impress, and for those who take on new duties early on in 2013, further advances are possible later in the year.

The progress the Wood Ox makes at work can also lead to a rise in income and some Wood Oxen may be helped by receiving an additional sum or gift. However, to make the most of this, the Wood Ox will need to remain disciplined and, where possible, budget for specific requirements, possibly including deposits he needs to put down. Also, when considering major purchases or entering into an agreement, he should check the terms carefully and, where appropriate, seek professional advice. Financially, he can do well this year, but he will need to be thorough and avoid risk.

Although the Wood Ox generally keeps himself active, with the possibility of long and often tiring days, it is important that he gives some consideration to his well-being this year and does not skimp on exercise or allow the quality of his diet to drop. To be at his best, he does need to look after himself and, if necessary, seek advice.

It is also important that he keeps his lifestyle in balance and allows time to enjoy his interests. Often these have a good social element too. The Wood Ox has a curious nature and if he sees a new interest or activity that appeals to him, he should find out more. Here again, quite a few Wood Oxen will find that what is started this year can develop into something of greater importance later on. March, June to early August and October could see the most social activity, but there will be many chances for the Wood Ox to meet many new people this year and make some good friends and contacts. For those who are enjoying or perhaps hoping for romance, the Snake year can be special and a chance meeting may become significant.

The Wood Ox's domestic life will be busy and a lot can be achieved over the year. Wood Oxen with a partner are especially likely to have many plans and hopes. Quite a few will also benefit from fortunate developments, especially as plans are set in motion. However, while the aspects are favourable, it is important that the Wood Ox seeks advice, especially on matters that could have important implications. Talking these through with relations or professional advisers can not only assist the Wood Ox in what he wants to do but also alert him to possible problems. The Wood Ox may like to retain a certain independence, but throughout the year he does need to avail himself of the help and support that are on offer. Certain plans and activities can be made a lot easier this way. Wood Oxen, take note.

Overall, the Year of the Snake can be an important one for the Wood Ox. It will offer him the chance to develop ideas and strengths as well as share meaningful times with others. To fully benefit the Wood Ox will need to act with determination and remain alert. The Snake year can spring surprises and bring unexpected possibilities. The Wood Ox has much to offer and in many areas will fare very well this year.

TIP FOR THE YEAR
Make the most of opportunities and use them to gain new experience and knowledge and advance your situation. This is a positive year for you. Use it well.

The Fire Ox

This will be a satisfying year for the Fire Ox, with many activities going well. A key feature of the Snake year is that it encourages learning and personal development, and by making the most of his ideas and opportunities, the Fire Ox will be able to get a lot out of it.

For the Fire Ox born in 1997 this can prove an especially important year. As well as having often significant exams to prepare for, many of these young Fire Oxen will be required to select subjects for more detailed study and give some thought to the longer term. A lot will be expected of the Fire Ox this year, but by giving his best and working consistently, he can not only make good headway but also make more of particular strengths. In some cases, he could be offered extra tuition or granted the use of special facilities, and by taking advantage of what is available, he can gain a great deal.

Throughout the year the Fire Ox should also be alert to opportunities to try new subjects, join activity groups or explore new interests. By being willing to try things out, he can not only derive a lot of pleasure from his pursuits but also get to know new people. For many Fire Oxen, this is a year of fine opportunity.

The young Fire Ox will also very much enjoy his existing interests and should aim to further these in some way over the year, perhaps by adding to his knowledge and skills or setting himself a project. By building on what he does, he will often delight in what he is able to accomplish. For some Fire Oxen, their interests can also bring travel opportunities which can add fun and adventure to the year.

The Fire Ox will also very much enjoy the companionship of his close friends this year. There could be some particularly lively occasions to look forward to and the Snake year can have its surprises as well. New activities can also introduce the Fire Ox to new people, with March to early April, June to early August and October often busy and enjoyable months socially.

With all his interests and activities, there will be a lot the Fire Ox wants to do and buy, with often limited means, so he will need to be disciplined in his spending and be wary about making too many impulse purchases. The greater his control, the more satisfying his actual purchases will be.

Over the year, he will be encouraged by the support he receives from those around him, although to benefit fully he does need to ask for help rather than keep thoughts to himself. When considering important matters such as future educational or work choices, he should listen carefully to the advice given and study the information he receives. What he learns can have a bearing on what he decides to do in the future.

Some Fire Oxen will decide to leave education this year and enter the world of work. For those who do, considerable effort and adjustment will be needed. Not only can securing a position be difficult, but when taking on a new role, there will be a new routine to get used to and new duties to learn. These can be daunting times, but if these Fire Oxen show commitment, they can soon become established. Taking advantage of apprenticeship schemes or continuing their education in some way can also help their situation and prospects. While offering many opportunities, the Snake year does require effort. If he is able to give this, the Fire Ox's actions this year can have important future value.

For Fire Oxen born in 1937, the Year of the Snake can also offer satisfying times. By setting themselves projects and purposeful pursuits, these Fire Oxen will often take considerable pleasure in what they do. For those who enjoy creative activities in particular, this is an ideal year to put their ideas and knowledge to good use. Some may enjoy writing about their experiences, while others will devote time to art, craftwork or gardening. By exploring their thoughts and ideas, they can make this an often personally rewarding time.

The more senior Fire Ox will also be grateful for the support of those around him and if at any time he feels he needs help or advice, he should ask.

As always, he will take considerable pleasure from following the activities of family members over the year and will particularly enjoy the celebrations and news concerning a younger relation. The bond he has with younger family members can mean a great deal.

For all Fire Oxen, whether born in 1937 or 1997, the Snake year can be satisfying, particularly as it will allow them to develop their ideas and personal interests. For the younger Fire Ox, this will also be an important year, not only in terms of furthering his knowledge and abilities but also in bringing out more of his strengths and potential. Overall, a positive and successful year.

TIP FOR THE YEAR
Make the most of your opportunities. With a willing attitude, you can find important benefits following on. Also, do seek the advice and support of others. With assistance, more can be achieved. This is a fine year for you. Enjoy it and use it well.

The Earth Ox

This can be an interesting year for the Earth Ox and he will have the chance to realize some of the hopes and plans he may have been nurturing for some time. The Snake year can also have its surprises and the Earth Ox should be adaptable and make the most of what arises *as it arises*.

One area which is encouragingly aspected is his own personal development. Over the years many Earth Oxen will have built up considerable expertise in certain areas and the Snake year will give them an excellent chance to put their knowledge and insights to effective use. This could be through setting themselves an ambitious but satisfying project, furthering their capabilities or meeting and conversing with fellow enthusiasts. Certain interest-related skills can reward the Earth Ox well this year and bring him the respect of others. Earth Oxen whose interests involve creativity and expression will find it worth putting forward any work they produce or entering an appropriate competition. Those who enjoy writing, art, craftwork or photography in particular can find their activities bringing much joy.

However, while the Earth Ox may have some favourite long-term interests, he should also be open to the new. A recreational pursuit he hears about, an activity or course in his area or a sudden idea he has could all be worth exploring. He could be surprised at what can open up for him. This is particularly the case for Earth Oxen who are recently retired and/or would welcome a new challenge. This is a year to keep alert and be open to opportunity.

Although the Earth Ox tends to keep his social life relatively quiet, he will also value the chances he has to go out over the year. Whether meeting friends or going to events that appeal to him, he will often enjoy what he does, and again, if he sees local events that interest him, he should follow these up. Snake years favour both culture and a broadening of the mind. March, late May to early August and October could be especially active times socially.

Earth Oxen who are lonely, have had recent difficulties or feel dispirited should also take the initiative this year and find a new interest or activity to pursue. This could include something they can do in their community or giving time to a charity or cause they support, but whatever they do, action on their part can give them a considerable uplift this year and, in many instances, introduce them to others.

The Earth Ox's domestic life will also see important developments, with the Earth Ox and those around him involved in significant decision-making. This could relate to work, a change of location, travel or some major projects on the home, but in all cases, time needs to be allowed for discussion and careful consideration of costs and implications. Here the Earth Ox's thoughtful and reasonable nature will be particularly valued, and important benefits will follow on from many of the decisions made over the year. Some decisions may also be influenced by sudden opportunities. In this respect, Snake years are encouraging and supportive of the Earth Ox.

In addition to advancing plans, there will be several domestic occasions the Earth Ox will especially enjoy. These could include celebrating a family achievement, a wedding, the birth of a grandchild or a special anniversary. There will be celebrations in many an Earth Ox household this year, and for those who move, a possible house-warming party as well.

In view of all the activity of the year, the Earth Ox will, however, have to manage his finances carefully. When involved in major undertakings, he should keep a close watch on costs, and if authorizing any work, obtain quotations and check what is included. The more thorough he is, the better. He should also deal with paperwork promptly and should he have problems or uncertainties, seek advice. This is a year for vigilance and good financial management.

For Earth Oxen in work, the Snake year can bring some important choices. Some Earth Oxen may decide to retire, while others could be involved in a considerable change of duties. Although such change can be daunting, it will often give these Earth Oxen more chance to use specialist skills as well as present an interesting new challenge. Few Earth Oxen will remain untouched by work developments this year. February, April, June and November could see important changes, but throughout the year if the Earth Ox sees an opportunity that appeals to him or has an idea he feels has potential, he should follow it up. As he will find, interesting developments can follow on.

Overall, the Year of the Snake offers considerable possibility for the Earth Ox, and by being active and alert and seizing his opportunities, he can derive much satisfaction from what he does. This is also a good year for personal development. By giving time to his interests and looking to extend his knowledge, the Earth Ox can find important benefits following on. Many Earth Oxen will also make some important decisions this year. Throughout the year, the Earth Ox will be well supported by those around him and benefit from opportunities. A full, interesting and personally rewarding year.

TIP FOR THE YEAR

Keep alert and be flexible as you set about your activities. New possibilities can arise which would be well worth considering. In addition, investigate new activities and interests, for these can often bring pleasure and personal benefit.

FAMOUS OXEN

Lily Allen, Hans Christian Andersen, Peter Andre, Gemma Arterton, Johann Sebastian Bach, Warren Beatty, Kate Beckinsale, David Blaine, Napoleon Bonaparte, Albert Camus, Jim Carrey, Charlie Chaplin, George Clooney, Natalie Cole, Bill Cosby, Diana, Princess of Wales, Marlene Dietrich, Walt Disney, Patrick Duffy, Jane Fonda, Edward Fox, Michael J. Fox, Peter Gabriel, Elizabeth George, Richard Gere, Ricky Gervais, Julia Gillard, William Hague, Handel, King Harald V of Norway, Adolf Hitler, Dustin Hoffman, Hal Holbrook, Anthony Hopkins, Billy Joel, King Juan Carlos of Spain, John Key, B. B. King, Keira Knightley, Mark Knopfler, Burt Lancaster, Rooney Mara, Kate Moss, Alison Moyet, Eddie Murphy, Jack Nicholson, Leslie Nielsen, Bill Nighy, Barack Obama, Gwyneth Paltrow, Oscar Peterson, Paula Radcliffe, Robert Redford, Lionel Richie, Wayne Rooney, Tim Roth, Rubens, Meg Ryan, Amanda Seyfried, Jean Sibelius, Bruce Springsteen, Meryl Streep, Lady Thatcher, Alan Titchmarsh, Scott F. Turow, Vincent van Gogh, Zoë Wanamaker, Sigourney Weaver, the Duke of Wellington, Arsène Wenger, W. B. Yeats.

26 JANUARY 1914 ∽ 13 FEBRUARY 1915   *Wood Tiger*

13 FEBRUARY 1926 ∽ 1 FEBRUARY 1927   *Fire Tiger*

31 JANUARY 1938 ∽ 18 FEBRUARY 1939   *Earth Tiger*

17 FEBRUARY 1950 ∽ 5 FEBRUARY 1951   *Metal Tiger*

5 FEBRUARY 1962 ∽ 24 JANUARY 1963   *Water Tiger*

23 JANUARY 1974 ∽ 10 FEBRUARY 1975   *Wood Tiger*

9 FEBRUARY 1986 ∽ 28 JANUARY 1987   *Fire Tiger*

28 JANUARY 1998 ∽ 15 FEBRUARY 1999   *Earth Tiger*

14 FEBRUARY 2010 ∽ 2 FEBRUARY 2011   *Metal Tiger*

THE

TIGER

THE PERSONALITY OF THE TIGER

It's
the zest,
the enthusiasm,
the giving the little bit more,
that makes the difference.
And opens up so much.

The Tiger is born under the sign of courage. He is a charismatic figure and usually holds very firm views. He is strong-willed and determined and sets about most of his activities with tremendous energy and enthusiasm. He is very alert and quick-witted and his mind is forever active. He is a highly original thinker and is nearly always brimming with new ideas or full of enthusiasm for some new project or scheme.

The Tiger adores challenges and loves to get involved in anything that he thinks has an exciting future or that catches his imagination. He is prepared to take risks and does not like to be bound either by convention or the dictates of others. He likes to be free to act as he chooses and at least once during his life he will throw caution to the wind and go off and do the things he wants to do.

The Tiger does, however, have a somewhat restless nature. Even though he is often prepared to throw himself wholeheartedly into a project, his initial enthusiasm can soon wane if he sees something more appealing. He can also be rather impulsive and there will be occasions in his life when he acts in a manner he later regrets. If he were to think things through or be prepared to persevere in his various activities, he would almost certainly enjoy a greater degree of success.

Fortunately the Tiger is lucky in most of his enterprises, but should things not work out as he hoped, he is liable to suffer from severe bouts of depression and it will often take him a long time to recover. His life often consists of a series of ups and downs.

He is, however, very adaptable. He has an adventurous spirit and rarely stays in the same place for long. In the early stages of his life he is likely to try his hand at several different jobs and he will also change his residence fairly frequently.

The Tiger is very honest and open in his dealings with others. He hates any sort of hypocrisy or falsehood. He is also well known for being blunt and forthright and has no hesitation in speaking his mind. He can be rebellious at times, particularly against any form of petty authority, and while this can lead him into conflict with others, he is never one to shrink from an argument or avoid standing up for what he believes is right.

The Tiger is a natural leader and can rise to the top of his chosen profession. He does not, however, care for anything too bureaucratic or detailed, and he does not like to obey orders. He can be stubborn and obstinate and throughout his life he likes to retain a certain amount of independence in his actions and be responsible to no one but himself. He likes to consider that all his achievements are due to his own efforts and he will not ask for support from others if he can avoid it.

Ironically, despite his self-confidence and leadership qualities, he can be indecisive and will often delay making a major decision until the very last moment. He can also be sensitive to criticism.

Although the Tiger is capable of earning large sums of money, he is rather a spendthrift and does not always put his money to best use. He can also be most generous and will often shower lavish gifts on friends and relations.

The Tiger cares very much for his reputation and the image that he tries to project. He carries himself with an air of dignity and authority and enjoys being the centre of attention. He is very adept at attracting publicity, both for himself and the causes he supports.

The Tiger often marries young and he will find himself best suited to those born under the signs of the Pig, Dog, Horse and Goat. He can also get on well with the Rat, Rabbit and Rooster, but will find the Ox and Snake a bit too quiet and serious for his liking, and he will be highly irritated by the Monkey's rather mischievous and inquisitive ways. He will also find it difficult to get on with another Tiger or a Dragon – both partners will want to dominate the relationship and could find it difficult to compromise on even the smallest of matters.

The Tigress is lively, witty and a marvellous hostess at parties. She takes great care over her appearance and is usually most attractive. She can be a very doting mother and while she believes in letting her children have their freedom, she makes an excellent teacher and will ensure that her children are well brought up and want for nothing. Like her male counterpart, she has numerous interests and likes to have sufficient independence and freedom to go off and do the things she wants to do. She has a most caring and generous nature.

The Tiger has many commendable qualities. He is honest, courageous and often a source of inspiration to others. Providing he can curb the wilder excesses of his restless nature, he is almost certain to lead a fulfilling and satisfying life.

THE FIVE DIFFERENT TYPES OF TIGER

In addition to the 12 signs of the Chinese zodiac there are five elements and these have a strengthening or moderating influence on the signs. The effects of the five elements on the Tiger are described below, together with the years in which they were exercising their influence. Therefore Tigers born in 1950 and 2010 are Metal Tigers, Tigers born in 1962 are Water Tigers, and so on.

Metal Tiger: 1950, 2010
The Metal Tiger has an assertive and outgoing personality. He is very ambitious, and while his aims may change from time to time, he will work relentlessly until he has obtained what he wants. He can, however, be impatient for results and become highly strung if things do not work out as he would like. He is distinctive in his appearance and is admired and respected by many.

Water Tiger: 1962

This Tiger has a wide variety of interests and is always eager to experiment with new ideas or satisfy his adventurous nature by going off to explore distant lands. He is versatile, shrewd and has a kindly nature. He tends to remain calm in a crisis, although he can be annoyingly indecisive at times. He communicates well with others and through his many capabilities and persuasive nature usually achieves what he wants in life. He is also highly imaginative and is often a gifted orator or writer.

Wood Tiger: 1914, 1974

The Wood Tiger has a friendly and pleasant personality. He is less independent than some of the other types of Tiger and more prepared to work with others to secure a desired objective. However, he does have a tendency to jump from one thing to another and can easily become distracted. He is usually very popular, has a large circle of friends and invariably leads a busy and enjoyable social life. He also has a good sense of humour.

Fire Tiger: 1926, 1986

The Fire Tiger sets about everything he does with great verve and enthusiasm. He loves action and is always ready to throw himself wholeheartedly into anything that catches his imagination. He has many leadership qualities and is capable of communicating his ideas and enthusiasm to others. He is very much an optimist and can be most generous. He has a likeable nature and can be a witty and persuasive speaker.

Earth Tiger: 1938, 1998

This Tiger is responsible and level-headed. He studies everything objectively and tries to be scrupulously fair in all his dealings. Unlike other Tigers, he is prepared to specialize in certain areas rather than get distracted by other matters, but he can become so involved in what he is doing that he does not always take into account the opinions of those around him. He has good business sense and is usually very successful in later life. He has a large circle of friends and pays great attention to both his appearance and his reputation.

PROSPECTS FOR THE TIGER IN 2013

The Tiger can get a lot from the Dragon year (23 January 2012–9 February 2013), but as it draws to a close he will need to be careful. Situations can be volatile, and rushing, taking risks or being overconfident can lead to problems. The Tiger will need to be on his mettle.

One of the Tiger's particular strengths is his innovative nature. He is capable of coming up with many fine ideas and in the closing months of the Dragon year his talents will be much appreciated. In his place of work, he may be able to suggest solutions to particular problems or take a lead in certain initiatives. It is worth him making the extra effort at this time, and if looking to progress or seeking a position, he could find September and November offering interesting possibilities.

The Tiger will also be in increasing demand as the Dragon year draws to a close and may have chances to meet family and friends he has not seen for some considerable time. Such occasions can not only mean a great deal, but some who have known the Tiger for a great many years may take the opportunity to pass on news or special advice which the Tiger would do well to heed.

With a lot to fit in at this time, it would be helpful for the Tiger to remain well organized and make arrangements in advance. This way he will have the chance to enjoy himself rather than proceed at a heady pace. He would also do well to watch his spending. Without care, his outgoings could be greater than anticipated.

Overall, the Dragon year will give the Tiger a chance to use his ideas and wide-ranging talents. However, in the remaining months he does need to be alert to all that is going on around him and, amid all the activity and demands, keep his lifestyle in balance.

The Tiger sets about his activities with considerable energy, and while he can look forward to many encouraging developments in the Snake year, which starts on 10 February, he may find it best to moderate his approach. The Snake year is one which favours a steadier pace.

However, while the Snake year can have a slightly restraining influence on the Tiger, it can still have its benefits. In particular it will give the Tiger the opportunity to plan ahead as well as appreciate certain activities more. This may not be the most progressive of years for him, but it can be highly satisfying.

In his work, the Tiger should view the Snake year as a time for consolidation, building up skills and being content with more modest headway. Tigers who are relatively new in their position should aim to become more established and learn about the different aspects of their work. By immersing themselves in what they do, they will not only find their work more fulfilling but also be building skills they will often be able to take further later on. Snake years encourage learning and personal development, and the effort the Tiger puts into developing his skills will be an investment in himself *and* his future.

Many Tigers will remain in their present position during the year and will have the chance to take on greater responsibility as the year progresses. However, for those who desire change or are looking for a position, the Snake year can bring important developments. By widening the scope of positions they are prepared to consider, many Tigers could take on a different form of work. Although this could involve considerable readjustment, it may give them a chance to add to their working knowledge and be something they can build on in the future. Some Tigers who are currently unemployed may also be able to take advantage of employment initiatives or retraining schemes, and it would be worth these Tigers keeping informed about what is available. April, May, September and October could see particularly important developments, but throughout the year the Tiger needs to keep alert and act when he sees openings that appeal to him.

In money matters, he will need to remain disciplined, keep careful control over his budget and make advance provision for more major expenses. With good management, he will be able to proceed with a lot of what he wants to do, and could also benefit from a gift or favourable terms on a major purchase, but the Snake year is very much one for planning ahead.

Many Tigers will take the opportunity to travel this year and, again, would do well to save up for this in advance and plan their time away. With their adventurous nature, Tigers often enjoy travelling, and for quite a few, this could be one of the highlights of their year.

With the Snake year favouring learning and personal development, the Tiger can also derive considerable pleasure from his interests over the year and may be attracted to a new recreational activity. The important factor this year is to allow time for himself and to enjoy relaxing rather than feel continually driven. The Tiger should step off the treadmill of activity every so often, especially if he leads a hectic lifestyle.

With his active and outgoing nature, the Tiger knows a great many people and will enjoy a lot of his socializing this year. However, while a lot will go well, the year can bring its problems. A disagreement or clash of personality may occur or a jealousy or rivalry surface. A new romance may founder. Should any Tiger place himself in an awkward or embarrassing position, problems could ensue. While usually so expert in his relations with others, the Tiger will find the Snake year does require care, tact and discretion. Tigers, take note. This can be a pleasing year, but it is not one for lapses or risks. March,

July, August and December could see the most social opportunities.

As always, the Tiger will play a very full part in his home life and will be pleased with how many domestic activities proceed. However, this is no year for rush and although the Tiger may be keen for certain ideas to go ahead, he will need to allow time for these to take shape. To hurry could lead to less satisfactory outcomes and some pressured situations. Again, this is a year for planning and proceeding at a more measured pace.

During the year the Tiger will also give important support to his loved ones, and when others may be facing decisions or have personal pressures, his advice and encouraging manner will be greatly appreciated. Also, with travel favourably aspected, time away with loved ones can do everyone a lot of good.

Overall, the Year of the Snake may lack the activity and buzz the Tiger favours, but it can still be personally satisfying. It will give the Tiger an excellent opportunity to add to his skills and often find greater fulfilment in what he does. Many of his personal activities can also develop well, but he does need to allow himself time to pursue these. In his relations with others, he will need to be aware and attentive, but with care, he will be generally pleased with how the year develops and how its more moderate pace allows him to appreciate that much more.

The Metal Tiger

The Metal Tiger keeps himself active and has widespread interests. He is never one to be idle and in the Snake year he will take satisfaction from the possibilities that open up for him. However, during the year he *will* need to show patience and accept that not all his activities and hopes can be hurried along or achieved as quickly as he might like.

At work, most Metal Tigers will be content to remain in their present position this year and put their skills and experience to good use. As new situations arise and pressures need to be dealt with, the Metal Tiger's judgement will be particularly valued, with colleagues often seeking his advice. Over the year many Metal Tigers will be an integral part of a team and enjoy the respect of many.

Some, however, could be offered the chance of early retirement or consider changing their role. These Metal Tigers do need to consider the implications of such a choice and seek the advice of loved ones and those able to offer expert advice. Important decisions should not be rushed and the Metal Tiger should be guided by what feels right for him.

Metal Tigers who do decide to seek a position elsewhere or are looking for work should also make the most of the assistance available to them. By being active, following up enquiries and showing resourcefulness, they can find new possibilities opening up. Admittedly, these could represent considerable change and involve readjustment, but at the same time they will offer an interesting personal challenge. Late March to early June, September and October could see important developments.

Financial prospects are encouraging and many Metal Tigers will receive a bonus, gift or funds from a maturing policy over the year. However, 'more thought, less speed' is very much the guiding principle of this year and to make the most of his position, the Metal Tiger will need to manage his finances carefully and rather than spend too readily, think over his plans and more major purchases.

With travel favourably indicated, he should, however, make provision for a holiday. Not only will he enjoy seeing places that are new to him, but time away can do him a lot of good. Also, if he receives invitations to stay with friends or relations, he should follow them up. Some of the shorter breaks of the year can give rise to a great deal of pleasure and a surprising amount can be fitted into just a few days.

With Snake years encouraging learning and personal development, the Metal Tiger should also consider taking certain personal interests further or starting something new. With his enquiring mind, he will often derive much satisfaction from what he sets out to do. Allied to this, if he considers he does not get sufficient exercise, he should take advice on the most appropriate activities he could start. By taking action, he not only stands to benefit physically but could also develop a new interest.

In his relations with others, the Metal Tiger is a direct and no-nonsense sort. He speaks honestly and, while many respect him for this, his candour can sometimes lead to problems. In the Snake year he does need to be mindful of this and choose his words carefully in any potentially difficult situation. Words spoken in haste could be regretted later.

However, while there is a need for increased mindfulness, the Metal Tiger will enjoy much of his socializing over the year. His interests can also have a pleasing social element, and for the unattached, a new friendship can add extra meaning to the year. March, July, August and December will be the busiest months socially.

In his domestic life, the Metal Tiger will take a great deal of pleasure in some home projects he decides to tackle, possibly adding new comforts, tidying certain areas or redesigning certain rooms. The Snake year will see much practical activity in many a Metal Tiger household. However, plans should not be rushed and only carried out when time allows.

The Metal Tiger will give valuable support to loved ones over the year and his assistance will be valued. However, while a lot in his home life will go well, there is a risk that certain issues will cause tension. Here good discussion and willingness to reach understanding will be of considerable help and handled well, these issues will not overshadow what can otherwise be a positive and rewarding home life.

One of the main benefits of the Snake year will be the opportunity it gives the Metal Tiger to make more of his interests and ideas. By setting himself satisfying pursuits and seizing his opportunities to add to his knowledge or take up a new interest, he can gain much pleasure from what he does. In his relations with others, the Snake year calls for care, but by being aware of this need for increased mindfulness, many Metal Tigers will be able to minimize the more awkward aspects and can look forward to a full and pleasing year.

TIP FOR THE YEAR

Consult others and listen to their views. Being too independent could lead to problems. Be mindful. Also, set aside time to enjoy your personal interests. These can bring you considerable pleasure and benefit.

The Water Tiger

This will be an interesting year for the Water Tiger. Progress may not be swift and the year will have its challenges, but the Water Tiger can still draw a lot of satisfaction from his activities.

As with all Tigers, in 2013 the Water Tiger will need to proceed carefully and steadily. Snake years do not favour rush and the Water Tiger should allow time to think over plans and activities and talk these through with others. The more preparation, the better.

One important feature of the year will be the chance the Water Tiger will have to develop his skills and interests. Whether in his work or his own interests, by going on training courses, undertaking private study, joining an organization or setting himself a new personal objective, he will be able to benefit from his actions. Where recreational pursuits are concerned, quite a few Water Tigers could be tempted by something new. The Water Tiger is blessed with an enquiring nature.

He would also do well to give some consideration to his well-being over the year. If sedentary for much of the day or tending to rely on convenience foods, he will benefit from seeking advice and making some modifications to his lifestyle.

At work, many Water Tigers will be content to remain where they are, especially in view of some of the more recent changes they may have experienced. These Water Tigers will often be glad to concentrate on their duties and use their skills to good effect. Though they may now have considerable experience behind them, when new procedures or objectives are introduced, they should take the time to familiarize themselves with what is involved, including taking up any training that may be offered. This may not be a necessarily progressive year, but it is not one for standing still.

While the Water Tiger enjoys positive relations with many of his colleagues, it may be that a disagreement, clash of personality or rivalry surfaces this year. If such a situation occurs, the Water Tiger should be careful it does not escalate or cast a shadow over what he does. Fortunately this will only apply to a few Water Tigers, but relations with colleagues can sometimes be problematic in the Snake year and the Water Tiger needs to be careful and aware.

For Water Tigers who would welcome change or are seeking work, the Snake year can bring some interesting possibilities. However, Snake years do move slowly and the job-seeking process can be long and protracted. In their quest, these Water Tigers should not be too restrictive in what they are prepared to consider. By thinking over different ways in which they could use their skills, they could identify new types of work to put in for. By seeking advice, taking care over their applications and preparing well for interview, they will see their discipline bringing results in the end. Late March to early June, September and October could see encouraging developments.

In money matters, the Water Tiger's astute nature can serve him well this year. If wanting to make a major purchase, by planning ahead, making comparisons and keeping alert, he could benefit from an attractive offer. It could also help his situation to carry out a review of his financial position. This could alert him to expenses which may no longer be necessary as well as allow him to manage his budget more effectively.

Where possible, he should try to take a holiday over the year. A visit to an area new to him could be of particular interest and he may be able to combine this with an attraction or event he is keen to see. Again, early planning can help.

The Water Tiger's various activities can also introduce him to many new people this year. However, while there will be good times to be had, Snake years can bring their problems and an indiscretion, misunderstanding or clash of personalities could cause an upset. Water Tigers, do bear this in mind and be careful. Similarly, those who find love this year will need to remain attentive and let any romance build gradually rather than rush into things.

In his home life, the Water Tiger will find his talents in demand. With busy lifestyles going on around him, work pressures to consider and family members facing important decisions, he will be called on to support and advise others. Here his ability to view matters from different perspectives and to come up with solutions will be particularly valued. And while the year will be busy, there will also be domestic plans, shared interests and joint family activities to enjoy.

Overall, the Snake year can be a satisfying one for the Water Tiger, particularly in the way that it allows him to further his interests and skills. This is an excellent time for personal development and what the Water Tiger starts now will often be something he can build on in future years. He will need to take care in his relations with others, but generally the Snake year will be a pleasant and constructive one for him.

Rather than rush and hurry, take things at a more moderate pace. Seize opportunities to add to your skills and knowledge. This can not only be satisfying now but also to your future advantage.

The Wood Tiger

The Wood Tiger is ambitious and likes to be active. However, he is also realistic and knows that some of his hopes and aspirations are for the future. The Year of the Snake will give him an excellent chance to work towards some of these, however, and can have far-reaching significance.

At work, many Wood Tigers will be affected by change. Although they may be settled where they are, they could find new methods being introduced and different objectives being set. Some of this will be challenging, but it can also give the Wood Tiger a chance to show his initiative, add to his skills and demonstrate his potential. As a result, he can do his prospects considerable good.

Many Wood Tigers will remain with their present employer this year, but for those who decide to move on or are seeking work, the Snake year can be significant. Obtaining a new position will not be easy, but by considering different possibilities, many Wood Tigers will secure an interesting new position. Not only can this represent change, but it can give the Wood Tiger experience in a new working environment, which can be an important factor in his subsequent progress. April, May, September and October could see encouraging developments.

With the increased pressures he may face over the year, it is also important the Wood Tiger keeps his lifestyle in balance. This includes allowing time for activities that let him rest and unwind. Some Wood Tigers will also enjoy going to sporting or other interest-related events, including those held in their local area. Should the Wood Tiger be sedentary for much of the day it would be worth him considering activities that would allow him to exercise more. Attention to his well-being can be of considerable benefit.

In financial matters he will fare reasonably well and may receive an additional sum or bonus during the year. However, with all his plans and commitments, he will need to be disciplined and keep careful control of his outgoings. There will, however, be opportunities to travel this year and where possible the Wood Tiger should allow for this in his budgeting.

With his outgoing manner, the Wood Tiger gets on well with most people and can look forward to some interesting social occasions and to widening his circle of acquaintances. However, the Snake year does require him to tread carefully. A difference of opinion or petty annoyance could arise and cast a shadow over this otherwise fine time. Relations with others, especially on a social basis, do need careful attention, and in any potentially awkward situation, the Wood Tiger needs to be guarded and discreet. He should also be very wary of placing himself in any situation which could cause embarrassment or rebound on him. Where new romances are concerned, it is better to proceed slowly than in haste. March, late June to the end of August and December could see the most social activity.

The Wood Tiger can, however, look forward to a busy and rewarding home life. There will be plans and ideas to pursue, and the Wood Tiger will take pleasure in the way certain projects develop. When carrying out these plans, the more co-operation there is, the better the outcome will be. Co-operation will also be needed when those in the Wood Tiger household, including the Wood Tiger himself, face pressures, decisions and unfamiliar situations. At such times, discussion and openness will help everyone. There may be moments of concern, but also some successes to mark. For Wood Tigers who are parents, the encouragement they can give to their children can do much to help their progress and during the year many will have good reason to be proud of the achievements of those around them.

Overall, the Year of the Snake can be a satisfying one for the Wood Tiger and he will often benefit from the knowledge and experience he can now gain. Particularly in his work situation, what he achieves now can be built on in the future. In his relations with others, time and care are needed, but with awareness (and the Wood Tiger is very good at gauging the feelings of others), he can do much to minimize the year's more negative aspects and can look forward to a full and rewarding domestic and social life. The Wood Tiger is both keen and determined and what he does this year will be instrumental in some of the successes he is soon to enjoy, especially in the auspicious Horse year which follows.

Set time aside to develop your knowledge and skills. Your efforts can open up new possibilities and prepare you for future opportunities. Also, keep your lifestyle in balance and preserve time for your loved ones.

The Fire Tiger

The Fire Tiger is enthusiastic, bold and enterprising. He busies himself in a great many things and is good at spotting opportunities. But sometimes he does spread his energies a little too widely and does not always get the full benefit of his actions. In the Snake year, if he remains disciplined and focused, his results can be both good and far-reaching.

At work, many Fire Tigers will now have more chance to establish themselves and their enthusiasm and in-depth knowledge will do a lot to help their standing and prospects. Some of the responsibilities they take on and situations they deal with can also underline their strengths and increase their skills and working knowledge. By showing commitment, raising their profile and working closely with others, they can make themselves very strong candidates for future promotion or employment elsewhere.

For Fire Tigers who are already keen to move elsewhere or are seeking work, the Snake year can again be significant. Obtaining a position will not be easy, but the Fire Tiger could be alerted to openings in a new type of work which not only offers interesting opportunities but also has the potential for future development. What some take on this year could be an introduction to an industry they will be involved with for many years. Late March to the end of May, September and October could see encouraging developments.

The Snake year is also excellent for personal development and if the Fire Tiger feels it would be useful to gain another qualification or a certain skill, he should follow this up. Positive action now can do much to prepare him for the opportunities that lie ahead.

He can look forward to an improvement in his financial situation over the year, but to benefit fully he will need to remain disciplined and keep a close watch on outgoings. With good control over his spending and budget, he will find he is in a better position to proceed with certain plans as well as put down any deposits required. If possible, he should also budget for a holiday or break over the year. A change of scene can do him good.

Another beneficial aspect of the year concerns the Fire Tiger's personal interests and he should make the most of any free time he has to develop his ideas, add to his knowledge and enjoy his recreational pursuits. This can help keep his lifestyle in balance and some activities may also give him the benefit of additional exercise.

The Fire Tiger will also enjoy the social opportunities of the year, especially the chances to talk to friends and share news as well as any concerns. Fire Tigers who would welcome new friends, perhaps having moved to a new area or seen a recent change in their personal circumstances, will often find their work situation or interests introducing them to others. For the unattached, there are interesting romantic possibilities, but time and patience are needed. This is not a year favouring haste.

Also, when in company, the Fire Tiger needs to be attentive and mindful. A slip, *faux pas* or disagreement could cause problems. If possible, he should avoid placing himself in a situation that could embarrass or cause difficulty. Without care, Snake years can have their difficult moments.

Most of the Fire Tiger's relations with others will go well, however, and he can also look forward to a full and active home life. Over the year some important decisions will be made and sometimes serendipity can assist in the process. If the Fire Tiger is considering a move or major purchase, something suitable could be found in a way that seems as if it was meant to be. The Fire Tiger does need to pay heed to what senior relations and professionals may advise, however. The input of others, together with his own efforts, can set things in motion. Domestically, this can be a pleasing year, but it does require good co-operation and support.

Overall, the Year of the Snake can be a significant one for the Fire Tiger. The experience and skills he can gain work-wise can give him a solid base on which to build, especially in the encouraging Horse year that follows. On a more personal level, the Fire Tiger will need to take careful note of the views and feelings of those around him. With support and co-operation, however, plans can proceed and many rewarding times be enjoyed. This is a useful year that will leave a powerful legacy.

TIP FOR THE YEAR

Gain experience and seize opportunities. Your efforts can not only help your present situation but also lead to future possibilities. Do *not* underestimate the importance of what you do now. Also, be mindful of others and enjoy quality time with your loved ones.

The Earth Tiger

This will be a quietly satisfying year for the Earth Tiger and by setting about his activities in his usual diligent way, he can look forward to some pleasing results.

Earth Tigers born in 1998 will now be moving on to an important stage in their education. Not only will there be much to learn but also the chance to study some subjects in greater depth. For the young Earth Tiger, there will be a lot to do, but by putting in the effort and using his time and resources well, he can make significant progress.

In his studying the Earth Tiger will be helped by his inquisitive mind. He could become particularly inspired by certain subjects and in the process demonstrate an aptitude that can be built on in the future. Snake years do have far-reaching effects.

With the more detailed study required this year, it is also important that the Earth Tiger seeks help if he feels he is struggling with any aspect of his education. If he is forthcoming, others will be better able to assist. Earth Tigers, when in doubt, do remember to ask.

Over the year the young Earth Tiger will delight in his interests and recreational pursuits. Those who are sportingly inclined will very much enjoy the games and activities they take part in and should take full advantage of the facilities and instruction available. Whatever the Earth Tiger's interests, the Snake year is an excellent one to explore ideas and discover new strengths. A key feature of the year is that it rewards personal development.

Throughout the year the Earth Tiger will also enjoy sharing many activities with his friends. As he gets to do more, he will also have the chance to meet new people and some important new friendships can be made. However, Snake years can bring their problems and jealousy, rivalry or a falling out could occur. This could cause much anguish for the Earth Tigers affected, but they should try to not let this overshadow the positive aspects of this generally encouraging year. Unfortunately the paths of friendship (and love) are not always smooth and this will be a lesson some Earth Tigers discover this year. In difficult situations, it will be best to tread carefully and keep things in perspective. Fortunately these words only apply to a minority and advice and support will be available.

More positively, there could be some exciting travel possibilities this year, with chances to visit new areas and some lively attractions. The Earth Tiger has an adventurous spirit and can enjoy some memorable moments.

Although he will often be kept occupied by studying and pursuing his interests, he should also participate in home life. Whether helping with certain tasks or being more forthcoming about his current activities, he will find his involvement is appreciated and can lead to better understanding and support.

For Earth Tigers born in 1938, the Snake year can be highly satisfying. The Earth Tiger is blessed with a curious and innovative mind and the more senior Earth Tiger will often have ideas and projects he is keen to tackle. For the most part, these will be related to his interests, and by spending time on these and drawing on his extensive knowledge, he will enjoy a lot of what he does. However, while the Snake year can be encouraging, it is not one for rush. In all his activities, the Tiger should proceed slowly and carefully and think his plans through. The greater his care, the more satisfying his results.

This also applies to any home or garden projects he may have in mind. These do need to be discussed and costed carefully. However, as many Earth Tigers will find, once plans are embarked upon, they could be helped along by sudden opportunities or advantageous offers.

The Snake year will also have its special moments, including opportunities to spend time with friends and relations that the Earth Tiger may not often see. These could include going to a family event or enjoying a holiday away. Whatever happens, the Snake year promises some interesting times. Many Earth Tigers will also see family numbers grow over the year.

For both younger and more senior Earth Tigers, the Snake year can be a generally satisfying one. In particular, it will give the Earth Tiger a good chance to use and enjoy his talents. Whether pursuing personal interests, carrying out plans or, for the younger Earth Tiger, studying, by seizing his opportunities and using his time well, the Earth Tiger can accomplish a great deal. Time needs to be allowed for results to filter through, but this is a year that rewards planning and effort. In general the Earth Tiger will be well supported, and travelling and sharing activities with his loved ones will bring him considerable pleasure.

TIP FOR THE YEAR

Seize your opportunities and use your skills to advantage, for a lot can be achieved this year. It is worth making the effort and drawing on the support and advice that is available to you. Young Earth Tiger, be disciplined in your studying, for your present work can often influence your future choices.

FAMOUS TIGERS

Paula Abdul, Amy Adams, Kofi Annan, Sir David Attenborough, Christian Bale, Queen Beatrix of the Netherlands, Victoria Beckham, Beethoven, Jamie Bell, Tony Bennett, Tom Berenger, Chuck Berry, Usain Bolt, Jon Bon Jovi, Sir Richard Branson, Matthew Broderick, Emily Brontë, Garth Brooks, Mel Brooks, Isambard Kingdom Brunel, Agatha Christie, Charlotte Church, Phil Collins, Robbie Coltrane, Bradley Cooper, Sheryl Crow, Tom Cruise, Penelope Cruz, Charles de Gaulle, Lana Del Rey, Leonardo DiCaprio, Emily Dickinson, David Dimbleby, Dwight D. Eisenhower, Queen Elizabeth II, Enya, Roberta Flack, Frederick Forsyth, Jodie Foster, Megan Fox, Lady Gaga, Crystal Gayle, Buddy Greco, Germaine Greer, Ed Harris, Hugh Hefner, William Hurt, Ray Kroc, Shia LaBeouf, Stan Laurel, Jay Leno, Matt Lucas, Groucho Marx, Karl Marx, Marilyn Monroe, Demi Moore, Alanis Morissette, Rafael Nadal, Robert Pattinson, Jeremy Paxman, Marco Polo, Beatrix Potter, Renoir, Kenny Rogers, the Princess Royal, Dylan Thomas, Liv Ullman, Jon Voight, Julie Walters, H. G. Wells, Oscar Wilde, Robbie Williams, Dr Rowan Williams, Tennessee Williams, Sir Terry Wogan, Stevie Wonder, William Wordsworth.

14 FEBRUARY 1915 ～ 2 FEBRUARY 1916   *Wood Rabbit*

2 FEBRUARY 1927 ～ 22 JANUARY 1928   *Fire Rabbit*

19 FEBRUARY 1939 ～ 7 FEBRUARY 1940   *Earth Rabbit*

6 FEBRUARY 1951 ～ 26 JANUARY 1952   *Metal Rabbit*

25 JANUARY 1963 ～ 12 FEBRUARY 1964   *Water Rabbit*

11 FEBRUARY 1975 ～ 30 JANUARY 1976   *Wood Rabbit*

29 JANUARY 1987 ～ 16 FEBRUARY 1988   *Fire Rabbit*

16 FEBRUARY 1999 ～ 4 FEBRUARY 2000   *Earth Rabbit*

3 FEBRUARY 2011 ～ 22 JANUARY 2012   *Metal Rabbit*

THE
RABBIT

THE PERSONALITY OF THE RABBIT

Whenever
Wherever
With whoever.
Always I try to understand.
Without this, one flounders.
But with understanding,
    at least you have a chance.
A good chance.

The Rabbit is born under the signs of virtue and prudence. He is intelligent, well mannered and prefers a quiet and peaceful existence. He dislikes any sort of unpleasantness and will try to steer clear of arguments and disputes. He is very much a pacifist and tends to have a calming influence on those around him. He has wide interests and usually a good appreciation of the arts and the finer things in life. He also knows how to enjoy himself and will often gravitate to the best restaurants and nightspots in town.

The Rabbit is a witty and intelligent speaker and loves being involved in a good discussion. His views and advice are often sought by others and he can be relied upon to be discreet and diplomatic. He will rarely raise his voice in anger and will even turn a blind eye to matters that displease him just to preserve the peace. He likes to remain on good terms with everyone, but he can be rather sensitive and takes any form of criticism very badly. He will also be the first to get out of the way if he sees any form of trouble brewing.

The Rabbit is a quiet and efficient worker and has an extremely good memory. He is very astute in business and financial matters, but his degree of success often depends on the conditions that prevail. He hates being in a situation which is fraught with tension or where he has to make sudden decisions. Wherever possible he will plan his various activities with the utmost care and a good deal of caution. He does not like to take risks and does not take kindly to change. Basically, he seeks a secure, calm and stable environment, and when conditions are right he is more than happy to leave things as they are.

The Rabbit is conscientious and because of his methodical and ever-watchful nature he can often do well in his chosen profession. He makes a good diplomat, lawyer, shopkeeper, administrator or priest, and he excels in any job where he can use his superb skills as a communicator. He tends to be loyal to his employers and is respected for his integrity and honesty, but if he ever finds himself in a position of great power he can become rather intransigent and authoritarian.

The Rabbit attaches great importance to his home and will often spend a lot of time and money maintaining and furnishing it and fitting it with all the latest comforts – the Rabbit is very much a creature of comfort! He is also something of a collector and there are many Rabbits who derive much pleasure from collecting antiques, stamps, coins, *objets d'art* or anything else which catches their eye or particularly interests them.

The female Rabbit has a friendly, caring and considerate nature, and will do all in her power to give her home a happy and loving atmosphere. She is also very sociable and enjoys holding parties and entertaining. She has a great ability to make the maximum use of her time and although she involves herself in numerous activities, she always manages to find time to sit back and enjoy a good read or a chat. She has a great sense of humour, is very artistic and is often a talented gardener.

The Rabbit takes considerable care over his appearance and is usually smart and well turned out. He also attaches great importance to his relations with others and matters of the heart are particularly important to him. He will rarely be short of admirers and will often have several serious romances before he settles down. He is not the most faithful of signs, but he will find that he is especially well suited to those born under the signs of the Goat, Snake, Pig and Ox. Due to his sociable and easy-going manner he can also get on well with the Tiger, Dragon, Horse, Monkey, Dog and another Rabbit, but he will feel ill at ease with the Rat and Rooster, as both these signs tend to speak their mind and be critical in their comments and the Rabbit just loathes any form of criticism or unpleasantness.

The Rabbit is usually lucky in life and often has the happy knack of being in the right place at the right time. He is talented and quick-witted, but he does sometimes put pleasure before work and wherever possible will opt for the easy life. He can at times be a little reserved and suspicious of the motives of others, but generally will lead a long and contented life and one which – as far as possible – will be free of strife and discord.

THE FIVE DIFFERENT TYPES OF RABBIT

In addition to the 12 signs of the Chinese zodiac there are five elements and these have a strengthening or moderating influence on the signs. The effects of the five elements on the Rabbit are described below, together with the years in which they were exercising their influence. Therefore Rabbits born in 1951 and 2011 are Metal Rabbits, Rabbits born in 1963 are Water Rabbits, and so on.

Metal Rabbit: 1951, 2011

This Rabbit is capable, ambitious and has very definite views on what he wants to achieve in life. He can occasionally appear reserved and aloof, but this is mainly because he likes to keep his thoughts to himself. He has a quick and alert mind and is particularly shrewd in business matters. He can also be very cunning in his actions. He has a good appreciation of the arts and likes to mix in the best circles. He usually has a small but very loyal group of friends.

Water Rabbit: 1963

The Water Rabbit is popular, intuitive and keenly aware of the feelings of those around him. He can, however, be rather sensitive and take things too much to heart. He is very precise and thorough in everything he does and has an exceedingly good memory. He tends to be quiet and at times rather withdrawn, but he expresses his ideas well and is highly regarded by his family, friends and colleagues.

Wood Rabbit: 1915, 1975

The Wood Rabbit is likeable, easy-going and very adaptable. He prefers to work in a group rather than on his own and likes to have the support and encouragement of others. He can, however, be rather reticent in expressing his views and it would be in his own interests to become a little more open and let others know how he feels on certain matters. He usually has many friends, enjoys an active social life and is noted for his generosity.

Fire Rabbit: 1927, 1987

The Fire Rabbit has a friendly, outgoing personality. He likes socializing and being on good terms with everyone. He is discreet and diplomatic and has a very good understanding of human nature. He is also strong-willed and provided he has the necessary backing he can go far in life. He does, not, however, suffer adversity well and can become moody and depressed when things are not working out as he would like. He has a particularly good manner with children, is very intuitive and there are some Fire Rabbits who are even noted for their psychic ability.

Earth Rabbit: 1939, 1999

The Earth Rabbit is a quiet individual, but nevertheless very astute. He is realistic in his aims and prepared to work long and hard in order to achieve his objectives. He has good business sense and is invariably lucky in financial matters. He also has a most persuasive manner and usually experiences little difficulty in getting others to fall in with his plans. He is held in high esteem by his friends and colleagues and his views are often sought and highly valued.

PROSPECTS FOR THE RABBIT IN 2013

The Year of the Dragon (23 January 2012–9 February 2013) will have been a variable one for the Rabbit and he may well have felt uncomfortable with its fast pace and sudden developments. The closing months will continue to see a lot of activity, but there will also be times the Rabbit can look forward to and enjoy.

The Rabbit's work situation could, though, be demanding at this time. His workload could increase and there could be challenging situations to deal with. The Rabbit will need to keep his wits about him, but he is resourceful and by using his skills and judgement well, he will often be able to impress. November is likely to see some key developments.

The need for vigilance also applies to money matters. With the closing months of the year a generally more expensive time, the Rabbit should watch his outgoings and make early provision for any increased outlay. This is no time for risk.

The most positive aspects concern the Rabbit's relations with others, and in the closing months of the year he will very much enjoy meeting his friends and socializing. With his easy manner and ability to relate to others, he will find himself in demand. August and December could be particularly busy months. For the unattached, romantic possibilities abound, while for those newly in love, this can be a time of much happiness.

In the Rabbit's home life the aspects are also promising. A lot is set to happen and the Rabbit and those around him will enjoy family get-togethers as well as domestic plans which suddenly (and sometimes fortuitously) move forward.

The Year of the Snake begins on 10 February and will be an improved one for the Rabbit. After the frenzy and pressure of the Dragon year, he will have more chance to concentrate on his objectives and advance his plans. This will be a satisfying and constructive year for him.

In his work, the year offers considerable scope. Whether the Rabbit decides to remain with his present employer or move on, the knowledge he has gained, the good working relations he enjoys and his own enterprising approach can all stand him in excellent stead. As a result, if promotion opportunities occur, staff are required for new projects or an interesting vacancy arises elsewhere, the Rabbit will be well placed to apply. In the Snake year he will feel more in control of his destiny and will be able to move his career forward in the way he wants.

The aspects are also encouraging for Rabbits who are seeking work. Although securing a position can be a long and wearying process, the Snake year can provide some interesting openings. Sometimes these could be in a different type of work from what the Rabbit has done before but nevertheless give him the opening he has been seeking for some time. Any new position will often involve training as well as familiarization with a new working environment, but by showing enthusiasm, these Rabbits can quickly make their mark. Work-wise, the Snake year is one of opportunity, with March, May, June and November being important months.

The progress the Rabbit makes at work can also help financially. The Rabbit will generally fare well in money matters this year and if he can use any upturn to reduce borrowings, he can improve his overall situation. Also, if making a major purchase at any time, by making comparisons and looking at options, he may not only choose well but also be able to secure favourable terms. His eye for quality and a good deal will be in fine form this year.

The Snake year favours travel and the Rabbit should try to make provision for a holiday if he can. Getting away and seeing places new can do him considerable good. If a holiday is not possible, a short break, possibly with relatives living some distance away, could be appreciated.

Another positive aspect of the year concerns cultural pursuits. Snake years favour learning and personal development, and with his enquiring mind, the Rabbit could become interested in a new pursuit or decide on a course of study. If he sees something that interests him and may be of benefit, he should follow it up.

With his sociable nature, the Rabbit will value the chances he has to go out over the year and will enjoy meeting his friends and attending parties and other social events. April, June, August and September could see considerable activity. However, while a lot will go well, there may be some matters which concern the Rabbit. In particular a close friend or family member may have a problem and the Rabbit may be unsure of the best way to help or advise. He may also be concerned about gossip or a particular rumour he hears. Fortunately the Rabbit is usually expert in handling personal relations, but in the Snake year he will need to tread carefully and in some situations be wary and circumspect.

The Rabbit's home life will see a lot of activity over the year and with those close to him often facing work, educational or other decisions, his good counsel will be frequently required. In addition to the assistance he gives family members, he will often take considerable pleasure in making improvements to his home and, if he has one, garden. His good taste and careful approach can lead to some particularly satisfying results. There could also be some personal or family achievements to mark later on in the year.

One of the main benefits of the Snake year is that it gives the Rabbit the chance to act upon his ideas. Whether improving his home, pursuing his interests or furthering his work skills, he will find it a time of considerable possibility. On a personal level he will be in demand, and while a rumour or the situation of a certain friend or family member may concern him, generally his home and social life will be a source of much pleasure. Overall, a satisfying and rewarding year.

The Metal Rabbit

This will be a pleasing year for the Metal Rabbit, particularly as it will allow him to further certain plans he has in mind. Unlike some years, when the Metal Rabbit may feel overwhelmed by various pressures, this will be a much steadier and more progressive time, with the Metal Rabbit more in charge of his own agenda.

One important aspect of the Snake year is that it favours personal development. Snake years are ideal for study, reflection and furthering knowledge, and many Metal Rabbits can benefit from this one either by extending a skill they have or taking up something new. This could be a project they set themselves, some research they decide to carry out or a local or online course they sign up for. Whatever they choose, by doing something definite, many will take great satisfaction from their activities and the benefits that will often follow on. A few Metal Rabbits may even delve into aspects of family history which could bring them into contact with distant relations or allow them to discover fascinating details about their past. The Snake year can certainly stimulate the Metal Rabbit's enquiring mind.

It also has a strong cultural edge and some Metal Rabbits may take the opportunity to visit museums, galleries and exhibitions. They will often be fascinated by the things they see. With travel favourably aspected, the Metal Rabbit may also be tempted to combine a holiday with visits to special attractions or places of interest. By following up his ideas, he can make this an enriching year.

The Metal Rabbit generally takes good care of himself, but if he feels he is lacking exercise or his diet is not sufficiently balanced, it would be worth him seeking advice and taking steps to remedy the situation. He could be introduced to disciplines such as *Tai Chi*, Pilates, yoga or some other form of exercise as a result, and such activities may not only benefit him but also, if he joins a class, bring considerable fun as well.

One of the Metal Rabbit's strengths is his ability to relate to people. Others generally feel at ease in his company, but this year there will be times when he will need to proceed with care. In particular, if a close friend has problems, he should think carefully about the best approach to take. Similarly, if he becomes involved in an awkward situation, he should keep the matter in perspective, check the facts and try to diffuse the problem through dialogue. He should remember that there are helplines and advice centres available if he feels these are appropriate. Fortunately most Metal Rabbits will escape the Snake year's trickier aspects, but nevertheless it would be worth the Metal Rabbit keeping his wits about him.

Despite these words of caution, the Snake year will contain some good social opportunities. Courses, interest groups or other activities the Metal Rabbit is involved with can often lead to meeting others. With travel favourably aspected, a holiday could also bring some fine social occasions. April, June, August and September are likely to see the most social activity.

The Metal Rabbit's home life will also be a source of much joy. In particular, he will be encouraged by the support and help he is given, especially concerning some of his decisions and projects. Whether these are work-related or involve other pursuits, his loved ones will often lend a helping hand and give good advice. The Snake year favours joint undertakings, and shared interests and household projects will go well. The year will also contain its highlights, including the possible marking of an academic or family success.

Many of the Metal Rabbits in work will have been involved in some stressful situations of late and affected by change. The Snake year will be a more settled time and give many a greater chance to focus on their responsibilities and use their talents to good effect. Many will remain with their present employer over the year, but for those who would prefer to move, perhaps to a position involving less commuting or a possible reduction in hours, as well as those currently looking for a position, the Snake year can present some interesting possibilities. Admittedly, these could involve switching to a different type of work, but what opens up could be a chance for the Metal Rabbit to use his abilities in new ways and this could present an interesting challenge. March, May to early July and November could see interesting developments.

The Metal Rabbit is usually careful in money matters and in view of the possibility of travel this year, together with plans for his home, he would do well to make allowance for his outgoings. He may also give assistance to another family member or have additional family expenses over the year. With good management, however, he will be satisfied with what he does and how he is able to help others.

Overall, the Year of the Snake can be a satisfying one for the Metal Rabbit. There will be good opportunities for him to develop his existing interests as well as to further his knowledge and skills. At work this can be a more fulfilling time, and while the Metal Rabbit may have concerns over someone close, generally he will be content with how the year develops and the benefits that many of his activities bring.

TIP FOR THE YEAR
Liaise with others. If you have concerns and would like advice or assistance, ask. With support and input, more will be possible. Also, enjoy your interests and look to further these in some way. Benefits will often follow on.

The Water Rabbit

The Water Rabbit is quietly ambitious. He proceeds without fuss but is very determined. In the Snake year he can look forward to making important progress as well as achieving certain long-held hopes. In this, his fiftieth year, he will not only be keen to get this new decade in his life off to a positive start but also to take some purposeful action towards his goals.

One area which will figure prominently will be his work situation. Although many Water Rabbits will have seen significant change in recent years, quite a few will still not be fully satisfied. Early on in the year, many will decide the time has now come to move their career to a new level. For those who are well established in a career, their reputation, contacts and in-depth experience can prove a great asset, and when promotion opportunities arise or they see a vacancy that interests them, they will be particularly strong candidates.

There will also be some Water Rabbits who are keen to move their career in a different direction and take on new challenges. For these Water Rabbits, as well as those currently seeking work, the Snake year can be one of important possibility. By considering the type of position .they would like and actively making enquiries, many will find an opening which will offer scope for further development. Sometimes this will involve retraining and readjustment, but these Water Rabbits will feel ready for change. Opportunities can arise at almost any time of the year, but March, May to early July and November could see key developments.

There will also be some Water Rabbits who decide to become self-employed during the year. Those who do so should take advantage of the advice and information available to them. With good support, they need not feel alone in their endeavour.

In addition to advancing his career, the Water Rabbit will often have other aspirations. These could include developing his interests and putting his knowledge to greater use. Whatever he would like to do, this is a year for action, and many Water Rabbits will be keen to make their fiftieth year special in some way.

Any who may have let their personal interests lapse recently or feel their lifestyle is not as balanced as it could be will find this an excellent year to address this. Allowing time for something they enjoy can be of great benefit. It could also be to the Water Rabbit's advantage to keep informed about what is available locally, including recreational facilities, courses, special interest groups and events and places to visit. By remaining aware, he can benefit from some interesting opportunities.

Travel is also favourably aspected and quite a few Water Rabbits will treat themselves to a special holiday to mark their fiftieth year. If there is somewhere specific they would like to visit, it would be worth making enquiries and investigating possibilities early on. Additional travel opportunities could occur unexpectedly, including invitations to visit others or a spur of the moment break. Snake years are full of interesting possibilities.

With all the travel and other plans and expenses the Water Rabbit will have, he would do well to keep a close watch on his financial situation and make advance provision for some of his outgoings. This can be an improved year financially, with work opportunities and the possibility of an additional sum of money, but it is still one for careful management.

The Water Rabbit will enjoy many of the social opportunities of the year and his interests will also bring him into contact with others. For the unattached, new friendships and romance can make their fiftieth year all the more special. April, June and August to early October could see the most social activity. However, while the Water Rabbit's social life will generally go well, Snake years can have their problem areas. The Water Rabbit may be concerned about rumour or gossip or the situation of a friend who is in difficulty. This may cause some anguish, but the Water Rabbit should keep the matter in perspective, check the facts, talk to those he trusts and, if relevant, consult advice centres. Support is there should he need it.

His domestic life will mean a great deal to him this year. In addition to the marking of his fiftieth birthday, there will be a lot to do and appreciate. Many Water Rabbits will decide to set about plans they have long had in mind, with a few even moving house. Others will decide to redecorate and make various improvements to their home. Where décor is concerned, their sense of style will be appreciated. Here again the Snake year can be productive and satisfying.

The Water Rabbit will also do a lot to support loved ones during the year and his advice, interest and affection will be valued. The more measured pace of the Snake year will allow him to spend more time with those around him, and domestically this can be a full and positive year.

Overall, the Water Rabbit will have much in his favour in 2013, and by acting determinedly, he can make important headway, both in his work situation and his personal interests. His home life also promises special times, and although some matters may concern him, possibly relating to a friend, with support, resolve and his own carefully thought through approach, a lot will go well and his fiftieth year will be a time of progress and positive change.

TIP FOR THE YEAR
Be resolute and purposeful and take action. This way you will be setting important wheels in motion and allowing good possibilities to open up. Also, set aside time for activities you enjoy. This is your fiftieth year and you can help make it special.

The Wood Rabbit
This is an encouraging year for the Wood Rabbit and with focus and persistence he can look forward to making good progress.

At work, many Wood Rabbits will have reached an interesting juncture. Although they will have experienced considerable change in recent years, many will now be keen to make more of particular strengths and move forward in their career.

All Wood Rabbits should take advantage of any training that is available to them as well as keep up to date with developments in their industry. This way they will not only be helping their present situation but also strengthening their prospects. They will also be helped by raising their profile in some way. This may mean assisting with initiatives where they work or, if appropriate, joining a professional body and networking more. Whatever they do, they will benefit from allowing others to see more of their capabilities. Any extra effort the Wood Rabbit puts in this year will be noticed *and* to his advantage.

During the year many Wood Rabbits will also benefit from staff movements in their current place of work. In particular, as senior colleagues move on, promotion opportunities could arise and the Wood Rabbit could find himself well placed to apply. Those who work for a large organization could also benefit from vacancies in other sections. It would be worth these Wood Rabbits keeping themselves informed and acting swiftly when a suitable opening occurs.

This also applies to those seeking work. Although the job-seeking process can be disheartening, by keeping alert for vacancies and staying in regular contact with employment agencies, many Wood Rabbits will be able to secure a position that can be a base on which to build in the future. This is a year which rewards steady, persistent effort and March, May, June and November could see encouraging developments.

The progress many Wood Rabbits make at work can also lead to a rise in income. However, to benefit fully, the Wood Rabbit will need to remain disciplined. With his existing commitments and the hopes he has for home and family, he needs to retain careful control over his outgoings and, where possible, make early provision for more expensive plans.

His domestic life will also see much activity and good co-operation will be needed. Here the Wood Rabbit's organizational abilities will be appreciated. Those close to him will also often seek out his advice, possibly over educational, work or more personal matters, and the Wood Rabbit will be glad to assist. He will value the close rapport he has with his family and the activities all can share. A few Wood Rabbits may also decide to move this year to accommodation which better meets their requirements. Again, this is a year when some of the Wood Rabbit's hopes and plans can be realized.

With his considerable personal skills, the Wood Rabbit knows a great many people and over the year will enjoy a variety of social occasions. His work situation can also lead to meeting others and making some important new friends and contacts. April, June, August and September will see the most social activity. However, in the Snake year the Wood Rabbit needs to keep alert. Sometimes a petty jealousy, rumour or misapprehension could concern him or he could find himself worrying about a friend's situation. At such times, he should think carefully about the best approach to take and, if applicable, seek the advice of someone he can trust. Snake years can sometimes pose tricky friendship or social issues and the Wood Rabbit needs to tread carefully and mindfully.

Throughout the year, although the Wood Rabbit will have many demands on his time, it is also important that he does not neglect his own interests or recreational pursuits. These can not only help keep his lifestyle in balance but sometimes give him the benefit of additional exercise. Some Wood Rabbits may decide on a personal project or challenge for the year and by setting regular time aside for this, they will draw considerable satisfaction from how their skills and ideas evolve.

Overall, the Snake year can be a significant one for the Wood Rabbit. By following up opportunities, he will be able to further his position and use his strengths to good effect. Personal interests and travel can also bring pleasure, although some friendships and social situations will require care. The Wood Rabbit's home life promises to be busy, with much to attend to but also some special times to enjoy. A generally positive and pleasing year.

TIP FOR THE YEAR
Set your plans into motion. You have much in your favour this year and determined effort can produce some good results.

The Fire Rabbit

This will be a significant year for the Fire Rabbit, and as it begins, he may well sense his fortunes are on the turn. After the changes and decisions he may have faced in recent years, he will now have more chance to carry out his plans and realize his aims. His determination and personal skills can help make this a fulfilling time.

For Fire Rabbits with a partner, this can be a busy and pleasing year. Quite a few will decide to move and a lot of their free time will be spent looking for a home and then setting it up as they want. For these Fire Rabbits, this can be an exciting time, especially as choices are considered, purchases made and plans take shape. Some may also start a family and the Snake year will see many plans and hopes come to fruition.

For the unattached Fire Rabbit, an existing friendship could become more meaningful or he could meet someone new. Fire Rabbits who have had some personal difficulty in recent years will now feel able to move ahead and the Snake year will offer brighter prospects. For relationships and romance, this can be a significant year, with many Fire Rabbits enjoying special developments.

With his genial and outgoing nature, the Fire Rabbit attaches great importance to his social life and will again enjoy going out and spending time with his friends. Interests he shares with others can often be a lot of fun and much mutual support can also be given over the year. Some Fire Rabbits may also decide to join an interest group or professional organization and this can again bring them into contact with others. April, June and August to early October could see the most social activity.

However, while the Fire Rabbit's personal and social life can be a source of much happiness, he will still need to keep his wits about him. A rumour, some gossip or a friend's problem may place him in a dilemma. At such times the Fire Rabbit should check the facts and think carefully over the best approach to take, seeking advice when necessary. In dealing with any delicate situation, he should avoid rush and pay heed to his instincts. Fortunately the more awkward aspects of the year will generally be short-lived, but the Fire Rabbit does need to be alert to potential problems and avoid placing himself in a situation which could rebound on him.

A more positively aspected area is travel and the Fire Rabbit will often enjoy going away and visiting places that are new to him and/or have long appealed to him. Sometimes he may be able to combine his travels with a special event. Some Fire Rabbits may also decide to go away on a whim, perhaps taking advantage of a last-minute travel opportunity. There could be further travel chances late on in the Snake year.

The Fire Rabbit is blessed with an enquiring mind and the Snake year will give him the chance to add to his knowledge and skills. Whether related to his work or his personal interests, possibilities can open up for him. For Fire Rabbits who have creative aspirations, this is an excellent year to promote what they do. Snake years favour creativity and self-expression and the Fire Rabbit's talents can be a source of pleasure and benefit.

The Snake year can also mark an interesting point in the Fire Rabbit's career. For Fire Rabbits who are already established in a certain line of work, there will be good chances to move ahead, and many will take on responsibilities they have been working towards for some time, either through being promoted where they are or moving to a different employer. The Snake year can bring some ideal opportunities, but the Fire Rabbit should act quickly when they arise. Their interest, reputation and experience will be important factors in their favour.

For Fire Rabbits who have been drifting recently and feeling unfulfilled, as well as those seeking work, the Snake year can again hold important developments. By keeping alert and emphasizing their experience and strengths to perspective employers, many will secure a position which could introduce them to a new type of work. This can sometimes represent considerable change, but also bring a new opportunity with the potential for development in the future. March, May to early July and November could see encouraging developments.

The headway the Fire Rabbit makes at work can also lead to an increase in income, but with his many outgoings, he will need to keep watch on spending and make provision for some of his plans. Should he enter into any major agreement he should check the terms and implications and, where appropriate, seek professional guidance. This is a year for discipline, diligence and good planning.

In general, the Year of the Snake can be a pleasing and significant one for the Fire Rabbit. His personal life is especially favourably aspected, with love, happiness and the realization of some hopes often helping to make this a special time. The Snake year will also encourage the Fire Rabbit to make more of himself. Whether in his work or his personal interests, this is a year for moving forward.

TIP FOR THE YEAR
Be open to opportunity and make the most of your ideas. By being active and willing, you can make this a positive and pleasing year. Use it well, for you can do well.

The Earth Rabbit

The element of Earth helps to reinforce a sign's practical qualities, and this is especially true for the Earth Rabbit. Keen to use his time well, he sets about his activities with focus. He is disciplined and resourceful and in the Snake year he will get to achieve and enjoy a great deal.

For Earth Rabbits born in 1939, this can be an especially rewarding time. Many will have particular ideas in mind for the next 12 months and if they discuss these with their loved ones, they can find a lot will come to fruition.

Their plans can concern several aspects of their life. Some Earth Rabbits will be keen to move to accommodation that better suits their requirements. These Earth Rabbits should allow ample time to view possible new homes and not make their decision until they are fully satisfied. Throughout the process they should consult those close to them, as well as professionals who are able to advise. Moving to a new home will take time and effort, but once settled, these Earth Rabbits will fully appreciate the benefits.

As always, the Earth Rabbit will take a keen interest in the activities of family members and during the year can look forward to some special family occasions. Whether celebrating the birth of a great-grandchild, an academic success or wedding, he will take pride in his loved ones. Domestically, this can be a busy and important year and the close bond the Earth Rabbit has with certain family members will mean a lot to him.

The Earth Rabbit will also take pleasure in the way he is able to use certain skills over the year. Those who are creatively or artistically inclined will find some of their activities going especially well. Here the Earth Rabbit's capacity for discovering the new and for experimenting will be undiminished.

The Earth Rabbit should also aim to keep himself informed about what is happening in his vicinity. There may be an activity or interest group he could join, a course that appeals to him or a special event he might enjoy. For those who move in particular, finding out about what is available can be a good way to meet others and get involved in something new. The Snake year offers variety and possibility.

Travel, too, is favourably aspected and many Earth Rabbits will enjoy the holidays they have carefully planned. With the Snake year's emphasis on culture, some may also decide to visit places of interest, exhibitions or events over the year and will appreciate the chance to see some often remarkable things.

In a great many of his activities the Earth Rabbit will enjoy the support of those around him. However, as is the way with Snake years, problems can arise. In particular the situation of a friend may worry the Earth Rabbit or a difference of opinion cause concern. At such times, the Earth Rabbit should be guided by instinct and, where necessary, seek advice.

He will also need to proceed carefully in financial matters. In view of his travel plans, a possible house move, and his other obligations and interests, he should watch his outgoings and make advance provision for plans and more major purchases.

For Earth Rabbits born in 1999, important opportunities can also open up over the year, including chances to study new subjects, learn additional skills or take existing interests further. These Earth Rabbits' resourceful nature will stand them in good stead and by making the most of their situation, they can not only gain personally but also find what they do leading on to other possibilities. This is a year to be open to opportunity and willing to try. The progress these Earth Rabbits feel they are making can also help build their confidence.

The young Earth Rabbit will also value the support of his close circle of friends over the year. However, while friendships will often work out well, problems can sometimes arise. If they do, the Earth Rabbit should try to deal with them at the time and ideally come to an agreement, understanding or compromise. Without care, rumours and differences of opinion can be upsetting. Only a minority of Earth Rabbits will be affected, but this is something the Earth Rabbit should bear in mind, and should the situation warrant it, he should seek advice.

For all Earth Rabbits, whether born in 1939 or 1999, the Snake year is filled with possibility. It is a time to act on hopes and plans and make the most of chances. By using his strengths to advantage, the Earth Rabbit will be pleased with many of the results he obtains, especially concerning his personal interests. On a personal level, he will enjoy good support and will be pleased with how many of his domestic plans proceed. Sometimes certain friendships may need special care, but generally this is a positive year and the Earth Rabbit will be satisfied with how it develops.

TIP FOR THE YEAR

Develop your strengths. Particularly where personal interests are concerned, this is a year to take what you do to a new level and set yourself interesting activities and projects. Young Earth Rabbit, be disciplined in your studying. What you undertake this year can be an important foundation on which to build in the future.

FAMOUS RABBITS

Margaret Atwood, Drew Barrymore, David Beckham, Harry Belafonte, Pope Benedict XVI, Ingrid Bergman, St Bernadette, Jeff Bezos, Kathryn Bigelow, Demián Bichir, Gordon Brown, Michael Bublé, Nicolas Cage, Lewis Carroll, Fidel Castro, John Cleese, Confucius, Marie Curie, Johnny Depp, Novak Djokovic, Albert Einstein, George Eliot, W. C. Fields, James Fox, Sir David Frost, Cary Grant, Ashley Greene, Edvard Grieg, Oliver Hardy, Seamus Heaney, Tommy Hilfiger, Bob Hope, Whitney Houston, Helen Hunt, John Hurt, Anjelica Huston, Chrissie Hynde, Enrique Inglesias, Henry James, Sir David Jason, Angelina Jolie, Michael Jordan, Michael Keaton, John Keats, Enda Kenny, Lisa Kudrow, Gina Lollobrigida, George Michael, Sir Roger Moore, Andrew Murray, Mike Myers, Brigitte Nielsen, Graham Norton, Michelle Obama, Jamie Oliver, George Orwell, Sarah Palin, Edith Piaf, Brad Pitt, Sidney Poitier, Romano Prodi, Ken Russell, Elisabeth Schwarzkopf, Neil Sedaka, Jane Seymour, Maria Sharapova, Neil Simon, Frank Sinatra, Sting, Quentin Tarantino, J. R. R. Tolkien, KT Tunstall, Tina Turner, Luther Vandross, Sebastian Vettel, Queen Victoria, Muddy Waters, Orson Welles, Hayley Westenra, Walt Whitman, Robin Williams, Kate Winslet, Tiger Woods.

3 FEBRUARY 1916 〜 22 JANUARY 1917   *Fire Dragon*

23 JANUARY 1928 〜 9 FEBRUARY 1929   *Earth Dragon*

8 FEBRUARY 1940 〜 26 JANUARY 1941   *Metal Dragon*

27 JANUARY 1952 〜 13 FEBRUARY 1953   *Water Dragon*

13 FEBRUARY 1964 〜 1 FEBRUARY 1965   *Wood Dragon*

31 JANUARY 1976 〜 17 FEBRUARY 1977   *Fire Dragon*

17 FEBRUARY 1988 〜 5 FEBRUARY 1989   *Earth Dragon*

5 FEBRUARY 2000 〜 23 JANUARY 2001   *Metal Dragon*

23 JANUARY 2012 〜 9 FEBRUARY 2013   *Water Dragon*

THE
DRAGON

THE PERSONALITY OF
THE DRAGON

I like giving things a go.
Sometimes I succeed,
sometimes I fail.
Sometimes the unexpected happens.
But it is the giving things a go
and the stepping forward
that make life so interesting.

The Dragon is born under the sign of luck. He is a proud and lively character and has a tremendous amount of self-confidence. He is also highly intelligent and very quick to take advantage of any opportunity. He is ambitious and determined and will do well in practically anything he attempts. He is also something of a perfectionist and will always try to maintain the high standards he sets himself.

The Dragon does not suffer fools gladly and will be quick to criticize anyone or anything that displeases him. He can be blunt and forthright in his views and is certainly not renowned for being either tactful or diplomatic. He does, however, often take people at their word and can occasionally be rather gullible. If he ever feels that his trust has been abused or his dignity wounded, he can sometimes become very bitter and it will take him a long time to forgive and forget.

The Dragon is usually very outgoing and is particularly adept at attracting attention and publicity. He enjoys being in the limelight and is often at his best when he is confronted by a difficult problem or tense situation. In some respects he is a showman and he rarely lacks an audience. His views are highly valued and he invariably has something interesting – and sometimes controversial – to say.

He also has considerable energy and is often prepared to work long and unsocial hours in order to achieve what he wants. He can, however, be rather impulsive and does not always consider the consequences of his actions. He also has a tendency to live for the moment and there is nothing that riles him more than to be kept waiting. The Dragon hates delay and can get extremely impatient and irritable over even the smallest of hold-ups.

The Dragon has an enormous faith in his abilities, but he does run the risk of becoming over-confident and unless he is careful he can sometimes make grave errors of judgement. While this may prove disastrous at the time, he does have the tenacity and ability to bounce back and pick up the pieces again.

The Dragon has such an assertive personality, so much willpower and such a desire to succeed that he will often reach the top of his chosen profession. He has considerable leadership qualities and will do well in positions where he can put his own ideas and policies into practice. He is usually successful in politics, show business, as the manager of his own department or business, and in any job that brings him into contact with the media.

The Dragon relies a tremendous amount on his own judgement and can be scornful of other people's advice. He likes to feel self-sufficient and there are many Dragons who cherish their independence to such a degree that they prefer to remain single throughout their lives. However, the Dragon will often have numerous admirers and many will be attracted by his flamboyant personality and striking looks. If he does marry, he will usually marry young, and will find himself particularly well suited to those born under the signs of the Snake, Rat, Monkey and Rooster. He will also find that the Rabbit, Pig, Horse and Goat make ideal companions and will readily join in with many of his escapades. Two Dragons will also get on well together, as they will understand each other, but the Dragon may not find things so easy with the Ox and Dog, as both will be critical of his impulsive and somewhat extrovert manner. He will also find it difficult to form an alliance with the Tiger, for the Tiger, like the Dragon, tends to speak his mind, is very strong-willed and likes to take the lead.

The female Dragon knows what she wants in life and sets about everything she does in a determined and positive manner. No job is too small for her and she is often prepared to work extremely hard to secure her objectives. She is immensely practical and somewhat liberated. She hates being bound by routine and petty restrictions and likes to have sufficient freedom to go off and do what she wants to do. She will keep her house tidy, but is not one for spending hours on housework – there are far too many other things that she prefers to do. Like her male counterpart, she has a tendency to speak her mind.

The Dragon usually has many interests and enjoys sport and other outdoor activities. He also likes to travel and often prefers to visit places that are off the beaten track rather than head for popular tourist destinations. He has a very adventurous streak in him and providing his financial circumstances permit – and the Dragon is usually sensible with his money – he will travel considerable distances during his lifetime.

The Dragon is a very flamboyant character and while he can be demanding of others and in his early years rather precocious, he will have many friends and will nearly always be the centre of attention. He has charisma and so much confidence that he can often become a source of inspiration to others. In China he is the leader of the carnival and he is also blessed with an inordinate share of luck.

THE FIVE DIFFERENT TYPES OF DRAGON

In addition to the 12 signs of the Chinese zodiac there are five elements and these have a strengthening or moderating influence on the signs. The effects of the five elements on the Dragon are described below, together with the years in which they were exercising their influence. Therefore Dragons born in 1940 and 2000 are Metal Dragons, Dragons born in 1952 and 2012 are Water Dragons, and so on.

Metal Dragon: 1940, 2000

This Dragon is very strong-willed and has a particularly forceful personality. He is energetic, ambitious and tries to be scrupulous in his dealings with others. He can also be blunt and to the point and usually has no hesitation in speaking his mind. If people disagree with him or are not prepared to co-operate, he is more than happy to go his own way. He usually has very high moral values and is held in great esteem by his friends and colleagues.

Water Dragon: 1952, 2012

This Dragon is friendly, easy-going and intelligent. He is quick-witted and rarely lets an opportunity slip by. However, he is not as impatient as some of the other types of Dragon and is prepared to wait for results rather than expect everything to happen at once. He has an understanding nature and is willing to share his ideas and co-operate with others. His main failing is a tendency to jump from one thing to another rather than concentrate on the job in hand. He has a good sense of humour and is an effective speaker.

Wood Dragon: 1964

The Wood Dragon is practical, imaginative and inquisitive. He loves delving into all manner of subjects and can quite often come up with some highly original ideas. He is a thinker and a doer and has the drive and commitment to put many of his ideas into practice. He is more diplomatic than some of the other types of Dragon and has a good sense of humour. He is very astute in business matters and can also be most generous.

Fire Dragon: 1916, 1976

This Dragon is ambitious, articulate and has a tremendous desire to succeed. He is a hard and conscientious worker and is often admired for his integrity and forthright nature. He is very strong-willed and has considerable leadership qualities. He can, however, rely a bit too much on his own judgement and fail to take into account the views and feelings of others. He can also be rather aloof and it would certainly be in his own interests to let others join in more with his various activities. He usually enjoys music, literature and the arts.

Earth Dragon: 1928, 1988

The Earth Dragon tends to be quieter and more reflective than some of the other types of Dragon. He has a wide variety of interests and is keenly aware of what is going on around him. He also has clear objectives and usually has no problems in obtaining support and backing for any of his ventures. He is very astute in financial matters and often able to accumulate considerable wealth. He is a good organizer, although he can at times be rather bureaucratic and fussy. He mixes well with others and has a large circle of friends.

PROSPECTS FOR THE DRAGON IN 2013

The Year of the Dragon (23 January 2012–9 February 2013) is a promising one for the Dragon himself and the remaining months will be busy and interesting.

In his home life the Dragon will see a great deal happening. Changes may be taking place in the lives of those around him and plans may need adjusting. Here good co-operation will help, as will some flexibility when making arrangements. Loved ones will often seek out the Dragon's opinions on certain matters, and his support may mean more than he may realize.

The closing months of the year will also see an increase in social activity for many Dragons. For the unattached, affairs of the heart could bring added excitement to the year's end.

In work matters too this can be a busy time, with many Dragons facing an increased workload. However, by focusing on what needs to be done and seizing the chance to display and develop their skills, they can do their standing considerable good. Those seeking work should keep alert. September and October could see some important opportunities.

The Dragon likes to keep busy and in the closing months of his own year he will certainly have a lot to do. To ease the pressure, he should stick to his priorities and resist the temptation to spread his energies too widely. By using his time well, he can enjoy a rewarding conclusion to his own year.

The Year of the Snake begins on 10 February and can be a successful one for the Dragon. It will give him a chance to build on recent activities and bring interesting new developments.

One of the Dragon's strengths is his willingness to be active and involved. He is not one to hold back and whenever he has ideas he wants to try or sees opportunities that interest him, he is prepared to go forward and see what happens. His keen approach can reward him well this year.

At work many Dragons will have the opportunity to build on their recent experience. Some may be asked to take on a more specialist role or concentrate on new initiatives, while others will be well placed for promotion. During the year the Dragon's special talents will often be recognized and many Dragons will make impressive headway.

The majority of Dragons will remain in their existing area of work. However for those who are keen to make a change or are seeking work, the Snake year can open up some important opportunities. By considering different ways in which they could use their experience, many could identify new types of work to put in for. February, April, May and November could see some good opportunities, but throughout the year the Dragon should keep alert and be quick to act should anything interest him. If certain applications do not go his way, he should not be discouraged. In this interesting year, success can come in curious ways and sometimes on the back of a disappointment.

Another benefit of the year will be the chances the Dragon will have to extend his capabilities. Often these will come as a result of new duties he takes on, but if he is offered training or is eligible for retraining or refresher courses, he should take full advantage of this. By keeping his skills up to date and acquiring new ones, he can improve both his current situation and his future prospects.

This also applies to his personal interests. Some Dragons may decide to learn a new skill, enrol on a course or gain a further qualification. This is an excellent year for personal growth and the Dragon will often be inspired by what he sets out to do.

His progress at work can help financially and many Dragons will enjoy an increase in earnings over the year. Some may also find an interest or an enterprising idea supplementing their means. However, the Dragon should manage his spending well, otherwise anything extra could be absorbed in everyday spending and the benefits not always felt. Good budgeting will help. Also, by keeping alert for opportunities, the Dragon could be fortunate in making certain acquisitions at a favourable price. Snake years do have an element of luck about them.

With his wide interests and outgoing personality, the Dragon knows a great many people and over the year will enjoy regular contact with his friends. Developments in his work and interests can also introduce him to new people and he will get on particularly well with some of those he meets. March, April, September and December will see the most social activity.

For Dragons hoping for or just starting a romance, this is a year for mindfulness. For a relationship to develop and strengthen, the Dragon will need to devote care and attention to it. Fortunately, most Dragons recognize the importance of nurturing relationships, but this is no time for inattention or taking the affection of another person for granted. Dragons, enjoy the romantic opportunities of the year, but do be mindful.

This need for awareness also applies to the Dragon's home life. In view of his many commitments, he does need to strike a sensible lifestyle balance and make sure quality time with his loved ones does not suffer. To help, when projects need tackling or decisions taking, the Dragon should share these rather than do too much single-handed.

He would also find it helpful to be forthcoming about his own activities and watch his sometimes independent-minded tendencies. Snake years do call for a certain mindfulness. However, for the most part the Dragon's home life will go well and he will enjoy carrying out some of his plans and some of the more spontaneous occasions of the year.

Overall, the Year of the Snake can be a rewarding one for the Dragon, especially as it will give him a greater chance to develop ideas and skills. With his busy lifestyle, he will need to give time and attention to those close to him, but provided he keeps his lifestyle in balance, this can be a pleasing and fulfilling year.

The Metal Dragon

This can be an interesting year for the Metal Dragon but the key message is to remain open-minded. Although the Metal Dragon may have definite ideas about his plans and intentions, he will need to show some flexibility and make the most of what arises. Provided he does not close his mind to possibilities, however, he can get a lot from the year.

For Metal Dragons born in 1940, the Snake year will bring the chance to pursue a range of different ideas. In his home, the more senior Metal Dragon could decide on projects and purchases that bring additional comforts or make certain tasks easier. Some may also decide to tidy up certain areas, perhaps thinning out storage areas or tending their garden. For domestic tasks, this can be a satisfying year, with the Metal Dragon and his loved ones appreciating the benefits of what is undertaken. However, where purchases are concerned, the Metal Dragon should take the time to compare options. It is important he does not remain wedded to his original idea if it turns out that something more suitable, and in some cases more economical, is available.

In setting about his activities, the Metal Dragon should also discuss his ideas with his loved ones. With additional help, more will be accomplished and better results obtained.

In addition to the practical undertakings of the year, the Metal Dragon will enjoy following the activities of younger family members. Not only will he be proud of their accomplishments but if he feels a close relation is struggling, some support or words of understanding will be particularly appreciated. Family members value the Metal Dragon's judgement.

There will also be opportunities for the Metal Dragon to travel during the year and while he may particularly delight in planning a holiday, he should also be open to some of the year's more spontaneous occasions. Whether taking advantage of a last-minute travel offer or a surprise invitation, he should make the most of the chances presented to him, even if some arise with little warning.

Another favourably aspected area concerns the Metal Dragon's personal interests. Not only will he continue to enjoy these, but he may have the chance to develop them further, perhaps by trying a different approach or buying new equipment. This can add new meaning to his activities. A few Metal Dragons may also decide to take up a new recreational pursuit. For those keen to improve their level of fitness, the gentle movements of *Tai Chi* may be worth considering.

The Metal Dragon's activities can also bring him into contact with others, and Metal Dragons who are members of a local activity or community group, or who decide to join one, will particularly enjoy the chance to be involved. By keeping informed about what is going on in his locality and maintaining regular contact with his friends, the Metal Dragon will often have things to look forward to. March to early May, September and December will see the most social activity.

Many Metal Dragons can also look forward to some positive financial developments this year. These could come through a gift, a maturing policy or an additional payment of some kind. In view of the plans and purchases the Metal Dragon will have in mind, anything extra could prove helpful. His eye for a good buy will also serve him well and he could be especially pleased with one of his more unusual purchases of the year.

For Metal Dragons born in 2000, the Snake year can again open up interesting possibilities. In his education, as the young Metal Dragon develops more skills, he will find he is able to do more, and whether in computing, the arts, sport or another sphere of interest, he should take advantage of the facilities available. It is also important that he keeps an open mind. Should a new subject or activity prove initially difficult, he should not give up too easily. It is by being stretched and overcoming difficulties that he will learn more. The Snake year requires a willing and determined approach.

The young Metal Dragon's personal interests can also develop well. Here again he should take advantage of the encouragement and instruction available to him as well as take his own ideas forward. For many, this can be an interesting time.

The Metal Dragon will enjoy the company of his friends over the year and enjoy making new ones. However, a word of warning: sometimes the young Metal Dragon's exuberance can lead to high jinks or a difference of opinion. At such times, he needs to be careful. This may be a good year, but it is not one for risk. Young Metal Dragons, do take note.

Overall, the Year of the Snake will contain many interesting possibilities for all Metal Dragons, whether born in 1940 or 2000. By proceeding with their ideas and seizing their opportunities, they will be pleased with what they are able to do. Throughout the year, the Metal Dragon will need to be flexible, but with an accommodating and willing attitude, he can make this a pleasing year and also benefit from moments of good fortune.

TIP FOR THE YEAR

Be active, interested and involved. Whether in your home and social life, your local community or, for the younger Metal Dragon, place of learning, the greater your participation, the more satisfaction and potential benefit you are likely to get. You have much to offer this year, but the initiative rests with you.

The Water Dragon

This can be a constructive year for the Water Dragon and with a positive approach, he can achieve a great deal.

One of the virtues of the Water Dragon is his ability to look ahead and work steadily towards the things he wants.

He is thorough and persistent and his strengths will serve him well this year.

For Water Dragons in work, this can be an important time. With the experience these Water Dragons will have built up, not only will many take on greater responsibilities this year but they will also have more chance to use their judgement and initiative. Snake years do offer scope and opportunity, and many Water Dragons will appreciate this.

Another factor in the Water Dragon's favour will be the good working relations he enjoys with those around him, with his colleagues giving good support and valuing his expertise.

The majority of Water Dragons will remain with their present employer over the year, but there will be some who will be hoping to reduce their commitments or just do something different. For these Water Dragons, as well as those seeking work, the Snake year can bring interesting developments. Obtaining a new position will require considerable effort, but here the Water Dragon's special talents can come into play. By keeping alert, investigating possibilities and making an extra effort with applications and at interview, his initiative can shine through, and often win through too. Sometimes what he is offered will only be temporary, but it will give the Water Dragon the chance to gain experience in another sphere and may lead on to something else. February, April, May and November could see encouraging developments, but generally the Water Dragon's skills, personality and drive can lead to opportunities throughout the year.

The progress he makes at work can help financially and many Water Dragons will enjoy some good fortune as well, possibly a gift or bonus payment. Some may also find ways to put an interest to profitable use. However, while the aspects are encouraging, the Water Dragon will need to manage his finances well and, if possible, use any upturn to reduce borrowings as well as make provision for forthcoming plans. Careful financial management can make a big difference this year.

The Water Dragon possesses an enquiring mind and not only will he take pleasure in pursuing various interests during the year but will often be tempted to do more, either by setting himself a new project or trying out something different. By following up his ideas, seizing his opportunities and using his time well, he will appreciate the way many of his activities develop.

His interests can also lead to some pleasing social occasions. As well as attending events in his area, he may choose to base a holiday around a particular interest.

A lot that he does over the year may have a good social element and he will once again appreciate the support of his friends. March, April, September, late November and December will see the most social activity. However while a lot will go well, any Water Dragon enjoying the early stages of romance should allow time to nurture this rather than rush or take another person's feelings for granted.

In the Water Dragon's home life it is also important that he remains attentive and gives time to his loved ones. Sometimes a busy work schedule can eat into home life and possibly cause difficulty. With awareness and good lifestyle balance, this can be avoided, but it is something all Water Dragons need to be conscious of during the year.

This warning apart, the Water Dragon can look forward to many pleasing family occasions, and those who are grandparents will enjoy the special bond with their grandchildren. Domestically, many Water Dragons will also enjoy carrying out projects they have been considering for some time. This can be a constructive time, and the more undertakings that can be carried out jointly, the better.

Overall, the Year of the Snake can be a pleasing one for the Water Dragon and his enthusiasm, skills and good sense can make it a constructive one too. Fortune in 2013 will very much favour the active and enterprising.

TIP FOR THE YEAR
This can be a full and satisfying year, but do keep your lifestyle in balance. Being too preoccupied could cause problems. Take note and be mindful. Nevertheless, work towards your goals with determination. You can obtain some fine results this year.

The Wood Dragon
The Wood Dragon is very adept at gauging situations and his talents will prove especially useful this year. During it, he can fare well and enjoy some good opportunities.

At work, many Wood Dragons will have the chance to consolidate their position, focus on their objectives and build on their experience. As the year progresses, new challenges can be set and these will also give the Wood Dragon opportunity to both develop and display his skills.

All Wood Dragons, whether new to their present role or more established, should take full advantage of any training offered as well as keep informed about developments in their industry. By keeping up to date, the Wood Dragon will not only be helping his present situation but can sometimes be alerted to future possibilities. With his ability to forge good working relations, he should also make the most of any chances to network. By being active and raising his profile, he can do his prospects a lot of good.

Most Wood Dragons will remain with their present employer over the year and make steady progress, but for those who feel unfulfilled or are seeking work, the Snake year can be significant. Although their quest may be difficult, the Wood Dragon's determination and initiative will help them win through. To help with applications, they should find out more about the employer and duties involved and emphasize any relevant experience they have. Interest, initiative and involvement will be key factors this year. February, April, May and November could see encouraging developments.

The Snake year can be a promising one financially, and by managing his situation well, the Wood Dragon will be able to go ahead with many of his plans. When he has specific purchases in mind, he should ask questions about suitability as well as compare terms. By being thorough, he can not only make more appropriate choices but also benefit from some attractive offers. He may also be able to supplement his earnings by putting an interest or skill to good use. The Snake year can provide good openings for the more entrepreneurial Wood Dragon.

Another encouraging feature of the year will be the opportunities the Wood Dragon will have to further his knowledge and skills. If he feels that another qualification or skill would help him to move forward, he should consider courses or study programmes. Similarly, if he is keen to extend his personal interests in some way or try something different, this is an excellent year to set time aside to do this. Snake years are constructive and encouraging.

The Wood Dragon should also make the most of his social opportunities. Interest-related events (especially those held locally) could particularly appeal, and any Wood Dragon who would welcome a more active social life would find it worth joining a group of enthusiasts. However, while the Wood Dragon will enjoy positive relations with many people, for those enjoying the early stages of romance, extra care and attention would be wise. To make assumptions or build high hopes early on could lead to disappointment. In the Snake year it is better for relationships to evolve in their own way. Romance should not be rushed.

The Wood Dragon's home life will see much activity and his good sense and understanding will be especially valued. There will be times when he may despair over all that is being asked of him, but being the good organizer he is, by concentrating on priorities, he will often be surprised at how many things he has successfully dealt with. There will also be quite a few family highlights, and whether enjoying special occasions with his loved ones, shared interests or travel, the Wood Dragon can find this a full and varied year.

Overall, this can be a satisfying year for the Wood Dragon. Whether at work or pursuing his personal interests, he will often find greater fulfilment in what he does.

On a personal level, this will be a busy time, with the Wood Dragon's qualities appreciated by those around him.

Seize your opportunities. A positive approach can bring considerable benefit and sometimes lead on to other possibilities. A pleasing and potentially rewarding year.

The Fire Dragon

With his ideas, aspirations and resolve, the Fire Dragon tends to be forward looking and his prospects for the Snake year are encouraging. Not only will he be able to build on recent successes but he will also have more chance to put his strengths to good use. A lot is set to go in his favour in 2013.

Many Fire Dragons will have seen great changes in their work situation in recent years. There will have been highs and lows, successes as well as some bitter disappointments. However, the Fire Dragon will have learned a great deal, both about his own capabilities and about how to deal with various situations. The Snake year will give him an excellent chance to build on this experience and make important headway.

Fire Dragons who are established in a certain type of work may be encouraged to take their skills further and be trained for a greater role. Also, as senior positions become available, the Fire Dragon will often find his in-house experience a great asset, and may take his career to a new level. The Snake year favours commitment and during it the Fire Dragon's capabilities can bring him some well-deserved success.

Fire Dragons who are keen to move on from their current work situation and those seeking work will find that securing a new position can be difficult. Here again, however, the Fire Dragon's persistence and other qualities can deliver. Any new position will require effort and sometimes readjustment, but the Snake year can open significant doors. Also, when given a chance, the Fire Dragon may not only quickly establish himself in a new place of work but also find it has more potential than he originally thought. For Fire Dragons who change their work early on in the year, further opportunities could arise late in 2013 or early 2014. Work-wise, this is an encouraging time, with February, April to early June and November being important months.

The Fire Dragon will also be helped by the good working relations he has with many people and over the year he should not only be an active member of any team but also use any chances to network and generally raise his profile. The effort he makes now can help both his present and future situation.

His progress at work can also lead to an increase in income and some Fire Dragons will find ways to supplement this through an interest or enterprising idea. Again the Fire Dragon's efforts this year can reward him well, but he should still keep careful control over his budget. Certain amounts will need to be set aside for his current commitments and his general spending should be watched. However, if there is something specific the Fire Dragon wants, by making enquiries and keeping alert, he could secure it on especially favourable terms. His canny sense can serve him well this year.

Although the Fire Dragon will have many demands on his time, it is important that he sets some time aside for recreation and, if sedentary for much of the day, additional exercise. Some Fire Dragons may also find it helpful to give consideration to the quality of their diet. For the Fire Dragon to be at his best this year, he does need to give some attention to his well-being.

He should also make sure his personal interests do not suffer due to other commitments. These provide a welcome contrast to his other activities and are good ways for him to keep his lifestyle in balance. Some can also have a good social element and give him a chance to spend time with friends and other enthusiasts. Any Fire Dragons who have let their interests lapse in recent times should aim to rectify this. Similarly, if the Fire Dragon sees something new that appeals to him, he should follow it up. A major benefit of the Snake year is that the Fire Dragon's actions during it can add to the quality of his life *and* be to his future benefit.

The Fire Dragon will again appreciate the social opportunities of the year and the support and advice of those around him. There will be good opportunities to get to know others during the year, and new contacts, friends and acquaintances will often prove helpful. However, for Fire Dragons who find romance, time and care will be needed. Snake years are not always easy for affairs of the heart, and relationships need to be nurtured.

The Fire Dragon's home life will see much activity, and with possible changes in the work situation and routines of family members, adjustments could be needed. Willingness to help and, at busy times, increased understanding can make an important difference. Throughout the year, family members will particularly value the Fire Dragon's thoughts and assistance as well as his ability to attend to a great many things.

Busy through the year will often be, there will also be a great deal to appreciate. Whether carrying out domestic projects, travelling, enjoying special occasions or celebrating personal successes, many Fire Dragons will find their home life special and meaningful.

Overall, the Year of the Snake can be an important one for the Fire Dragon, particularly as it will give him the chance to develop his skills and move forward. Over the year his qualities, determination and inner belief can make a real difference. Importantly, the experience he gains now can be built on in the future. However while this is a favourable year, he does need to keep his lifestyle in balance and preserve time for himself and his interests as well as to enjoy with those who are close to him.

TIP FOR THE YEAR
As a Fire Dragon, you know you have it within you to accomplish a great deal. This year, remain determined. Your qualities and resolve can serve you well. Be bold, be enterprising and make your talents count.

The Earth Dragon

The Earth Dragon is set to do well this year. Not only is this a good time for personal development, but he will also find himself making some long-term decisions. He can look forward to good support in a lot of what he does and whenever considering anything of importance, he would do well to run his thoughts past his loved ones and those with relevant experience. The Earth Dragon may like to make his own decisions (a typical Dragon trait), but over the year he can gain a lot by drawing on the help that is available to him.

An encouraging feature of the year will be the opportunities the Earth Dragon has to meet new people. He should aim to widen his social circle and, especially in his work, build up contacts and become better known. With his genial and sincere manner, he is set to impress, and, as so many people have discovered, the more people you know, the more possibilities open up. This will be very true for the Earth Dragon in 2013.

Throughout the year it could also be helpful for the Earth Dragon to keep himself informed about what is going in his locality. There could be events that appeal to him or he could discover special interest or professional groups he could join, or facilities (including sporting) he could use. Late February to April, September and December could be potentially rewarding months as well as see much social activity.

Although the Earth Dragon will enjoy good relations with many of those around him, for those who are in the early stages of a romance or who start one during the Snake year, this is a time for care and mindfulness. Affairs of the heart are not always easy or straightforward in Snake years and the Earth Dragon will need to remain attentive and allow the relationship to develop in its own time. To be hasty or have high expectations in the early stages could lead to it foundering. Earth Dragons, take note and be patient.

For those with a partner, the Snake year can be busy and interesting. Not only will there be plans and hopes to share but, as situations change, new opportunities too. As their work situation changes, some Earth Dragons may feel it makes sense to move and will spend some of the year looking for somewhere suitable to live. Others will be keen to make improvements to their home and will often be excited as choices are made and plans go ahead. With work-related decisions or any other matter that may be concerning him, the Earth Dragon does need to be forthcoming and talk things over with his partner and more senior relations. Just as he does so much for those around him, he also needs to give them the chance to reciprocate. Earth Dragons, do take note and consult others. This busy and interesting year is very much a time for sharing and joint effort.

The Earth Dragon will have many financial commitments this year and while his efforts at work can lead to a rise in earnings, he will need to keep a close watch on outgoings and take his time over more substantial purchases. By keeping alert, however, he could make some acquisitions on highly favourable terms and enjoy an element of good fortune.

As far as his work situation is concerned, the Snake year is filled with possibility. For the many Earth Dragons who are already established in a specific line of work, there will be good opportunities to extend their role and take on new responsibilities. Sometimes these could be more extensive and challenging than the Earth Dragon initially thought, but the experience gained can be an important factor in his subsequent progress. Also, with the good relations he enjoys with his colleagues, he can not only be an important member of many a team but also benefit from the support of a more senior colleague. The skills and potential of many Earth Dragons will certainly be recognized and encouraged in the Snake year.

Most Earth Dragons will remain with their present employer over the year, but for those who feel it could be to their advantage to move on, as well as those seeking work, there can be interesting developments in store. By keeping alert and being fully involved in the job-seeking process, they will not only be in a better position to learn about possible vacancies but also to receive additional help from employment advisers and certain friends and colleagues. Finding work will involve effort and persistence, but a new position the Earth Dragon gains during the year will often be something he can build upon in the future. Work-wise, the Snake year can be both constructive and instructive. While openings could arise at almost any time, February, April, May and November could see some particularly encouraging developments.

Although many Earth Dragons keep themselves active, it is also important that the Earth Dragon gives some consideration to his well-being over the year, including his level of exercise and quality of diet. Neglecting this could leave him lacking in energy or prone to minor ailments. In this busy and favourable year, some attention to his own well-being can be of great benefit.

Overall, the Year of the Snake can be a good one for the Earth Dragon. It will not only give him the chance to use and acquire skills but also to realize certain plans and hopes. These can relate to his accommodation and his personal interests as well as the many good times he will be able to share with those who are special to him. The

Earth Dragon has much in his favour this year and can look forward to some encouraging and well-deserved progress.

TIP FOR THE YEAR
Set about your aims with determination and seize your opportunities. This is a positive time for you and a lot can follow on from it. Also, draw on the advice and support of those around you. Their input can assist in many ways.

FAMOUS DRAGONS

Adele, Maya Angelou, Jeffrey Archer, Joan Armatrading, Joan Baez, Count Basie, Maeve Binchy, Sandra Bullock, Alexandra Burke, Michael Cera, Courteney Cox, Bing Crosby, Russell Crowe, Roald Dahl, Salvador Dali, Charles Darwin, Neil Diamond, Bo Diddley, Matt Dillon, Christian Dior, Placido Domingo, Fats Domino, Kirk Douglas, Faye Dunaway, Dan Fogler, Sir Bruce Forsyth, Sigmund Freud, Graham Greene, Rupert Grint, Che Guevara, James Herriot, Paul Hogan, Joan of Arc, Boris Johnson, Sir Tom Jones, Immanuel Kant, Martin Luther King, John Lennon, Abraham Lincoln, Elle MacPherson, Michael McIntyre, Queen Margrethe II of Denmark, Florence Nightingale, Nick Nolte, Sharon Osbourne, Al Pacino, Gregory Peck, Pelé, Edgar Allan Poe, Vladimir Putin, Nikki Reed, Keanu Reeves, Ryan Reynolds, Sir Cliff Richard, George Bernard Shaw, Martin Sheen, Alicia Silverstone, Ringo Starr, Karlheinz Stockhausen, Shirley Temple, Maria von Trapp, Louis Walsh, Andy Warhol, Mark Webber, Raquel Welch, the Earl of Wessex, Sam Worthington.

23 JANUARY 1917 〜 10 FEBRUARY 1918   *Fire Snake*

10 FEBRUARY 1929 〜 29 JANUARY 1930   *Earth Snake*

27 JANUARY 1941 〜 14 FEBRUARY 1942   *Metal Snake*

14 FEBRUARY 1953 〜 2 FEBRUARY 1954   *Water Snake*

2 FEBRUARY 1965 〜 20 JANUARY 1966   *Wood Snake*

18 FEBRUARY 1977 〜 6 FEBRUARY 1978   *Fire Snake*

6 FEBRUARY 1989 〜 26 JANUARY 1990   *Earth Snake*

24 JANUARY 2001 〜 11 FEBRUARY 2002   *Metal Snake*

10 FEBRUARY 2013 〜 30 JANUARY 2014   *Water Snake*

THE

SNAKE

THE PERSONALITY OF THE SNAKE

I think
And think some more.
About what is,
About what can be,
About what may be.
And when I am ready,
Then I act.

The Snake is born under the sign of wisdom. He is highly intelligent and his mind is forever active. He is always planning and always looking for ways in which he can use his considerable skills. He is a deep thinker and likes to meditate and reflect.

Many times during his life he will shed one of his famous Snake skins and take up new interests or start a completely different job. The Snake enjoys a challenge and he rarely makes mistakes. He is a skilful organizer, has considerable business acumen and is usually lucky in money matters. Most Snakes are financially secure in their later years, provided they do not gamble – the Snake has the distinction of being the worst gambler in the whole of the Chinese zodiac!

The Snake generally has a calm and placid nature and prefers the quieter things in life. He does not like to be in a frenzied atmosphere and hates being hurried into making a quick decision. He also does not like interference in his affairs and tends to rely on his own judgement rather than listen to advice.

At times the Snake can appear solitary. He is quiet, reserved and sometimes has difficulty in communicating with others. He has little time for idle gossip and will certainly not suffer fools gladly. He does, however, have a good sense of humour and this is particularly appreciated in times of crisis.

The Snake is certainly not afraid of hard work and is thorough in all that he does. He is very determined and can occasionally be ruthless in order to achieve his aims. His confidence, willpower and quick thinking usually ensure his success, but should he fail it will often take a long time for him to recover. He cannot bear failure and is a very bad loser.

The Snake can also be evasive and does not willingly let people into his confidence. This secrecy and distrust can sometimes work against him and are traits that all Snakes should try to overcome.

Another characteristic of the Snake is his tendency to rest after any sudden or prolonged bout of activity. He burns up so much nervous energy that he can, if he is not careful, be susceptible to high blood pressure and nervous disorders.

It has sometimes been said that the Snake is a late starter in life and this is mainly because it often takes him a while to find a job in which he is genuinely happy. However, he will usually do well in any position that involves research and writing and where he is given sufficient freedom to develop his own ideas and plans. He makes a good teacher, politician, personnel manager and social adviser.

The Snake chooses his friends carefully and while he keeps a tight control over his finances, he can be particularly generous to those he likes. He will think nothing of buying expensive gifts or treating his friends or loved ones to the best theatre seats in town. In return he demands loyalty. The Snake is very possessive and can become extremely jealous and hurt if he finds his trust has been abused.

The Snake is also renowned for his good looks and is never short of admirers. The female Snake in particular is most alluring. She has style, grace and excellent (and usually expensive) taste in clothes. A keen socializer, she is likely to have a wide range of friends and the happy knack of impressing those who matter. She has numerous interests and her opinions are often highly valued. She is generally a calm person and while she involves herself in many activities, she likes to retain a certain amount of privacy in her undertakings.

Affairs of the heart are very important to the Snake and he will often have many romances before he finally settles down. He will find that he is particularly well suited to those born under the signs of the Ox, Dragon, Rabbit and Rooster. Provided he is allowed sufficient freedom to pursue his own interests, he can also build up a very satisfactory relationship with the Rat, Horse, Goat, Monkey and Dog, but he should try to steer clear of another Snake as they could very easily become jealous of each other. The Snake will also have difficulty in getting on with the honest and down-to-earth Pig, and will find the Tiger far too much of a disruptive influence on his quiet and peace-loving ways.

The Snake certainly appreciates the finer things in life. He enjoys good food and often takes a keen interest in the arts. He also enjoys reading and is invariably drawn to subjects such as philosophy, political thought, religion or the occult. He is fascinated by the unknown and his enquiring mind is always looking for answers. Some of the world's most original thinkers have been Snakes, and although he may not readily admit it, the Snake is often psychic and relies a lot on intuition.

The Snake is certainly not the most energetic member of the Chinese zodiac. He prefers to proceed at his own pace and to do what he wants. He is very much his own master and throughout his life he will try his hand at many things. He is something of a dabbler, but at some time – usually when he least expects it – his hard work and efforts will be recognized and he will invariably meet with the success and the financial security he so desires.

THE FIVE DIFFERENT TYPES
OF SNAKE

In addition to the 12 signs of the Chinese zodiac there are five elements and these have a strengthening or moderating influence on the signs. The effects of the five elements on the Snake are described below, together with the years in which they were exercising their influence. Therefore Snakes born in 1941 and 2001 are Metal Snakes, Snakes born in 1953 and 2013 are Water Snakes, and so on.

Metal Snake: 1941, 2001
This Snake is quiet, confident and fiercely independent. He often prefers to work on his own and will only let a privileged few into his confidence. He is quick to spot opportu-

nities and will set about achieving his objectives with an awesome determination. He is astute in financial matters and will often invest his money well. He also has a liking for the finer things in life and a good appreciation of the arts, literature, music and food. He usually has a small group of extremely good friends and can be generous to his loved ones.

Water Snake: 1953, 2013

This Snake has a wide variety of interests. He enjoys studying all manner of subjects and is capable of undertaking quite detailed research and becoming a specialist in his chosen area. He is highly intelligent, has a good memory and is particularly astute when dealing with business and financial matters. He tends to be quietly spoken and a little reserved, but he does have sufficient strength of character to make his views known and attain his ambitions. He is very loyal to his family and friends.

Wood Snake: 1965

The Wood Snake has a friendly temperament and a good understanding of human nature. He is able to communicate well and often has many friends and admirers. He is witty, intelligent and ambitious. He has numerous interests and prefers to live in a quiet, stable environment where he can work without too much interference. He enjoys the arts and usually derives much pleasure from collecting antiques and other items that appeal. His advice is often highly valued, particularly on social and domestic matters.

Fire Snake: 1917, 1977

The Fire Snake tends to be more forceful, outgoing and energetic than some of the other types of Snake. He is ambitious, confident and never slow in voicing his opinions, and he can be very abrasive to those he does not like. He does, however, have many leadership qualities and can win the respect and support of many with his firm and resolute manner. He usually has a good sense of humour, a wide circle of friends and a very active social life. He is also a keen traveller.

Earth Snake 1929, 1989

The Earth Snake is charming, amusing and has a very amiable manner. He is conscientious and reliable in his work and approaches everything he does in a level-headed and sensible way. He can, however, tend to err on the cautious side and never likes to be hassled into making a decision. He is adept in dealing with financial matters and is a shrewd investor. He has many friends and is very supportive towards the members of his family.

PROSPECTS FOR THE SNAKE IN 2013

In the Year of the Dragon (23 January 2012–9 February 2013) the Snake will need to expect the unexpected. Although he may like to follow carefully laid plans, Dragon years go their own way and can cause the Snake to alter course, rethink activities or adjust as new situations arise. Life may not always be straightforward as this Dragon year draws to a close, but with flexibility, the Snake can gain a great deal from the closing months.

In his work he will face new pressures and challenges and may sometimes feel buffeted by events. This can be an especially busy time, but one of the key benefits of the Dragon year is the experience it can offer. What the Snake can accomplish at this time can considerably help his prospects in his own year. Extra effort will not be wasted and any position secured now (even if on a temporary basis) can often lead to other possibilities.

With the closing months of the year being a generally expensive time, the Snake will need to keep track of his spending and also look after his valuables carefully. A loss could prove upsetting. Also, should he be troubled by gossip or rumour, he should check the facts and correct any untruths. Dragon years can sometimes bring tricky moments.

Domestically, it is important that the Snake is forthcoming and shares his thoughts and concerns with others. With so much happening in his home life and an increase in social activity (especially from mid-November), he could be grateful for additional help with certain activities and decisions. However, while busy, the closing weeks of the year can bring special times to enjoy with family and friends.

The Year of the Snake holds great possibilities for the Snake himself. His own year begins on 10 February and as it starts he would do well to reflect on the Chinese proverb, 'With aspirations, you can go anywhere; without aspirations, you can go nowhere.' This is very much a year for the Snake to act on his aspirations. With determination backed by the encouraging aspects of the year, he can enjoy considerable good fortune.

Any Snake who starts the year in low spirits or disappointed by recent progress should try to draw a line under what has happened and focus his attention on the present. This can be the start of a new chapter in his life and he should take action to bring about the improvements he wants. With aspirations, a lot can become possible this year.

Work prospects are especially encouraging. For Snakes who are established in a career, there will be some excellent opportunities to progress. As more senior staff move on, the Snake will often be well positioned to take on a greater role. Snakes who work in a large organization may see a position in another department which would give them the chance to gain experience in another capacity. This is certainly a time to keep alert and act when opportunities arise. Particularly for those who have languished in the same position for some time, this is a year to look to move on.

Some Snakes may be keen to make more substantial change, including in some cases becoming self-employed. By being thorough in their enquiries, getting expert advice and using their initiative, many will realize their objectives and relish the chance to do something different. A trait of the Snake is that he is patient, but when the time comes, he seizes the moment, and this will be very much the case this year.

For Snakes seeking work, this can be an important year. By actively following up any vacancies that interest them, many will secure an opening they can build on. This will require considerable effort, but if the Snake shows self-belief and purpose, his qualities will shine through and his own year will provide him with the opportunity he has been seeking. Opportunities could arise at almost any time, but March, June, July and September could see particularly encouraging developments.

The Snake's financial situation can also see an improvement. However, while generally astute in financial matters, he cannot afford to be lax. Without care, he could find his spending creeping up and his judgement not as good as usual. To do well with purchases, investments and financially related decisions, he will need to check terms, implications and liabilities. This can be a successful year financially, but lapses and haste can lead to misjudgement. Snakes, take note and do be thorough.

With his enquiring nature, the Snake always tries to make time to follow up anything that intrigues him and in his own year he will particularly enjoy developing ideas and trying out new activities. For many Snakes, their own year can be inspiring, and the creatively inclined may find some of their ideas and work particularly well received. Time spent on personal interests and recreational pursuits will also allow the Snake to reconnect with himself, which is especially important for the Snake psyche.

The Snake's social life is also encouragingly aspected and although he may be selective in his socializing, he will enjoy many of the times he does go out. Both new and existing interests can help bring him into contact with others, and some new acquaintances will become good friends. For unattached Snakes, their own year can be special. Quite a few will meet their soul mate, and in circumstances which will seem as if it was destined to be. April, May, August and September could see the most social activity.

The Snake's home life will also bring him much pleasure and the year will often be marked by special occasions. There could be a special birthday in the Snake's family or an anniversary or success to celebrate. The Snake will be the key instigator in a lot that happens, and whether suggesting home improvements, supporting loved ones or arranging family activities and a possible holiday, he can make this a full and satisfying year. However, while a lot will go well, difficulties could still arise, sometimes caused by tiredness or lack of communication. At such times, the Snake should talk through problems and tackle issues rather than risk them souring an otherwise promising year. Fortunately, problems will be few, but they should not be ignored. Late 2013 could see some exciting developments in many a Snake household, with the possibility of additional travel.

Overall, the Snake year can be special and fulfilling for the Snake himself. With his deep-thinking ways and preference for planning, he will be pleased with the way many of his activities proceed, and his skills and ideas will bring success as well as open up new opportunities. The Snake does need to take charge, overcome his sometimes reticent nature and *seize the moment*, but his own year is one of the best for him and in so many respects this has the potential to be a great and wonderful time for him.

The Metal Snake

There is a Chinese proverb that will hold good for many a Metal Snake this year: 'Come prepared and succeed; come unprepared and fail.' The Metal Snake usually prepares well and his actions can make this a personally rewarding and successful year.

For Metal Snakes born in 1941, the Snake year has many possibilities, but one area which will be particularly pleasing will be their personal interests. These Metal Snakes will not only enjoy pursuing these but will also delight in the way their ideas now develop. Over the year, they could obtain new equipment, learn new techniques or set themselves a particular goal, but whatever they do, they will find the Snake year both encouraging and inspiring.

In addition the Metal Snake could benefit from what is available locally. There could be an interest or community group he could join, a course he could enrol on or facilities he could use. By remaining aware and seizing his opportunities, he can get more from the year and often add something to his lifestyle.

A feature of Snake years is that they favour culture, and with his enquiring nature, the Metal Snake may well decide to visit places of interest and attend special events. A few Metal Snakes may also delve into family or local history or another subject area that appeals to them. Over the year, the Metal Snake may often become fascinated by what he does and the new knowledge he acquires.

Some activities can also have a good social element, with the Metal Snake enjoying the chance to meet, talk and exchange ideas. Particularly for any who may be alone, an existing or new interest can not only be a reason to go out but also provide an ideal opportunity to get to know others. Late March to early June, August and September will see the most social activity.

The Metal Snake's home life is pleasingly aspected, but it will be very much a case of sharing activities and being forthcoming. With flexibility, many plans can be advanced and hopes realized, even if sometimes in a different way or to a different timescale than first envisaged. The Metal Snake will also appreciate the travel opportunities of the year and whether visiting relations or enjoying a break away, a change of scene will do him good.

In money matters, he will need to exercise care and allow time to check the details of any transactions he may conduct or forms he has to complete. If he has uncertainties, it is important that he gets these addressed before proceeding. Also, if there is something special he is hoping to buy, he should remain alert. His own year contains an element of luck and he may benefit from some fortunate discoveries.

For Metal Snakes born in 2001, the Year of the Snake is also one of considerable opportunity. During the year the young Metal Snake will not only move on to more advanced studies but may also change school. This can be a pivotal year in his education and he can create a solid foundation from which to develop and grow. Metal Snakes who do change school in particular will find that by giving their best and making a commitment they will be helping to give their prospects important momentum. This is no time to waste.

Quite a few young Metal Snakes will also have opportunities to develop particular skills and talents. The musically inclined could learn an instrument while the more sporting may prefer more active pursuits. Again, to fully benefit, the young Metal Snake should take advantage of what is available.

As he will now be tackling more complex work, it is also important that the young Metal Snake is forthcoming and talks over any concerns to those at home or teachers at school. This way he can be better supported.

Many Metal Snakes will have the chance to travel this year and, whether on an educational visit or a holiday, can look forward to seeing some fascinating places. The Snake year can whet the imagination of the young Metal Snake and open his mind to future possibilities.

Overall, the Year of the Snake has considerable scope for both younger and more senior Metal Snakes. By making the most of their chances and furthering their ideas, interests and skills, they can get a great deal of satisfaction from their activities. They will also be well supported and, with this being the Snake year, quite a few could also be encouraged by strokes of luck and good fortune. An interesting and personally rewarding year.

TIP FOR THE YEAR
Be open to the new. The Snake year can open up excellent possibilities. Embrace these and be prepared to move forward. Much can flow from what you do now.

The Water Snake

This will be a special year for the Water Snake. Not only is this his year and one marking a new decade in his life, but he will find many of his ideas and activities developing well. During the year he can also benefit from some particularly fine opportunities and his quietly determined nature will help him make the most of many a situation.

He will also be assisted by the support of those around him, and while he sometimes keeps his thoughts to himself, it is especially important this year that he is receptive to the advice of others. Not only will greater openness on his part lead to more happening, but also more success.

One area which will bring especial pleasure will be the Water Snake's personal interests. By spending time on these and using his skills to advantage, he can find interesting developments often following on. Snake years very much favour originality, and here the Water Snake's ability to think creatively can impress. For Water Snakes who are interested in writing, art, music or some other form of expression in particular, this has the potential to be a successful and inspiring year. For any Water Snake who would welcome new challenges, this is an excellent time for widening skills and trying something new.

It can also be to the Water Snake's advantage to find out what is available locally. Some Water Snakes could discover courses or interest groups they could join or recreational facilities they could use. For many, this will be a year filled with interesting possibility.

The Water Snake's home life will also be important this year. Not only will his loved ones be keen to mark his sixtieth birthday in style but could also have some surprises in store. Their affection and kindness will mean a great deal to the Water Snake as well as underline the important role he plays in the lives of those close to him. Some parts of his year will prove memorable and special.

In addition to any birthday celebrations, quite a few Water Snakes will decide to travel this year, perhaps to a destination they have long favoured. If they plan ahead, they will not only be able to look forward to this all the more, but often also able to do more while away.

The Snake year has a practical element to it and many Water Snakes will decide to tackle some home projects over the year, including some they may have been considering for some time but have put off. There could be disruption involved and some practical undertakings may take longer than anticipated, but when everything is done, the Water Snake will often appreciate the benefits. He may even have a purge on clutter and mount an efficiency drive as well. For many Water Snakes, their own year can be a call to get things done.

Throughout the year the Water Snake will do much to assist others, and with some younger relations facing important decisions, the advice he is able to give will be particularly valued. He may also be able to look forward to an additional celebration during the year, perhaps an academic success, a wedding or the birth of a grandchild.

He will once again value his close circle of friends and socially this can be a pleasant time. April, May and August to October could see some good social occasions and even if some Water Snakes prefer to keep their social life low key, if they see events that appeal to them, they should make the effort to go. This is, after all, their own year and one to enjoy.

For Water Snakes who are alone, their own year can be made special by the chance of romance or an important new friendship. The Year of the Water Snake can be eventful for many a Water Snake, and for the unattached, could see a transformation in their situation.

The Water Snake's work prospects can also take an interesting course. One of the Water Snake's strengths is his creativity and this year his ideas will often be well received. He may find himself being given special duties which suit his skills well. There will be excellent chances to progress and the Water Snake's reputation and experience will stand him in good stead.

For Water Snakes who would welcome a new challenge, as well as those seeking work, the Snake year can bring some sometimes unusual opportunities. By not being too restrictive in the type of position they are considering, these Water Snakes could be offered work which could use their abilities in different ways. There could be quite a bit of adjustment involved, but the Water Snake will feel ready for the opportunity. This is a year to be open to possibility and March, June, July and September could see encouraging developments.

In view of all his plans and activities, this can be an expensive time for the Water Snake. Where possible, he should make early provision for forthcoming expenses and travel and, when considering transactions, check the terms and implications. However, while the Snake year calls for good financial management, many Water Snakes will benefit from some financial luck this year, possibly including a maturing policy or a gift.

Overall, the Year of the Water Snake can be an exciting and memorable one for the Water Snake himself. With the chance of travel and possible celebrations to mark his sixtieth birthday, he may feel inspired this year and set about his activities with renewed determination. Personal interests, especially those which draw on the Water Snake's ideas and creative talents, could bring especial pleasure and success. At work, the Water Snake will have the chance to use his skills to excellent effect and sometimes enjoy the challenge of something new. His own year is filled with possibility, and central to it will be the love, support and encouragement of those around him.

TIP FOR THE YEAR
Make the most of your ideas and talents. This is your own year and by doing the things you are good at, you will be well rewarded. Believe in yourself, act determinedly and enjoy the good fortune that comes your way.

The Wood Snake

'A long journey will not deter one with high aspirations', as the Chinese proverb reminds us. Many a Wood Snake will feel as if he has already been on a long journey. The last few years will have seen a lot happen, some good, some bad, and the Wood Snake may be wondering how recent efforts and decisions will develop. Pleasingly, 2013 is a promising year for him and many Wood Snakes will reap some well-deserved and sometimes overdue rewards.

One of the important factors in the Wood Snake's favour is the experience he has built up. The Snake year will give him the chance to develop this and there will be several opportunities to take on greater responsibilities. These could entail adjustments to routine and a few Wood Snakes may be required to change location, but with their background and desire to progress, they could take advantage of some very good opportunities.

The Wood Snake's position will be helped by the good working relations he has with many around him, and senior colleagues will often be encouraging. In addition the Wood Snake should use any chances he has to build up contacts.

Many Wood Snakes will stay with their present employer this year, but for those who feel there are better opportunities elsewhere or are seeking work, the Snake year can again hold interesting developments. The job-seeking process will not be easy, but Snake years proceed in curious ways and some Wood Snakes could discover an ideal opportunity by chance. In 2013 the Wood Snake will need to show some flexibility and make the most of opportunities *as they arise*. As many will find, a lot this year happens for a reason and the chances they are given now will often have future potential. March, June and July to mid-October could see interesting possibilities.

The Wood Snake is also blessed with a creative mind. He thinks deeply and is capable of producing some very fine ideas. In the Snake year he will be able to put some of these into practice. This could be in his place of work, but also applies to his personal interests. Either way, his experience and inventiveness can reward him well this year. He should not be too restrictive in his activities and if there is something new that appeals to him, he should find out more. This is a year offering scope and opportunity.

The Wood Snake's social life is favourably aspected and although his commitments may mean he is not able to go out as often as in other years, when he sees events that appeal to him or has invitations to go out, he should do his best to go. This can do him good as well as provide balance to his lifestyle. For the unattached, especially those who have been nursing some sadness or recent hurt, the Snake year can see a considerable brightening in their situation and, for some, a chance romance adding excitement and hope to the year. Late March to May, August and September could see the most social activity.

Progress at work can help financially and some Wood Snakes may also find an interest or personal success supplementing their means. However the Wood Snake will need to remain disciplined and keep a watch on outgoings. To do all he wants, he does need to budget accordingly. Also, should he have concerns over a financial matter, he should check the details and seek advice where necessary. Although this is a good year, it still requires vigilance.

The Wood Snake can look forward to a full and pleasing domestic life. In addition to his own successes, other family members could have news to share and occasions to mark. At busy periods, some adjustment and flexibility will be needed. However, busy though home life may be, the Snake year will also contain many rewarding times, with the Wood Snake appreciating the love and support of those close to him.

Overall, the Year of the Snake can be a personally rewarding one for the Wood Snake, with his efforts, skills and experience serving him well. It will also give him chance to benefit from his ideas and special talents, and whether in his work, personal interests or in some other sphere, by being active and putting himself forward, he can look forward to some very positive results. He will also be well supported by those around him and his successes this year will be considerable and well deserved.

TIP FOR THE YEAR

You have much to offer and with belief, determination and the support of others, you can move forward and act on your ideas. Your talents, experience and background can reward you well.

The Fire Snake

The Fire Snake has a very determined nature and his efforts and resolve can lead to some fine achievements this year. To get it off to a good start, he would do well to give some thought to what he would like to see happen. His thoughts could concern his home or his personal life, his work or his interests, as well as any other aspirations he may have, but having ideas in mind will give him something to work towards. With purpose and direction, he can make this a highly successful year.

Almost all areas of his life can see encouraging developments, but one factor that will be very much in the Fire Snake's favour will be his willingness to learn. At work in particular, many Fire Snakes will have the opportunity to take on new responsibilities. Although these may be daunting and require the Fire Snake to quickly master new skills, by focusing on what needs to be done, he will not only have the chance to prove himself in a new capacity but also establish himself in his new role, which he may have been working towards for some time.

The majority of Fire Snakes will have chances to progress with their present employer over the year, but some may consider their prospects are better elsewhere. These Fire Snakes should keep alert and make enquiries as well as talk to those who are able to advise. Their initiative can often lead to them being offered a new position with the potential for future development. Effort and determination will be recognized and rewarded this year.

This also applies to Fire Snakes seeking work. Although the job-seeking process can be wearying, they should remember that this *is* the Snake year and a special one. Their initiative, resolve and strong self-belief will impress and they too may well be offered a position on which they can subsequently build. March, June, July, September and early October could see some important opportunities.

Throughout the year the Fire Snake should also liaise well with his colleagues and use any chances to build up contacts. More senior colleagues could be especially helpful in supplying advice, support and references.

The progress the Fire Snake makes at work will often lead to an increase in income, but with his existing commitments and some major plans ahead (possibly including a move), he will need to manage his situation carefully. With discipline, a lot will be possible this year, but early planning will be helpful. Also, if the Fire Snake has concerns over any financial matter, he should check the facts and, if appropriate, seek advice.

He would also do well to allow time to develop his interests. In this active year he does need to keep his lifestyle in balance and some 'me time' will be essential. Fire Snakes who are keen to make more of their skills should explore new ideas. This is a year of exciting possibility.

The Fire Snake will also appreciate the social opportunities of the year. April, May and late July to September could see much activity, and for the unattached, this can be a year of exciting romantic developments, with an existing friendship becoming more serious or someone special entering the Fire Snake's life. Snake years can be promising and significant. Support the Fire Snake may be given can also be important, and should a friend have expertise in a matter he needs to know about, the Fire Snake should ask.

He can also look forward to some exciting developments in his home life. In view of some of his hopes for the year, early planning will be useful. Some Fire Snakes could have the chance to move to more suitable accommodation, while others will be keen to carry out specific plans for their home. Where practical activities are concerned, chance and a certain element of luck could come into play. This is a year favouring togetherness, joint effort and planning, and in many a Fire Snake household there will also be good news to enjoy. Domestically, a busy but rewarding year.

The Fire Snake has strength, ambition and much to offer, and in the Year of the Snake his abilities can bring some deserved success. This is a time when his determination and talents can reward him well. Overall, a busy year, but importantly, one bringing good opportunities.

TIP FOR THE YEAR

Give some thought to what you want to see happen this year and then work towards it. With purpose and direction, you can see important chances opening up for you. This is a favourable and lucky year. Use it well.

The Earth Snake

The Earth Snake is set to do well this year. With his keen, eager nature and desire to make more of himself, he will find good chances emerging and will benefit from many of the year's developments.

The Earth Snake's relations with others are particularly well aspected and he will be helped by his ability to relate so well to so many people. Affairs of the heart will be especially important for many Earth Snakes this year. For those in a serious relationship, their love for each other can help make this a special time. There will be plans and hopes to realize and some memorable moments to enjoy. In addition some Earth Snakes will make important decisions this year, possibly marrying, settling down together, setting into new accommodation or starting a family. For quite a few, this can be a significant time.

This also applies to Earth Snakes who may be alone, as a chance encounter could add a new dimension to their life. Although not all may be seeking it, Cupid's arrow could be heading in their direction in 2013, with April, May, August and September seeing an increase in social activity and chances to meet others.

Throughout the year, family members can also be important, and although the Earth Snake will want to take responsibility for his own decisions, it is important he talks over his current activities and seeks advice. This way he can not only benefit from others' experience but also the assistance they may be able to offer. Family members will also be keen to share in his successes and support him.

The Snake year is also an excellent one for personal development and will see many of the Earth Snakes who are involved in studying complete their courses and obtain the qualifications they have been working towards. Again, effort and personal discipline will reward them well, and their achievements will be something they can be proud of and build on.

However, all Earth Snakes, no matter what their current situation, should continue developing their knowledge and skills. Often they will have the chance to do this through their work, but those who have personal interests they would like to take further should allow themselves time to make more of their talents. This could be by mastering new techniques, setting themselves projects or promoting their ideas. Some could be particularly encouraged by feedback they are given or success they enjoy. The Year of the Snake has great potential for the Earth Snake.

The aspects are also encouraging for work prospects. Earth Snakes who are already at work will often find the skills they have built up will lead to the offer of extra responsibilities. In addition, if promotion opportunities arise or there is the chance of increased involvement, the Earth Snake should put himself forward. With his commitment and readiness to learn and contribute, he can make important headway. Throughout the year, these Earth Snakes should also work closely with their colleagues and use any chances to build up contacts and become better known. Their actions and personality can impress others, including those with influence.

For Earth Snakes who are looking to make a change or seeking work, the Snake year can bring important opportunities. To benefit, these Earth Snakes should not be too restrictive in their search but put themselves forward whenever they see a potentially interesting opening. Their quest may at times be disheartening, but they have a lot to offer and may be able to gain a base on which to build in the future. March, June, July and September could see some important developments.

The progress many Earth Snakes will make at work can help financially. However, with an often active lifestyle, as well as his existing commitments, the Earth Snake will need to manage his money well. Succumbing to too many temptations could result in having to cut back on other activities. This is a year for sensible budgetary control.

Overall, the Year of the Snake can be both a special and rewarding one for the Earth Snake. His personal life is especially well aspected and he will benefit from the support and goodwill of those around him. Affairs of the heart are capable of bringing him much happiness. Importantly, the year will also give him the chance to develop his skills. Whether in his work or personal interests, by seizing his opportunities, he can make good headway. This is the Year of the Snake and the Earth Snake should regard it as a chance to prove himself and move forward. A good year and one of long-term significance.

Be active. With determination, backed by your considerable personal qualities, you can accomplish a great deal. However, you do need to seize opportunities as they arise. Also, value your relations with those around you. Their love and support can make this fine year all the more special.

FAMOUS SNAKES

Muhammad Ali, Ann-Margret, Kim Basinger, Ben Bernanke, Björk, Tony Blair, Michael Bloomberg, Michael Bolton, Brahms, Pierce Brosnan, Casanova, Chubby Checker, Jackie Collins, Tom Conti, Viola Davis, Cecil B. de Mille, Robert Downey Jr, Bob Dylan, Michael Fassbender, Sir Alex Ferguson, Sir Alexander Fleming, Mahatma Gandhi, Greta Garbo, Art Garfunkel, J. Paul Getty, Dizzy Gillespie, W. E. Gladstone, Goethe, Princess Grace of Monaco, Stephen Hawking, Audrey Hepburn, Jack Higgins, Elizabeth Hurley, James Joyce, Stacy Keach, Ronan Keating, J. F. Kennedy, Chaka Khan, Carole King, Courtney Love, Rory McIlroy, Mao Tse-tung, Chris Martin, Henri Matisse, Robert Mitchum, Piers Morgan, Alfred Nobel, Mike Oldfield, Jacqueline Onassis, Sarah Jessica Parker, Pablo Picasso, Mary Pickford, Daniel Radcliffe, Franklin D. Roosevelt, Mickey Rourke, J. K. Rowling, Jean-Paul Sartre, Franz Schubert, Shakira, Charlie Sheen, Paul Simon, Delia Smith, Ben Stiller, Taylor Swift, Madame Tussaud, Shania Twain, Dionne Warwick, Mia Wasikowska, Charlie Watts, Kanye West, Oprah Winfrey, Virginia Woolf.

11 FEBRUARY 1918 ∼ 31 JANUARY 1919	*Earth Horse*
30 JANUARY 1930 ∼ 16 FEBRUARY 1931	*Metal Horse*
15 FEBRUARY 1942 ∼ 4 FEBRUARY 1943	*Water Horse*
3 FEBRUARY 1954 ∼ 23 JANUARY 1955	*Wood Horse*
21 JANUARY 1966 ∼ 8 FEBRUARY 1967	*Fire Horse*
7 FEBRUARY 1978 ∼ 27 JANUARY 1979	*Earth Horse*
27 JANUARY 1990 ∼ 14 FEBRUARY 1991	*Metal Horse*
12 FEBRUARY 2002 ∼ 31 JANUARY 2003	*Water Horse*

THE
HORSE

THE PERSONALITY OF THE HORSE

There are many worn paths,
but the most rewarding
is the one you decide on and forge yourself.

The Horse is born under the signs of elegance and ardour. He has a most engaging and charming manner and is usually very popular. He loves meeting people and likes attending parties and other large social gatherings.

The Horse is a lively character and enjoys being the centre of attention. He has many leadership qualities and is much admired for his honest and straightforward manner. He is an eloquent and persuasive speaker and has a great love of discussion and debate. He also has a particularly agile mind and can assimilate facts remarkably quickly.

He does, however, have a fiery temper and although his outbursts are usually short-lived, he can often say things that he will later regret. He is also not particularly good at keeping secrets.

The Horse has many interests and involves himself in a wide variety of activities. He can, however, get involved in so much that he can often waste his energies on projects that he never has time to complete. He also has a tendency to change his interests rather frequently and will often get caught up in the latest craze or 'in thing' until something more exciting turns up.

The Horse also likes to have a certain amount of freedom and independence. He hates being bound by petty rules and regulations and as far as possible likes to feel that he is answerable to no one but himself. But despite this spirit of freedom, he still likes to have the support and encouragement of others in his various enterprises.

Due to his many talents and likeable nature, the Horse will often go far in life. He enjoys challenges and is a methodical and tireless worker. However, should things go against him and he fail in any of his enterprises, it will take a long time for him to recover and pick up the pieces again. Success to the Horse means everything. To fail is a disaster and a humiliation.

The Horse likes to have variety in life and will try his hand at many different things before he settles down to one particular job. Even then, he will probably remain alert to see whether there are any better opportunities for him to take up. He has a restless nature and can easily get bored. He does, however, excel in any position that allows him sufficient freedom to act on his own initiative or brings him into contact with a lot of people.

Although the Horse is not particularly bothered about accumulating great wealth, he handles his finances with care and will rarely experience any serious financial problems.

The Horse also enjoys travel and loves visiting new and faraway places. At some stage during his life he will be tempted to live abroad for a short period of time and due to his adaptable nature will find that he will fit in well wherever he goes.

The Horse pays a great deal of attention to his appearance and usually likes to wear smart, colourful and rather distinctive clothes. He is very attractive to others and will often have many romances before he settles down. He is loyal and protective to his partner, but despite his family commitments he still likes to retain a certain measure of independence and have the freedom to carry on with his own interests and hobbies. He will find that he is especially well suited to those born under the signs of the Tiger, Goat, Rooster and Dog. He can also get on well with the Rabbit, Dragon, Snake, Pig and another Horse, but he will find the Ox too serious and intolerant for his liking. He will also have difficulty in getting on with the Monkey and the Rat – the Monkey is very inquisitive and the Rat seeks security, and both will resent the Horse's rather independent ways.

The female Horse is usually most attractive and has a friendly, outgoing personality. She is highly intelligent, has many interests and is alert to everything that is going on around her. She particularly enjoys outdoor pursuits and often likes to take part in sport and keep-fit activities. She also enjoys travel, literature and the arts, and is a very good conversationalist.

Although the Horse can be stubborn and rather self-centred, he does have a considerate nature and is often willing to help others. He has a good sense of humour and will usually make a favourable impression wherever he goes. Provided he can curb his slightly restless nature and keep tight control over his temper, he will go through life making friends, taking part in a multitude of different activities and generally achieving many of his objectives. His life will rarely be dull.

THE FIVE DIFFERENT TYPES
OF HORSE

In addition to the 12 signs of the Chinese zodiac there are five elements and these have a strengthening or moderating influence on the signs. The effects of the five elements on the Horse are described below, together with the years in which they were exercising their influence. Therefore Horses born in 1930 and 1990 are Metal Horses, Horses born in 1942 and 2002 are Water Horses, and so on.

Metal Horse: 1930, 1990
This Horse is bold, confident and forthright. He is ambitious and a great innovator. He loves challenges and takes great delight in sorting out complicated problems. He likes to have a certain amount of independence and resents any outside interference in his affairs. He has charm and a certain charisma, but he can also be very stubborn and rather impulsive. He usually has many friends and enjoys an active social life.

Water Horse: 1942, 2002
The Water Horse has a friendly nature and a good sense of humour and is able to talk intelligently on a wide range of topics. He is astute in business matters and quick to take advantage of any opportunities that arise. He does, however, have a tendency to get easily distracted and can

change his interests – and indeed his mind – rather frequently, and this can often work to his detriment. He is nevertheless very talented and can often go far in life. He pays a great deal of attention to his appearance and is usually smart and well turned out. He loves to travel and also enjoys sport and other outdoor activities.

Wood Horse: 1954

The Wood Horse has a most agreeable and amiable nature. He communicates well with others and is able to talk intelligently on many different subjects. He is a hard and conscientious worker and is held in high esteem by his friends and colleagues. His opinions are often sought and, given his imaginative nature, he can often come up with some very original and practical ideas. He is usually widely read and likes to lead a busy social life. He can also be most generous and often holds high moral views.

Fire Horse: 1966

The element of Fire combined with the temperament of the Horse creates one of the most powerful forces in the Chinese zodiac. The Fire Horse is destined to lead an exciting and eventful life and to make his mark in his chosen profession. He has a forceful personality and his intelligence and resolute manner bring him the support and admiration of many. He loves action and excitement and his life will rarely be quiet. He can, however, be rather blunt and forthright in his views and does not take kindly to interference in his own affairs or to obeying orders. He is a flamboyant character, has a good sense of humour and will lead a very active social life.

Earth Horse: 1918, 1978

This Horse is considerate and caring. He is more cautious than some of the other types of Horse, but is wise, perceptive and extremely capable. Although he can be rather indecisive at times, he has considerable business acumen and is very astute in financial matters. He has a quiet, friendly nature and is well thought of by his family and friends.

PROSPECTS FOR THE HORSE IN 2013

The fast-moving Dragon year (23 January 2012– 9 February 2013) will suit the Horse well. With his lively nature and many interests, he will have a lot to do and find many of his activities satisfying. However, this is no time to throw caution to the wind. In the closing months of the Dragon year the Horse will need to think over his decisions carefully and liaise well with those around him. He can accomplish a lot at this time, but he will need support.

His home will be busy, with certain plans getting underway and some important purchases being considered. There may be considerable anticipation in many a Horse household at this time. A loved one could also have a surprise in store which will mean a great deal to the Horse. On a social level he will be in demand and, with affairs of the heart favourably aspected, for some unattached Horses, the closing months of the Dragon year could contain interesting romantic possibilities.

There will also be travel prospects towards the end of the year, and with this being such an active time, the Horse will need to keep a close watch on spending and avoid risk.

At work, many Horses will face additional pressures and some may take on additional responsibilities. Although this will often be a challenging time, it can still offer the Horse the chance to move his career forward and add to his experience. September and November could see some good possibilities arising.

Overall, the Year of the Dragon will have been an interesting one for the Horse and the closing months will see a flurry of activity, with many occasions for him to enjoy.

In the cycle of Chinese years, some are progressive while others are problematic. For the Horse, the Snake year, which begins on 10 February, is sandwiched between the two. While not a particularly auspicious year, it is not a bad one either. In essence, it is a middling year which will give the Horse a chance to take stock, immerse himself in his activities and add to his skills.

For Horses who may have recently changed their work or are in the process of doing so, the Snake year will offer the opportunity to become more established. To help, the Horse should make the most of any training and support available to him, as well as be an active member of any team. He should also use his personal skills to advantage, working closely with colleagues, meeting others in his line of work and becoming better known. He may not only make a favourable impression but also be encouraged to move forward, especially when changes in staff occur.

For Horses who want to move on from where they are or are seeking work, the Snake year will require considerable effort. With competition likely to be fierce, these Horses will need to show commitment and resourcefulness in their quest. Finding out more about the duties involved in any position they are putting in for and emphasizing their experience will help. A hallmark of the Horse is his determination, and by giving that little bit extra, many Horses may secure a new opening during the year. April, June, September and November could see some interesting opportunities.

In money matters, this is a year for caution. While the Horse will be able to proceed with many of his purchases and plans, at all times he needs to remain vigilant and check the details of any terms and conditions he may be taking on. In addition, he should be thorough when dealing with paperwork. A delay, mistake or lost document could cause problems. The greater care, the better.

Although many Horses keep themselves active, it could also be to the Horse's advantage to give some consideration to his lifestyle and well-being. If he feels he lacks regular exercise or relies on convenience foods, he would do well to consider ways of remedying this. Even small changes could help. Also, if the Horse has a series of particularly pressured days followed by late nights, he should allow time to rest and catch up. A benefit of the slower-moving Snake year is that it will give many Horses the chance to get their lifestyle into better balance.

The Horse can also derive considerable pleasure from his interests and should again allow time to enjoy these. With the Snake year encouraging personal development, if the Horse would like to learn a new skill or extend an interest, this would be an excellent time to do so. Indeed, new skills can be one of the lasting legacies of the year.

With his outgoing nature, the Horse will again enjoy socializing this year. However, while a lot can go well in this respect, Snake years can create problems and the Horse will need to be on his guard. Lapses or indiscretions could undermine rapport, and for any Horse who is tempted to stray or take risks, there could be consequences to face. These words of warning only apply to a few, but these Horses should *take careful note*. Also, Horses who are enjoying romance or who find love this year need to remain attentive and allow time for the relationship to develop. Where relations with others are concerned, the Horse needs to tread carefully this year. March, May, October and December will see the most social activity.

Home life will also be busy, with many Horse households seeing much practical activity. Many of the home improvements will be satisfying, and the more that can be undertaken jointly, the better. Throughout the year it is also important that there is good communication, and should the Horse feel under pressure or have concerns at any time, he should allow others to help and advise. A spirit of openness can be to the advantage of all. In addition, the Horse should make sure quality time is spent with his loved ones. Shared interests and, if possible, a short break or holiday could be particularly appreciated. In the Snake year, increased mindfulness will make a difference.

Overall, the Year of the Snake can be a reasonable one for the Horse. Although it may lack the buzz and dynamism of some years, it will give the Horse a chance to concentrate on his activities. At work, many Horses will be able to develop their skills and make steady headway. Personal interests and household undertakings can also be satisfying, and by making an effort to keep his lifestyle in balance and give time to his own needs, the Horse can benefit from his actions. Although his relations with others will often go well, he will need to remain attentive and careful. But while a quieter year than some, it can be pleasantly satisfying.

The Metal Horse

There is a word that can be especially important for the Metal Horse this year: 'focus'. With focus, a lot can be accomplished, but should focus be lacking, valuable time and opportunities could be lost. How the Metal Horse fares this year is very much in his own hands.

For the many Metal Horses currently studying for qualifications, there will be work to prepare and important exams to take. With a lot resting on the outcome, these Metal Horses will need to remain disciplined and allow ample time for preparation and revision. This is a year that rewards focus and dedication. Should inspiration flag at any time, these Metal Horses would do well to remind themselves what their qualifications can open up for them.

In addition, the Metal Horse should set aside time to pursue his personal interests. His enthusiasm and interest in the world around him can once again reward him well.

Snake years can present some very good opportunities for the Metal Horse and he should consider developing his skills at this time.

For Metal Horses in work this can be also an important year. However, to do well, again they will need to be focused. If they involve themselves in what is going on and show themselves willing to learn, many will have the chance to take on greater responsibilities and in the process gain the skills necessary for future progress.

For Metal Horses seeking work, the Snake year can have important developments in store. Although the job-seeking process can be difficult, the Metal Horse's steely determination can win through. Although what he is offered might sometimes be different from what he was envisaging, it can still be a valuable foothold on the employment ladder. Quite a few Metal Horses could take on a position almost by chance that turns out to determine their future career. April, June, September and November could see key developments, but whenever the Metal Horse sees a vacancy that interests him, he should act quickly.

With his busy lifestyle, this will be an expensive year for him, especially as he may also decide to travel. In order to proceed with his plans, he will need to keep a close watch on spending. This year requires careful financial management. The Metal Horse should also be wary of risk and check the details and implications of any agreement he enters into.

The Metal Horse attaches a lot of importance to his social life and once again will enjoy many social occasions this year. With changes in his circumstances, there could be the opportunity to forge an additional set of friends.

Socially, the Metal Horse will be in demand. However, where affairs of the heart are concerned, this is a time to tread carefully. Some romances will flourish, but some may founder. Without sufficient time, care and attention, problems can arise. In the Snake year, the warnings are there. If the Metal Horse remains true and nurtures the relationship, however, this can be a wonderfully happy year. Again, much rests in the Metal Horse's own hands. March, May, October and December could see the most social opportunity.

Although the Metal Horse will often be busy with his own pursuits, he should also involve family members in his activities. While they recognize the Metal Horse may want a certain independence, they will be keen to assist. Throughout the year the Metal Horse should remember that support is there should he need it.

Overall, the Year of the Snake will be a demanding one for the Metal Horse and it will require considerable effort to make progress. However, the Metal Horse has a very redoubtable nature, and by making the most of his situation, he can lay down foundations to build on in the future. His personal interests and social life will keep him busy, but where romance is concerned, this is a year for mindfulness. Overall, an important year with far-reaching benefits.

TIP FOR THE YEAR
Focus on what you need to do. With commitment, your rewards will be so much greater and will help as you look to move ahead.

The Water Horse

This will be a quieter year than some, but the Water Horse will appreciate the chance to focus on his activities rather than feel rushed or pressured.

One of the Water Horse's strengths is his enquiring mind, and Water Horses born in 1942 will find their thirst for knowledge well satisfied this year. Not only will they often enjoy reading up on their chosen subjects and following the latest developments, but also trying out new products and equipment. Some may decide to update their computer, master new software, enjoy some gadgetry or install equipment in their home that makes certain tasks easier. Whatever they do, many will also have the opportunity to set themselves interesting projects and personal objectives. The Snake year can whet their inventive streak and many will enjoy trying out ideas and immersing themselves in different pursuits.

The Water Horse will also appreciate his close circle of friends and the chance to meet up and exchange views. Local activities can also bring him into contact with others, with March, May, late September, October and December seeing the most social activity.

However, while the Water Horse is the master of discretion and has a fine personal manner, even he is not immune from the trickier aspects of the year, and should he find himself in an awkward situation, he will need to tread carefully. Minor issues can suddenly escalate, casual remarks be misconstrued and a moment of indiscretion lead to anguish. Water Horses, take note and be on your guard.

The Water Horse also needs to be vigilant in money matters this year and when making more major purchases, it would be worth him taking the time to compare different products as well as check the terms and conditions. Extra care will lead to better decisions and sometimes save unnecessary outlay. Paperwork also needs care. Although this can be irksome, insufficient attention could be to the Water Horse's disadvantage. Again, Water Horses, take note.

In his home life the Water Horse will be grateful for the support of those around him, although to benefit fully he does need to be receptive to their views and suggestions. A combined approach will lead to better results. During the year many Water Horses can look forward to celebrating the news and success of a younger relation. Domestically, this is a pleasing time.

For Water Horses born in 2002, this can also be an interesting year. As their education develops, more chances will open up for them. By taking advantage of the opportunities that are available, these Water Horses will not only enjoy learning more but also the sense of achievement their new accomplishments bring.

Throughout the year, the young Water Horse should be forthcoming and tell others if he has a particular idea or there is something he would like to try out. Similarly, he should draw on the assistance of those around him if he has concerns or is finding something difficult. This is not a year to suffer in silence or deny himself the help and support that is available to him.

Also, while he can have a great deal of fun with his friends, sometimes a petty jealousy or disagreement could surface. Where possible, the Water Horse should try to resolve any problems quickly and, if necessary, seek help. While much can go well, Snake years are not without their problems and the young Water Horse needs to remember that support is there should he need it.

Overall, this will be a satisfying year for the Water Horse, especially as he will be able to carry out many of his ideas and plans. When dealing with finance and some social situations, extra care will be needed, but generally a lot will be in the Water Horse's favour this year and there will be some pleasing personal accomplishments to enjoy, especially relating to home and interest-related activities.

TIP FOR THE YEAR
Delight in your enquiring nature. Follow up your ideas and develop your skills and interests. This is a particularly encouraging year for personal pursuits. Seize your opportunities and use your time well, as you can gain a lot from this year.

The Wood Horse

The Wood Horse reads situations well. He is not only quick to spot opportunities but also relies a lot on instinct. When he has misgivings, he holds back until he has clarified his thoughts and it is the right moment to act. His canny sense will serve him well this year, as it will be a variable one for him. Even though it will bring some good opportunities and pleasing times, there will also be lulls when progress may be slow and sluggish. However, it is by making the most of such times that the Wood Horse can benefit from his actions as well as help his future prospects.

One of the key features of the Snake year is that it encourages personal development and in 2013 the Wood

Horse should use any chance he has to further his skills and knowledge. Particularly where personal interests are concerned, by looking to do more, he can not only get considerable satisfaction from his activities but also find new possibilities opening up. To assist in this, some Wood Horses may buy additional equipment or, if their activities are computer-related, get software to make certain processes easier. Whatever they do, many will delight in the way certain activities and ideas move forward over the year.

Also, if the Wood Horse should become intrigued by a new subject or recreational pursuit, or sees a course that appeals to him, he should follow it up. By using his time well, particularly in some of the year's quieter moments, he can gain a lot from the Year of the Snake.

In addition, if the Wood Horse lacks regular exercise, this would be an excellent time to consider ways he could remedy this. If he seeks advice, he could well learn of a suitable pursuit to take up, perhaps yoga, Pilates, *Tai Chi* or something similar. Snake years favour personal development.

The Wood Horse's work situation may also see some important developments. In view of their experience, many Wood Horses will find themselves with new objectives to meet and possibly some challenging situations to deal with. While some months will be demanding, by drawing on his extensive knowledge and focusing on what needs to be done, the Wood Horse will not only acquit himself well but also enjoy some notable triumphs. This is a year when his judgement, instinct and commitment will help in a lot of what he has to do.

The majority of Wood Horses will remain with their present employer this year and will have the chance to take on greater responsibilities. However, for those who decide to change their working commitments, perhaps in order to reduce their commuting time, as well as those seeking work, the Snake year can open up some interesting possibilities. Although securing a position will be difficult, by widening the scope of what they are prepared to consider and indicating their willingness to learn and adapt, many Wood Horses will be given an opportunity (even if initially only on a temporary basis) which will allow them to use their skills in new ways. April, June, September and November could see encouraging developments.

Financially, the Wood Horse is likely to be involved in some large transactions this year. Often these will be related to his home. Whether repairs or purchases, he will need to make allowance for them and, where applicable, obtain several quotations and check that these meet his requirements. Many Wood Horses will also spend money on their personal interests as well as have additional family and travel expenses. To help, these Wood Horses should plan ahead and keep track of their spending. Financially, this is a year for discipline and care. Also, should anything concern the Wood Horse at any time, it would be helpful for him to seek additional advice.

In his home life, he can look forward to some interesting developments. Some Wood Horses will use some of the year's quieter times to go ahead with projects they have long been considering. By sharing decisions and carrying out projects jointly, the Wood Horse and those around him will be pleased with the results. Throughout the year it is also important that the Wood Horse talks to family members about his various interest-related activities and ideas. This way others will be able to give more informed advice and support. The Wood Horse does a lot for others and in the Snake year he should give others a chance to do something for him in return. Also, in many a Wood Horse household there will be a key event to celebrate, possibly a personal milestone, success or anniversary which will be a source of pride to the Wood Horse.

The Wood Horse will also enjoy his socializing over the year. Whether attending local events, meeting up with friends or pursuing his interests, he will find the Snake year bringing good social opportunities. March, May, October and December will be active months. Certain of the Wood Horse's friends could also be especially helpful with some activities he is undertaking or decisions he has to take. However, while a lot will go well, the Wood Horse needs to be wary of indiscretions or placing himself in potentially awkward situations. Lapses may undermine the good relationships he has built up. This will only apply to a minority, but Wood Horses, take note.

Overall, the Snake year may be quieter than some, but it will give the Wood Horse a chance to proceed in the way he wants. As a result, he can broaden his interests and skills and advance some of his plans. He will need to be mindful of others and liaise well with those around him, but his ability to read people and situations well will stand him in good stead and he will enjoy much of this quiet but pleasantly encouraging year.

TIP FOR THE YEAR

Seize your opportunities and put your ideas into practice. What you do this year can often work out well and open up new possibilities. Also, share what you do with others. Their support can be helpful to you as well as strengthen the rapport you share.

The Fire Horse

The Fire Horse has tremendous drive. He is not one to sit on the sidelines. When he wants things done, he just gets on and does them. Determined and resourceful, he leads a full life and seizes his opportunities. However, in the Snake year he can expect a slowdown in activity. Snake years proceed in more measured ways and while the Fire Horse may sometimes be champing at the bit, this year he will need to show greater patience than usual. The year can still be constructive, but may lack the activity and immediate results the Fire Horse tends to favour.

At work, many Fire Horses will find that as new methods are introduced they will have the opportunity to vary their role or take on new responsibilities. While the Snake year may not be one for sweeping progress, there will still be a chance to make headway. All Fire Horses, whether relatively new to their position or well-established, should keep themselves informed of work developments as well as take advantage of any training they are offered. Keeping themselves up to date will not only help their present situation but also help them to detect trends and possibilities worth pursuing later. In this respect, the effort the Fire Horse puts into his current situation can have considerable bearing on his future prospects, especially next year.

There will, though, be some Fire Horses who feel unfulfilled where they are and decide to make a change. For these Fire Horses, as well as those seeking work, the Snake year can be significant. Obtaining a new position will not be easy and there will be disappointments in their quest. However, by widening the scope of positions they are prepared to consider and being active in the job-seeking process, they can see their resolve rewarded, and once in a new position, they will revel in the opportunity. This could mean considerable adjustment and a steep learning curve, but the Fire Horse can quickly establish himself in a new type of work and build on this in the future. April, June, September and November could see important developments.

As a result of changes in their work situation, many Fire Horses will successfully widen their skills during the year, but this need not be restricted to their work – the Fire Horse should give some thought to how he could make more of his interests too. If new skills or equipment could help, he should find out more. Also, if there is an idea or project he has been thinking over, now would be an excellent time to take this further. Any Fire Horse who, due to other commitments, has let personal interests fall away in recent years would find this an ideal year to start something new. This can not only be satisfying but help keep the Fire Horse's lifestyle in balance. The Snake year encourages personal growth and the Fire Horse's positive actions during it can have both present *and* future benefit. Also, should the Fire Horse feel himself lacking in regular exercise, it would be worth giving consideration to this area too.

With his various activities and commitments, the Fire Horse will need to keep a close watch on spending during the year. Where more expensive purchases are concerned, he should take the time to consider his choices carefully as well as check terms and obligations. In matters of finance this is a year for managing outgoings carefully and being thorough.

As far as the Fire Horse's social life is concerned, this may be a quieter year than usual. The Fire Horse may be more selective in his socializing, but when he has the chance to meet up with his friends or attend social events, he should do his best to go. This can help him relax and do him good.

For Fire Horses who find romance this year, care will be needed. Rather than rush into any commitment, the Fire Horse should allow time to get to know the other person better. Haste may lead to heartache. Also, the Fire Horse should be wary of acting in ways that could cause problems. Without care, a lapse or moment of indiscretion could lead to personal difficulty and regret. Fire Horses, take note.

In his home life the Fire Horse will often be kept busy. Not only will he be involved in his own activities, but will also help and advise those close to him, particularly as some could have major decisions to take. In addition there could be a household problem to deal with. At all times the Fire Horse's talent for coping with a great many things will be appreciated, as will his ability to organize. Though busy, he will draw much satisfaction from certain home projects and purchases over the year as well as enjoy the interests he shares with his loved ones. There could also be interesting travel opportunities, especially late on in the year.

Overall, the Year of the Snake will be a varied but interesting one for the Fire Horse. Although some projects may take longer than he would like, he will have the chance to focus on his current situation and build on his skills. This may not be a progressive year, but it can be a constructive one. Also, the slower nature of the Snake year will give the Fire Horse more chance to appreciate his personal interests and develop these in some way. He will play a special part in the lives of those close to him and his qualities and strengths will be appreciated. By adjusting to the slower pace of the Snake year, he can find a lot can follow on from what he does during it.

TIP FOR THE YEAR
Avoid haste. Spend time developing your skills. What you do now can prepare the way for future opportunities and some fine personal successes, especially in 2014, the auspicious Year of the Horse.

The Earth Horse

There is a Chinese proverb that the Earth Horse would do well to bear in mind this year: 'Constant effort yields certain success.' The Snake year can be an important one for him. This is a time for effort, personal development and laying the foundations for future success.

The Earth Horse has an ambitious streak and tends to reflect on his future. If he feels it could be helpful to acquire another qualification or skill, he should see what is possible this year. It could be that there is a course he could take or an online study programme. If training is offered in his place of work, he should take full advantage of it. By using this year to extend his skills he will be investing in himself *and* his future. Any Earth Horses who have been contemplating a career change or are set on making more of a particular strength will find that research and study could alert them to new possibilities or suitable openings. Time spent on personal and career development can be especially important this year.

The Earth Horse's work situation can also see interesting developments. For Earth Horses who have been in the same position for some time, this is a year to build on their proven experience and look to move on. This includes putting in for promotion or, if working in a large organization, enquiring about vacancies in other sections. In many cases their in-house experience will stand them in good stead and lead to a change of role and the assumption of new duties. Admittedly, any progress may be modest rather than substantial, but a key benefit of the year will be the way the Earth Horse can add to his experience and gain greater insight into the organization and industry in which he works.

Also, Earth Horses who do change their duties during the year will often have the chance to work with other colleagues and make new contacts. The effort the Earth Horse puts into this, and into networking in general, will be helpful, and some Earth Horses will particularly benefit from the encouragement of more senior colleagues.

Most Earth Horses will remain with their present employer this year, but for those who are keen to move on or are seeking work, the Snake year can be important. Obtaining a new position will involve considerable effort and there will be disappointments along the way. However, by keeping informed of vacancies and acting quickly on those that are of interest, these Earth Horses will find their initiative and keenness rewarded. Over the year, many will secure a new position that has the potential for further development. April, June, September and November could see interesting possibilities.

In money matters, the Earth Horse will need to be disciplined and manage his finances well, including making early provision for plans and purchases and keeping careful control of outgoings. He should take careful note of the terms and obligations of any new agreement he may enter into as well as keep paperwork and guarantees safe. Without extra vigilance, problems and delays could occur.

The Earth Horse should also give time to his personal interests over the year. Again, if he is able to add to his skills or extend what he does in some way, this can add something special to what he sets out to do. Any Earth Horses who feel they could benefit from a new challenge or would welcome something different to do should consider taking up a new interest and see what is available locally. Again, what they do now can open up both present and future possibilities.

The Earth Horse will appreciate his socializing this year and can look forward to a range of pleasant social occasions. Changes in his work situation and personal interests can give him further chances to meet others and make new friends. For the unattached, romance can also figure significantly. However, as with all Horses this year, the Earth Horse does need to guard against indiscretions or jeopardizing any relationship with some lapse. These words only apply to a few, but without care, unwise actions can lead to personal difficulty. Earth Horses, take note.

The Earth Horse's home life promises to be full and interesting. In particular, he will do a lot to help and advise those close to him and many will be grateful for what he is able to do. When pressures or problems arise, his ability to suggest solutions will be especially helpful.

Over the year, the Earth Horse will particularly enjoy the various domestic activities and plans that can be shared. The more co-operation, the better. This is a year encouraging involvement and a joint approach. The Earth Horse will also value quality time with his loved ones. Some breaks or a holiday can be particularly enjoyable and even if it is not possible to travel far, a change of scene can do everyone good.

Overall, the Year of the Snake can be a pleasant and satisfying one for the Earth Horse. Modest progress is possible, but the real gains will come from the way the Earth Horse is able to build on his skills and, in some cases, take up new interests. By putting in the effort and furthering his knowledge, he can find interesting possibilities opening up for him both now and in the near future. This is a year for laying the groundwork for future success, especially in 2014, the Year of the Horse. This is a time to learn, prepare and enjoy.

TIP FOR THE YEAR

Two tips! Value your relations with others. Spend time with those who are special to you and share your activities and thoughts. Also, look to develop your work skills. What you do now can be an investment in your future. Use this year well, for its benefits can be significant.

FAMOUS HORSES

Roman Abramovich, Neil Armstrong, Rowan Atkinson, Samuel Beckett, Ingmar Bergman, Leonard Bernstein, Joe Biden, James Blunt, Helena Bonham Carter, David Cameron, James Cameron, Jackie Chan, Ray Charles, Chopin, Nick Clegg, Sir Sean Connery, Billy Connolly, Catherine Cookson, Elvis Costello, Kevin Costner, Cindy Crawford, James Dean, Clint Eastwood, Thomas Alva Edison, Harrison Ford, Aretha Franklin, Bob Geldof, Samuel Goldwyn, Billy Graham, Gene Hackman, Rolf Harris, Rita Hayworth, Jimi Hendrix, Janet Jackson, Calvin Klein, Petra Kvitova, Lenin, Annie Lennox, Pixie Lott, Rachel McAdams, Sir Paul McCartney, Nelson Mandela, Angela Merkel, Michael Moore, Ben Murphy, Sir Isaac Newton, Louis Pasteur, Katie Price (Jordan), Dennis Quaid, Gordon Ramsay, Lou Reed, Rembrandt, Ruth Rendell, Jean Renoir, Theodore Roosevelt, Helena Rubenstein, Adam Sandler, David Schwimmer, Martin Scorsese, Kristen Stewart, Barbra Streisand, Kiefer Sutherland, Patrick Swayze, John Travolta, Kathleen Turner, Usher, Vivaldi, Robert Wagner, Denzil Washington, Emma Watson, Billy Wilder, Andy Williams, Brian Wilson, the Duke of Windsor, Caroline Wozniacki, Jacob Zuma.

---

1 FEBRUARY 1919 ～ 19 FEBRUARY 1920   *Earth Goat*

17 FEBRUARY 1931 ～ 5 FEBRUARY 1932   *Metal Goat*

5 FEBRUARY 1943 ～ 24 JANUARY 1944   *Water Goat*

24 JANUARY 1955 ～ 11 FEBRUARY 1956   *Wood Goat*

9 FEBRUARY 1967 ～ 29 JANUARY 1968   *Fire Goat*

28 JANUARY 1979 ～ 15 FEBRUARY 1980   *Earth Goat*

15 FEBRUARY 1991 ～ 3 FEBRUARY 1992   *Metal Goat*

1 FEBRUARY 2003 ～ 21 JANUARY 2004   *Water Goat*

THE
GOAT

THE PERSONALITY OF THE GOAT

Amid the complexities of life,
it is the ability to appreciate that is so special.

The Goat is born under the sign of art. He is imaginative, creative and has a good appreciation of the finer things in life. He has an easy-going nature and prefers to live in a relaxed and pressure-free environment. He hates any sort of discord or unpleasantness and does not like to be bound by a strict routine or rigid timetable. He is not one to be hurried against his will, but despite his seemingly relaxed approach to life, he is something of a perfectionist and when he starts work on a project he is certain to give his best.

The Goat usually prefers to work in a team rather than on his own. He likes to have the support and encouragement of others and if left to deal with matters on his own he can get very worried and tend to view things rather pessimistically. Wherever possible he will leave major decision-making to others while he concentrates on his own pursuits. If, however, he feels particularly strongly about a certain matter or has to defend his position in any way, he will act with great fortitude and precision.

The Goat has a very persuasive nature and often uses his considerable charm to get his own way. He can, however, be rather hesitant about letting his true feelings be known and if he were prepared to be more forthright he would do much better as a result.

The Goat tends to have a quiet, somewhat reserved nature, but when he is in company he likes he can often become the centre of attention. He can be highly amusing, a marvellous host at parties and a superb entertainer. Whenever the spotlight falls on him, his adrenaline starts to flow and he can be assured of giving a sparkling performance, particularly if he is allowed to use his creative skills in any way.

Of all the signs in the Chinese zodiac, the Goat is probably the most gifted artistically. Whether it is in the theatre, literature, music or art, he is certain to make a lasting impression. He is a born creator and is rarely happier than when occupied in some artistic pursuit. But even in this he does well to work with others rather than on his own. He needs inspiration and a guiding influence, but when he has found his true *métier*, he can often receive widespread acclaim and recognition.

In addition to his liking for the arts, the Goat is usually quite religious and often has a deep interest in nature, animals and the countryside. He is also fairly athletic and there are many Goats who have excelled in some form of sporting activity or who have a great interest in sport.

Although the Goat is not particularly materialistic or concerned about finance, he will find that he will usually be lucky in financial matters and will rarely be short of the necessary funds to tide himself over. He is, however, rather self-indulgent and tends to spend his money as soon as he receives it rather than make provision for the future.

The Goat usually leaves home when he is young but he will always maintain strong links with his parents and the other members of his family. He is also rather nostalgic and is well known for keeping mementoes of his childhood and souvenirs of places that he has visited. His home will not be particularly tidy, but he knows where everything is and it will be scrupulously clean.

Affairs of the heart are particularly important to the Goat and he will often have many romances before he finally settles down. Although he is fairly adaptable, he prefers to live in a secure and stable environment and he will find that he is best suited to those born under the signs of the Tiger, Horse, Monkey, Pig and Rabbit. He can also establish a good relationship with the Dragon, Snake, Rooster and another Goat, but he may find the Ox and Dog a little too serious for his liking. Neither will he care particularly for the Rat's rather thrifty ways.

The female Goat devotes all her time and energy to the needs of her family. She has excellent taste in home furnishings and often uses her considerable artistic skills to make clothes for herself and her children. She takes great care over her appearance and can be most attractive to others. Although she is not the most organized of people, her engaging manner and delightful sense of humour create a favourable impression wherever she goes. She is also a good cook and usually derives much pleasure from gardening and outdoor pursuits.

The Goat can win friends easily and people generally feel relaxed in his company. He has a kind and understanding nature and although he can occasionally be stubborn, he can, with the right support and encouragement, live a very satisfying life. And the more he can use his creative skills, the happier he will be.

THE FIVE DIFFERENT TYPES OF GOAT

In addition to the 12 signs of the Chinese zodiac there are five elements and these have a strengthening or moderating influence on the signs. The effects of the five elements on the Goat are described below, together with the years in which they were exercising their influence. Therefore Goats born in 1931 and 1991 are Metal Goats, Goats born in 1943 and 2003 are Water Goats, and so on.

Metal Goat: 1931, 1991

This Goat is thorough and conscientious in all that he does and is capable of doing very well in his chosen profession. Despite his confident manner, he can be a great worrier and he would find it helpful to discuss his concerns with others rather than keep them to himself. He is loyal to his family and employers and will have a small group of particularly close friends. He has good taste and is usually highly skilled in some of aspect of the arts. He is often a collector of antiques and his home will be very tastefully furnished.

Water Goat: 1943, 2003

The Water Goat is very popular and makes friends with remarkable ease. He is good at spotting opportunities but does not always have the necessary confidence to follow them through. He likes to have security both in his home life and work and does not take kindly to change. He is articulate, has a good sense of humour and is usually very good with children.

Wood Goat: 1955

This Goat is generous, kind-hearted and always eager to please. He usually has a large circle of friends and involves himself in a wide variety of activities. He has a very trusting nature but can sometimes give in to the demands of others a little too easily and it would be in his interests if he were to stand his ground more often. He is usually lucky in financial matters and, like the Water Goat, is very good with children.

Fire Goat: 1967

This Goat usually knows what he wants in life and often uses his considerable charm and persuasive personality to achieve his aims. He can sometimes let his imagination run away with him and has a tendency to ignore matters that are not to his liking. He is rather extravagant in his spending and would do well to exercise a little more care when dealing with financial matters. He has a lively personality, many friends, and loves attending parties and social occasions.

Earth Goat: 1919, 1979

This Goat has a considerate and caring nature. He is particularly loyal to his family and friends and invariably creates a favourable impression wherever he goes. He is reliable

and conscientious in his work but sometimes finds it difficult to save and never likes to deprive himself of any little
luxury he might fancy. He has numerous interests and is
often very well read. He usually derives much pleasure
from following the activities of the various members of his
family.

PROSPECTS FOR THE GOAT IN 2013

The Year of the Dragon (23 January 2012–9 February 2013)
will have been a busy one for the Goat and as it draws to a
close he will have a lot to do and some interesting times to
enjoy.

Whether assisting those at home, dealing with practical
matters, making plans or arranging special occasions, the
genial Goat will find himself in demand at this time. The
last few months of the year in particular will see a flurry of
activity. Although the Goat may sometimes despair over all
he has to do, he will be pleased with how a lot of his activities work out and will appreciate spending time with his
loved ones. His social life, too, is set to become busier in the
closing months of the year.

The Dragon year is generally a fast-moving one and
during it the Goat will have seen considerable change taking
place at work. This could have brought pressure and uncertainty, but also opened up new opportunities. This pattern
will continue to the end of the Dragon year. This will be a
busy and volatile time, but will offer the Goat the chance to
learn and move ahead. September, October and early
January could see particularly interesting developments.

The closing months of the Dragon year will also bring an increase in expenditure, and while the Goat will enjoy what he spends his money on, as well as be generous to others, he will need to watch his outgoings. Without care, they could be greater than anticipated.

In general, the Year of the Dragon will be an active one for the Goat, but despite the pressures it may bring, it will contain some rewarding times and leave the Goat with some accomplishments he can build on.

The Year of the Snake begins on 10 February and during it the Goat can enjoy considerable good fortune. Not only will he feel more inspired than of late, but will also find many of his activities going well.

One of the most positive aspects of the year concerns the Goat's relations with others. With his outgoing nature, he will appreciate his chances to meet friends and socialize. There will be news and gossip to follow and good opportunities to meet new people. Many a Goat will see quite an increase in his social circle this year and in the process meet some people who can be helpful and important. There will be social opportunities at most times of the year, but March, April, August and December could see the most activity.

For any Goats who are feeling lonely, perhaps having moved to a new area or experienced some recent difficulty in their personal life, the Snake year can mark a turning point. By putting the past behind them and concentrating on the present, they could find new activities, new people and new chances all helping to make a difference to their outlook and lifestyle. Snake years are supportive of Goats, and for those who have languished for a while or experienced recent misfortune, better times *are* on the way.

For the unattached, affairs of the heart can also make this a special time. For those already enjoying romance, relationships can become more permanent. Wedding bells will sound for many a Goat this year. Cupid's arrow could also be aimed at quite a few. Even if one romance founders, another could soon take its place. Goats will be popular company this year.

The Goat's home life is also favourably aspected. Support is very important for the Goat and as he makes progress and has significant decisions to make, he will be particularly glad of the advice and reassurance of those close to him. It is important that he is forthcoming, as that way he can benefit from what others say or do.

He can also look forward to some fine family occasions and, whether marking his own success or sharing in the good news of others, he will greatly enjoy these. There will be times that will mean a great deal, and some Goats could see the realization of long-cherished hopes.

Travel, too, is well aspected, and if possible the Goat should take a holiday with his loved ones at some time during the year. A rest and change of routine could be very welcome, and careful planning could lead to the Goat especially enjoying some of the sights he sees or cultural events he attends.

Snake years also encourage personal interests, and for Goats who are creatively inclined or enjoy the arts, this can be a rewarding time. During the year all Goats should aim to make more of their ideas and talents.

For those whose work involves some form of creative input, this can be a particularly successful year. By using their strengths to advantage, they can enjoy some notable successes as well as further their career. Even though some Goats may be shy and retiring, this is a year to have faith in themselves and make the most of their opportunities.

Also, no matter what area of work the Goat may be in, the Snake year is one for progress, and if promotion opportunities become available or the Goat sees a vacancy that appeals to him, he should put himself forward. This is no time for standing still and many Goats will be able to move on to a greater and more fulfilling role.

For Goats seeking work, again this is a year of interesting developments. While the job-seeking process can be wearying, by making enquiries and exploring possibilities (including training initiatives or government-sponsored schemes), they will find doors opening. Some may be offered work that is different from what they have done before but find it allows them to use their skills in new ways. This is a year to be open to possibility, with February, March, September and November seeing encouraging developments.

The Goat can also look forward to an increase in income over the year. However, with an often busy lifestyle, his spending can be considerable and he would do well to keep a close watch on outgoings. Many Goats will be tempted to travel this year and should make provision for this.

One of the most encouraging features of the Snake year is that it gives the Goat a chance to use and enjoy his abilities. In both his work and personal interests, his ideas, skills and gift of expression can make a real difference and allow him to make headway and gain encouraging results. Over the year the Goat really does need to put himself forward and should remember the maxim, 'Nothing ventured, nothing gained.' In 2013 the Goat *should* venture. His personal life can also bring him considerable pleasure, with the love of others and, for some, the excitement of romance helping to make this year special. Goats have a lot in their favour in 2013 and it rests with them to make things happen. With determination, they can.

The Metal Goat

The Chinese have a proverb, 'If a spider works hard spinning webs, it will eventually catch insects. Hard work will pay off.' This will be very true for the Metal Goat this year. This is an exciting time for him and a lot is set to go well.

One of the chief benefits of the year will be the experience and knowledge the Metal Goat is able to gain. Those in education should set about their studying in a disciplined and well-planned manner. By allowing sufficient time for coursework, revision and research, they will not only understand and appreciate more of the subjects they are studying but often gain better results. Consistency and application *will* pay off.

These Metal Goats should also make the most of the assistance available to them. Not only can this help with their studying, but when considering future options, some guidance could prove especially helpful. With so much riding on the Metal Goat's current work and decisions, it is important that he remembers there are experts around who can instruct and encourage. The Metal Goat has many rooting for him, but to benefit, he will need to be prepared to ask.

Snake years favour culture and the arts, and Metal Goats who are interested in these areas should make the most of their skills and ideas. With many Metal Goats possessing creative flair, this can be an inspiring time, with work they put forward often being well received.

No matter what the Metal Goat's interests, the Snake year can provide many fine recreational opportunities. He will often have a great mix of things to do and enjoy. In addition, he can look forward to a lot of socializing during the year and his circle of friends is set to increase as his circumstances change. March, April, August and December will see much social activity.

Affairs of the heart can also add excitement to this already busy year. For some Metal Goats, existing romances can become more meaningful, while for others, new romances can make this an interesting although not always easy time. With his outgoing manner, the Metal Goat could have quite a few people competing for his attention and his heart may be drawn in several directions. However, while some relationships may peter out after a short while, quite a few Metal Goats will meet someone who will become special on a longer-term basis.

Although the Metal Goat will be kept busy with his various activities, he should also give time to his home life, including spending time talking to more senior relations. Not only will they be interested and supportive, but they can sometimes provide advice, resources or assistance that can make a difference to the Metal Goat's situation. In turn, he can reciprocate by assisting with certain household tasks or using some of his skills and knowledge to help with particular projects. With co-operation and good communication, relations between the Metal Goat and his family members will often be positive and mutually beneficial.

This can also be an important year for work prospects. Metal Goats who are already in a position may have impressed others recently and may now be encouraged to do more and in some cases take on a greater role. These Metal Goats should take advantage of any training they are offered as well as take the time to familiarize themselves with the different aspects of their work. Involvement, effort and commitment will pay off.

For those who are currently unfulfilled or seeking work, the Snake year can have interesting developments in store. Although the job-seeking process may not be easy, by thinking carefully over what they actually want to do and making enquiries, these Metal Goats could be alerted to possibilities worth considering or a different way to get into the type of work they favour. The Snake year will require these Metal Goats to put effort into their quest and show flexibility, but they may be able to obtain a position that can be a valuable platform for future progress. February to early April, September and November could see interesting possibilities.

Throughout the year, however, the Metal Goat will need to keep a close watch on his finances. With an active social life, plus his commitments and interests, he will need to manage his money well and, in some cases, be disciplined about how much is spent on certain activities or occasions. Some restraint may be needed if he is to do all he wants.

Generally, the Snake year can be a full and pleasing one for the Metal Goat. It can bring excellent chances to further his skills and gain useful experience and additional qualifications. What the Metal Goat achieves this year can be something positive he can take further in future years. On a personal level this will be a busy and often creative time and the Metal Goat can look forward to an active social life, with affairs of the heart adding excitement and sparkle. Overall, a year of great potential, but to make the most of it the Metal Goat will need effort and commitment.

TIP FOR THE YEAR
What you do now can have far-reaching consequences. When making decisions, do draw on the advice and expertise available to you. With support and the right information, your choices can be made a lot easier. This can be a valuable year. Enjoy it and reap the benefits.

The Water Goat

The Water element can not only make a sign more communicative and aware but also heighten its intuitive ability. This is especially true for the Water Goat. He is particularly adept at sensing things, following hunches and being in tune with what is going on. In 2013, which marks a new decade in his life, his abilities will serve him well.

For Water Goats born in 1943, this can be an inspiring time. Born under the sign of art, the Water Goat has fine taste. Whether he enjoys music, art, writing, visiting places of interest or being out in the countryside (or garden), by spending time in ways he appreciates, he will delight in a lot of what he does this year.

He will also often be tempted to take certain interests further, and by adding to his knowledge or pursuing his ideas, he can take great satisfaction in his activities. Some can have added benefits, including the chance to meet other enthusiasts or join a local interest group. Both new and existing interests can bring the Water Goat real pleasure and benefit this year. Also, should he see a competition which draws on his talents or specialist knowledge, he should consider entering it. He may fare particularly well. Similarly, if any creatively inclined Water Goats see opportunities to put their art, writing or craftwork forward, they could again enjoy an encouraging response.

Another pleasing aspect of the year will be the travel opportunities that arise and many Water Goats will decide to treat themselves to a special holiday to mark their seventieth year. This could include realizing a long-held ambition to visit specific places or attend certain events. The Water Goat's seventieth year can be rich in possibility.

With his outgoing and enquiring nature, he will also enjoy good relations with many people and very much appreciate the social opportunities that arise over the year, particularly if he would welcome company or new friends. Often his interests, including new ones he takes up over the year, can have a good social element. With his caring nature and desire to contribute, he may also decide to help in his community or support a cause, and this can again bring him into contact with others. March, April, August and December could be particularly pleasurable months socially.

The Water Goat's family and close friends will also be keen to mark his seventieth birthday in style and many Water Goats will be genuinely touched by the affection shown them and the surprises loved ones have in store. Some will also have the opportunity to meet up with friends and relations they may not have seen for some while. Some parts of the year will have an exciting and celebratory feel. In addition, there could be further news that will delight the Water Goat, often concerning the deserved success of a younger relation and made all the more heartening because of the effort involved.

In most respects this will be a pleasing year for the Water Goat but, as always, problems can raise their head. If they do, it is important the Water Goat talks to his loved ones and others who are able to give advice. With assistance, problems can often be defused.

Similarly, this is not a year to be lax or make assumptions over financial matters. The Water Goat should be thorough when dealing with paperwork and seek advice if anything concerns him. Delays could be to his disadvantage. Water Goats, take note.

For Water Goats born in 2003, this can be a year of discovery and fun. Not only will they cover a lot of ground in their schoolwork but also be encouraged to develop new skills. With a willing attitude, many will be excited by what they get to try out this year. Even if some activities may initially be difficult, with application and support the young Water Goat can make good progress and see some definite strengths emerging.

He will also value the camaraderie of his close circle of friends. Not only will he enjoy mutual interests but also being able to share news and secrets. The young Water Goat will develop well over the year, both in outward confidence and in what he learns and discovers.

Overall, the Year of the Snake can be an encouraging one for the Water Goat and give him the chance to enjoy his skills, interests and creativity. This can be an inspiring time. Also, with it marking a new decade in the Water Goat's life, there will be celebrations and surprises in store.

This can be a special and successful year. Be sure to put your talents to good use and make the most of your ideas. Much good can follow on from what you do now.

The Wood Goat

The Wood Goat may have felt buffeted by events in recent years. There will have been pressures and difficult decisions, and not everything will have gone as smoothly as he would have liked. However, the Snake year will see a steadying in his position and will give him more chance to proceed in the way he wants, as well as enjoy some positive developments.

As the Snake year begins, the Wood Goat should give some thought to what he would like to see happen over the next 12 months. This will not only give him something to work towards but also make him more alert to opportunities. 'Well begun is half done', as the Chinese proverb states, and by deciding on his personal objectives for the year the Wood Goat will be helping to get it off to a positive start.

During the year he will also be helped by the support and advice of those close to him. To get full benefit, though, he does need to be forthcoming.

At work the aspects are encouraging. Many Wood Goats will have come under intense pressure in recent years and not be satisfied with their situation. However, the Snake year will give them more chance to concentrate on their area of expertise and many will benefit from promotion opportunities and/or the chance to take on new responsibilities, including becoming involved with new initiatives and assisting junior colleagues.

Throughout the year the Wood Goat should also make the most of his innovative nature. If he has ideas about how certain procedures could be improved, solutions to problems or suggestions that could be of benefit, he should put them forward. His input can make a significant difference.

The majority of Wood Goats will make headway with their present employer over the year, but for those who feel the time is right for change or are seeking work, the Snake year can open up possibilities. These Wood Goats should not be too restrictive in the type of work they look for. By being flexible and investigating what is available, many could secure a position which not only offers an interesting work challenge but also gives them new incentive. February, March, September and November could see good opportunities, but throughout the Snake year the Wood Goat should act quickly if he identifies a suitable opening.

The progress he makes at work can also help financially, but with his commitments, planned purchases and the possibility of travel, he will need to watch his spending and make advance provision for larger outgoings. He also needs to deal with financial paperwork carefully. This may be a favourable year, but insufficient attention to what could be important matters could be to his disadvantage. Wood Goats, take note.

The Snake year favours culture and the arts, and as many Wood Goats are interested in this area, they should use any chances they get to follow this up, including attending events and visiting places that appeal to them. In addition the Wood Goat should set time aside for his own pursuits. Creative activities are favourably aspected this year and the Wood Goat will often be inspired by ideas he has and projects he starts. Any Wood Goats who have let their interests lapse would find this an excellent year to take up something new. Wood Goats who lack regular exercise would particularly benefit from starting a suitable activity. The Wood Goat will feel more in control of what he does this year and his interests can bring him both pleasure and benefit.

The Wood Goat has a circle of close friends and over the year will particularly value their support and enjoy the social events he attends. As the year develops, some Wood Goats could find themselves involved in activity groups or helping their community or someone in need. The Wood Goat has a caring nature and certain of his activities will have added meaning this year.

Any Wood Goat who starts 2013 in low spirits or feeling lonely will find the Snake year can bring an improvement in his situation. By going out more and joining in with local activities, these Wood Goats will often get to make new friendships. For a few, the Snake year can also bring romance. March, April, late July, August and December could see the most social activity.

As always, the Wood Goat will value his home life, and as this is a year favouring communication, if he talks over his ideas with those around him, a lot can happen. There will also be special occasions that everyone can appreciate, perhaps celebrating personal achievements or taking a holiday or short break. Domestically, this can be a pleasing and positive year. Admittedly, there will be pressures and possible regrets too, but with support, these can often be dealt with and extra help given.

Overall, the Snake year has great potential for the Wood Goat. It will allow him to make more of his own special talents and by deciding what he wants and then taking positive action, he can make good progress. This is a positive year, but it does rest with the Wood Goat to seize the initiative. He will value the support of those around him, however, and his home and social life will bring him especial pleasure.

TIP FOR THE YEAR
Enjoy and develop your interests and make the most of your strengths and ideas. You can accomplish a lot this year and should seize your opportunities. Good luck and enjoy this special and encouraging year.

The Fire Goat
The Fire Goat has considerable resolve and always tries to make the best of his situation. Admittedly, recent conditions may not have made this easy, but in 2013 his talents and personal strengths will come into their own. Any Fire Goat who has been disappointed with recent progress or had personal difficulties should aim to draw a line under what has gone before and concentrate on the present. With a positive approach (and Fire Goat resolve),

he can do a lot to bring about the improvements he wants.

At work, the Fire Goat may well have reached an important stage in his career. Many Fire Goats will have specialized in a certain area and built up a good knowledge of the industry they work in. In the Snake year they will be able to take this further, with many benefiting from promotion opportunities or internal reorganization or using their experience to gain a better position elsewhere. This is very much a year for moving forward and the Fire Goat's proven abilities will help.

For Fire Goats who feel there are limited opportunities where they are or desire change, this is a year to take the initiative. By keeping alert for openings to pursue, many will be able to improve their position and will welcome the new developments. Admittedly, making a change will take considerable effort, but this is very much a time when interesting possibilities can suddenly open up.

The same is true for Fire Goats seeking work. Again, their quest will not be easy and there will be disappointments along the way, but if they are willing to consider different types of work and draw on the advice and resources available to them (including, for some, retraining and refresher courses), their perseverance will often lead to an interesting new position with potential for the future. February, March, late August, September and November could see encouraging developments, but throughout the year all Fire Goats should keep alert for opportunities.

While the Fire Goat will often be kept busy with various commitments, it is important that he allows time to enjoy and develop his personal interests. These not only help keep his lifestyle in balance and provide another outlet for his talents, but sometimes have additional benefits, possibly including exercise or the chance to socialize. Fire Goats seeking a new challenge should aim to take up something different this year. The Snake year is rich in possibility and especially rewards personal development and creativity.

Many Fire Goats can look forward to an increase in earnings this year and some may also find ways to put an interest or skill to profitable use. However, in view of his existing commitments and the wide variety of plans he wants to carry out, the Fire Goat should budget with care and save up for large purchases and possible travel. He should also attend to financial paperwork carefully and promptly. The extra attention he gives will be well worth his while.

Socially, he can look forward to a variety of occasions and will often appreciate them as well as benefit from chances just to relax and enjoy himself. March, April, August and December could see the most social opportunity.

Fire Goats who start the year in low spirits and would welcome new friends or activities should keep informed about what is available in their area. Positive action can reward them well. Many will relish the chance to meet others, and for the unattached, there may be some exciting romantic possibilities.

The Fire Goat's home life is also pleasingly aspected. The Snake year will see personal effort rewarded and some plans and hopes coming to fruition. However, to make the most of the favourable aspects, the Fire Goat's household needs to pool together, share activities and responsibilities and freely discuss ideas and any concerns or niggles. At some point during the year, the Fire Goat should also try to take a holiday with his loved ones. A rest and change of scene could do everyone good.

Overall, the Year of the Snake is one of considerable possibility for the Fire Goat. His resolve, ideas and talents can take him forward and lead to some deserving (and sometimes overdue) successes. This is a time for initiative. The Fire Goat will enjoy good support and his personal life and interests can help make this a pleasing and satisfying year.

TIP FOR THE YEAR
Take action. Make those dreams happen. Keep alert for opportunities and use your ideas and experience to advantage. You have a lot in your favour this year and can make your efforts count. Much is possible. Good luck.

The Earth Goat

The Earth Goat has a great personal manner. He understands, listens and empathizes. Over the year his talents will serve him well. His relations with others can be a particularly important factor this year.

In his home life he will be very much in demand, with both younger and more senior relations grateful for his time and support. Admittedly, there may be issues which concern him, but throughout the year his level-headed manner and ability to gauge what is right will be appreciated. He will also be the driving force behind a lot that happens in his domestic life, including home projects and important purchases. A lot of his suggestions can work out well, but while he may be willing, it is important that household responsibilities are shared and he does not end up tackling too much single-handed. If he is under pressure, tired or would welcome a helping hand, *he should ask*. Also, when facing work or other decisions, he should involve others, as he can benefit from their advice. In some cases, a frank discussion can lead to new possibilities emerging. This is very much a year for combined effort.

With the aspects so favourable, there will be news to celebrate in many an Earth Goat household and the Snake year can be marked by some special times. Also, where possible, the Earth Goat should try to arrange a holiday with his loved ones. Even if it is somewhere not too far away, a break can do everyone a lot of good.

The Earth Goat will also appreciate his social life. Although his commitments may mean he is more selective in his socializing this year, he will again enjoy his opportunities to meet friends and attend events. Some people he has known for some time could be especially grateful for his views, and his friends will again value his insights. Although he may not always appreciate it, this year he will play an important part in the lives of quite a few.

However, while he will do much to assist others, he should not underestimate the help they can give him in return. This also applies to new acquaintances. Many of these will respond well to the Earth Goat's engaging manner and some will become part of his social circle over the year.

The aspects are also encouraging for any Earth Goat who is alone and would welcome new friends or romance. Chance can play an important part this year, with a meeting in fortuitous circumstances often becoming significant. On a personal level, Snake years can be a time of exciting possibility for the Earth Goat and mark a distinct change in fortunes.

The Earth Goat can also gain much satisfaction from his personal interests. If there is a project he would like to tackle, an objective he is keen to reach or a skill he wants to learn, he should allow himself time to do this. His efforts and enthusiasm can lead to a lot opening up for him. Many Earth Goats will be able to put their creative talents to effective use this year.

As far as work is concerned, the Snake year can bring some important opportunities. Although many Earth Goats will now be established in a certain type of work, unexpected possibilities may open up. For those in large organizations, there could be the chance to move to another section or be awarded a promotion which will bring a substantial change in duties. A lot of learning and adjustment could be involved, but what is achieved could not only be an important step forward but also a chance for the Earth Goat to prove himself in another capacity. This can be to his present *and* future benefit.

This also applies to Earth Goats who are currently seeking a position or considering switching careers. Although their quest will require great effort and persistence, the Snake year can proceed in curious ways and many will be offered a position which is different from what they have done before but nevertheless represents a substantial opportunity. Work-wise, the Snake year may not always follow the pattern the Earth Goat anticipates, but its longer-term significance should not be underestimated.

Progress at work can also help financially, but in view of the Earth Goat's commitments and possibly expensive home plans, he will need to manage his spending with care. When making purchases, he should take the time to consider the suitability and cost of what he is considering, and should he have doubts or questions, it is important he seeks advice and clarification before proceeding. This is a time for vigilance.

Overall, the Year of the Snake is a promising one for the Earth Goat. In his work he will have the chance to move forward and learn, and what he achieves now will be important in the longer term. His personal interests can bring him much pleasure and his ideas will often work out well. However, one of the most important aspects of the year is the Earth Goat's relations with others. He can look forward to some special times with his family and close friends, and colleagues and new acquaintances can also be helpful. The Earth Goat's personal qualities will impress many this year and help make this a pleasurable and successful time.

TIP FOR THE YEAR

Look to move forward. The effort you make now can have considerable bearing on both your present situation and the possibilities that can soon open up. Also, enjoy your relations with others and spend quality time with your loved ones. Their love, support and encouragement can help you get so much from this favourable year.

FAMOUS GOATS

Pamela Anderson, Jane Austen, Jenson Button, Lord Byron, Vince Cable, Coco Chanel, Mary Higgins Clark, Nat 'King' Cole, Jamie Cullum, Robert de Niro, Catherine Deneuve, Charles Dickens, Ken Dodd, Sir Arthur Conan Doyle, Douglas Fairbanks, Will Ferrell, Dame Margot Fonteyn, Jamie Foxx, Noel Gallagher, Bill Gates, Robert Gates, Mel Gibson, Whoopi Goldberg, Mikhail Gorbachev, John Grisham, Oscar Hammerstein, George Harrison, Billy Idol, Julio Iglesias, Sir Mick Jagger, Steve Jobs, Norah Jones, Nicole Kidman, Sir Ben Kingsley, Christine Lagarde, John le Carré, Matt LeBlanc, Franz Liszt, James McAvoy, Sir John Major, Michelangelo, Joni Mitchell, Rupert Murdoch, Randy Newman, Sinead O'Connor, Michael Palin, Eva Peron, Pink, Marcel Proust, Keith Richards, Julia Roberts, Nicolas Sarkozy, Philip Seymour Hoffman, William Shatner, Gary Sinise, Jerry Springer, Lana Turner, Mark Twain, Rudolph Valentino, Vangelis, Barbara Walters, John Wayne, Fay Weldon, Bruce Willis.

20 FEBRUARY 1920 ⌒ 7 FEBRUARY 1921 *Metal Monkey*

6 FEBRUARY 1932 ⌒ 25 JANUARY 1933 *Water Monkey*

25 JANUARY 1944 ⌒ 12 FEBRUARY 1945 *Wood Monkey*

12 FEBRUARY 1956 ⌒ 30 JANUARY 1957 *Fire Monkey*

30 JANUARY 1968 ⌒ 16 FEBRUARY 1969 *Earth Monkey*

16 FEBRUARY 1980 ⌒ 4 FEBRUARY 1981 *Metal Monkey*

4 FEBRUARY 1992 ⌒ 22 JANUARY 1993 *Water Monkey*

22 JANUARY 2004 ⌒ 8 FEBRUARY 2005 *Wood Monkey*

THE
MONKEY

THE PERSONALITY OF
THE MONKEY

The more open to possibility,
the more possibilities open.

The Monkey is born under the sign of fantasy. He is imaginative, inquisitive and loves to keep an eye on everything that is going on around him. He is never backward in offering advice or trying to sort out the problems of others. He likes to be helpful and his advice is invariably sensible and reliable.

The Monkey is intelligent, well read and always eager to learn. He has an extremely good memory and there are many Monkeys who have made particularly good linguists. The Monkey is also a convincing talker and enjoys taking part in discussions and debates. His friendly, self-assured manner can be very persuasive and he usually has little trouble in winning people round to his way of thinking. It is for this reason that he often excels in politics and public speaking. He is also particularly adept in PR work, teaching and any job that involves selling.

The Monkey can, however, be crafty, cunning and occasionally dishonest, and he will seize any opportunity to make a quick profit or outsmart his opponents. He has so much charm and guile that people often don't realize what he is up to until it is too late. But despite his resourceful nature, he does run the risk of outsmarting even himself. He has so much confidence in his abilities that he rarely listens to advice or is prepared to accept help from anyone.

He likes to help others, but prefers to rely on his own judgement when dealing with his own affairs.

Another characteristic of the Monkey is that he is extremely good at solving problems and has a happy knack of extricating himself (and others) from the most hopeless of positions. He is the master of self-preservation.

With so many diverse talents, the Monkey is usually able to make considerable sums of money, but he does like to enjoy life and will think nothing of spending his money on some exotic holiday or luxury he has had his eye on. He can, however, become very envious if someone else has what he wants.

The Monkey is an original thinker and despite his love of company, he cherishes his independence. He has to have the freedom to act as he wants and any Monkey who feels hemmed in or bound by too many restrictions will soon become unhappy. Likewise, if anything becomes too boring or monotonous, the Monkey will soon lose interest and turn his attention to something else. He lacks persistence and this can often hamper his progress. He is also easily distracted, a tendency that he should try to overcome. By concentrating on one thing at a time, he will almost certainly achieve more in the long run.

The Monkey is a good organizer and even though he may behave slightly erratically at times, he will invariably have a plan at the back of his mind. On the odd occasion when his plans do not work out, he is usually quite happy to shrug his shoulders and put it down to experience. He will rarely make the same mistake twice and throughout his life he will try his hand at many different things.

The Monkey likes to impress and is rarely without followers or admirers. Many are attracted by his good looks, his sense of humour, or simply because he instils so much confidence.

Monkeys usually marry young and for it to be a success their partner must allow them time to pursue their many interests and indulge their love of travel. The Monkey has to have variety in his life and is especially well suited to those born under the sociable and outgoing signs of the Rat, Dragon, Pig and Goat. The Ox, Rabbit, Snake and Dog will also be enchanted by his resourceful and outgoing nature, but he is likely to exasperate the Rooster and Horse, and the Tiger will have little patience with his tricks. A relationship between two Monkeys will work well – they will understand each other and be able to assist each other in their various enterprises.

The female Monkey is intelligent, extremely observant and a shrewd judge of character. Her opinions are often highly valued and, having such a persuasive nature, she invariably gets her own way. She has many interests and involves herself in a wide variety of activities. She pays great attention to her appearance, is an elegant dresser and likes to take particular care over her hair. She can be a doting parent and will have many good and loyal friends.

Provided the Monkey can curb his desire to take part in everything that is going on around him and concentrate on one thing at a time, he can usually achieve what he wants in life. Should he suffer any disappointment, he is bound to bounce back. He is a survivor and his life is usually both colourful and eventful.

THE FIVE DIFFERENT TYPES OF MONKEY

In addition to the 12 signs of the Chinese zodiac there are five elements and these have a strengthening or moderating influence on the signs. The effects of the five elements on the Monkey are described below, together with the years in which they were exercising their influence. Therefore Monkeys born in 1920 and 1980 are Metal Monkeys, Monkeys born in 1932 and 1992 are Water Monkeys, and so on.

Metal Monkey: 1920, 1980

The Metal Monkey is very strong-willed. He sets about everything he does with dogged determination and often prefers to work independently rather than with others. He is ambitious, wise and confident, and is certainly not afraid of hard work. He is very astute in financial matters and usually chooses his investments well. Despite his somewhat independent nature, he enjoys attending parties and social occasions and is particularly warm and caring towards his loved ones.

Water Monkey: 1932, 1992

The Water Monkey is versatile, determined and perceptive. He also has more discipline than some of the other Monkeys and is prepared to work towards a particular goal rather than be distracted by something else. He is not always open about his true intentions and when questioned can be particularly evasive. He can be sensitive to criticism but also very persuasive and usually has little trouble in getting others to fall in with his plans. He has a very good understanding of human nature and relates well to others.

Wood Monkey: 1944, 2004

This Monkey is efficient, methodical and extremely conscientious. He is also highly imaginative and is always trying to capitalize on new ideas or learn new skills. Occasionally his enthusiasm can get the better of him and he can get very agitated when things do not quite work out as he had hoped. He does, however, have a very adventurous streak and is not afraid of taking risks. He also loves travel. He is usually held in great esteem by his friends and colleagues.

Fire Monkey: 1956

The Fire Monkey is intelligent, full of vitality and has no trouble in commanding the respect of others. He is imaginative and has wide interests, although sometimes these can distract him from more useful and profitable work. He is very competitive and always likes to be involved in everything that is going on. He can be stubborn if he does not get his own way and he sometimes tries to indoctrinate those who are less strong-willed than himself. He is a lively character, attractive to others and most loyal to his partner.

Earth Monkey: 1968

The Earth Monkey tends to be studious and well read, and can become quite distinguished in his chosen line of work. He is less outgoing than some of the other types of Monkey and prefers quieter and more solid pursuits. He has high principles, a very caring nature and can be most generous to those less fortunate than himself. He is usually successful in handling financial matters and can become very wealthy in old age. He has a calming influence on those around him and is respected and well liked. He is, however, especially careful about whom he lets into his confidence.

PROSPECTS FOR THE MONKEY
IN 2013

The Year of the Dragon (23 January 2012–9 February 2013) will have been a busy one for the Monkey and in the closing months there will be no shortage of things for him to do, think about and plan.

At work, many Monkeys will find their workload increasing as changes take place and more is asked of them. This can be an exacting time, but the Monkey's skills can serve him well. Many Monkeys will achieve their objectives and quite a few will also benefit from the opportunities that will arise. Those looking to make headway in their career or secure a position should watch developments closely and actively pursue any openings that interest them. A lot is set to happen in the closing months of the Dragon year.

The Monkey could also be fortunate in some purchases at this time and if he wants something specific, he should remain alert. However, as this can be an expensive time, he does need to keep track of his outgoings.

He can look forward to an increase in social activity as the year draws to a close, with August, December and early January often busy. For the unattached, romantic prospects are promising. Domestically, a lot will be happening, and to fit in all he would like, the Monkey should consult others and make arrangements early on. The better organized he is, the more chance he will have to enjoy all that takes place.

The Year of the Snake begins on 10 February and will be a reasonable one for the Monkey. However, to do well, he will need to accept that this is no time for rush or risk. Progress can be made, but this will come over time. The Snake year favours a steady and considered approach.

In his work, the Monkey will need to remain focused and concentrate on his objectives. To spread his attention too widely, dabble in a variety of different activities or look too far ahead could undermine his position. Although the Monkey may like to involve himself in a great many things and has commendable enthusiasm, in the Snake year he *will* need to channel his energies wisely.

He can also benefit from working closely with colleagues and being an active member of any team. By using his skills to advantage and getting himself better known, he can not only help his present situation but also his future prospects. He should also take advantage of any training offered as well as keep informed of developments in his industry. With involvement and participation, he will (in time) be rewarded well.

This will also be an important year for Monkeys who decide to move on or are looking for work. Although the job-seeking process will be challenging and there will be disappointments along the way, the Monkey's determination will often win through. It will take considerable effort, but if he makes enquiries and investigates possibilities, openings will be found and positions offered. Quite a lot of learning and some adjustment could be required, but by making the commitment, these Monkeys can establish themselves in a new type of work which has the potential for future development. April, June, July and September could see interesting opportunities, but the key this year will be focus, determination and the willingness to develop.

The Monkey can look forward to a rise in income over the year and some Monkeys will also benefit from extra funds, perhaps a gift, bonus or the fruition of a policy. In addition some may find ways to put an interest or idea to profitable use. With effort and enterprise, the Monkey can fare well. However, he will need to manage his situation carefully, including, where possible, reducing borrowings and saving towards specific requirements, and avoid making financial decisions too hurriedly. This is a year rewarding care and attention.

The Monkey's personal interests are favourably aspected and although he will often have a lot to do, it is important he allows time for activities he enjoys. Some will develop in an encouraging manner, and with the Snake year's emphasis on culture, if the Monkey sees events or exhibitions which appeal to him, he should try to go.

He will also appreciate his social opportunities and the Snake year can provide an interesting mix of things to do. March, April, September and December could be particularly full and active months. However, while a lot will go well, the Snake year does require the Monkey to be on his guard. An unfortunate remark or oversight could cause embarrassment. Similarly, where matters of the heart are concerned, the Monkey needs to be his attentive self. This is no time to take the feelings of close friends or romantic partners for granted. Monkeys, take note, and where romance and close relationships are concerned, be true and mindful.

This need for awareness also applies to the Monkey's home life. Sometimes, with pressures of work or concerns over his situation, the Monkey could become preoccupied or lack his usual patience. When under pressure, it is important that he is forthcoming about his concerns and involves others. This way not only can those around do much to support and understand, but also help more with some of the tasks and chores the Monkey feels he has to do. Throughout the Snake year the Monkey should draw on the assistance available to him rather than keep his thoughts to himself or feel certain responsibilities are just his preserve. Also, while the Monkey and his family will all have various commitments, some quality time together can do everyone good. Time and awareness will be important factors in home life this year and will also help as domestic plans are successfully advanced.

With his keen and active nature, the Monkey always tries to make the most of his situation. He is determined, resourceful and good at spotting opportunities. However, in the Snake year progress will not be easy or swift, and this is a time for the Monkey to concentrate on what he *can* do rather than what he *would like* to do. By making the most of his current opportunities, including learning and adding to his skills, he can prepare the way for better chances in the near future. This is a constructive rather than progressive year. In his relations with others, the Monkey will also need to be his attentive and thoughtful self. This is a time to tread carefully, liaise, listen and be aware. The Monkey has many admirable qualities and while this may not be the best of years for him, his efforts will ensure it is not necessarily a bad one either.

The Metal Monkey

There is a Chinese proverb that could be especially helpful for the Metal Monkey this year: 'Set long-term goals, but work on short-term tasks.' The Metal Monkey has a particularly ambitious streak and will cherish high hopes both for himself and his future. However, as he recognizes, certain aspirations are still some way from being realized and this year he will have to make the best of his current situation. The Snake year is very much a time to concentrate on short-term tasks.

At work the Metal Monkey will have seen a lot happen in recent years and while he will have made some progress and broadened his experience, he will also have faced disappointments and uncertainty. For many Metal Monkeys, the Snake year will herald a more settled time. In particular, it will give them the chance to concentrate more fully on their actual duties and to use their skills to better effect.

Those working in a large organization could have the opportunity to take on specific responsibilities or help with new initiatives. A valuable feature of the year will be the way the Metal Monkey is encouraged to use and develop his strengths, and what he can demonstrate now can help his future progress. Metal Monkeys who work in a creative environment in particular would find it worth putting forward their ideas. Many will have the chance to impress.

Many Metal Monkeys will remain with their present employer over the year, but for those who feel unfulfilled as well as those seeking work, the Snake year can take an interesting course. The job-seeking process will be difficult and there will be times when these Metal Monkeys will despair of making a breakthrough. However, a chance will come and it may be unexpected. An application they did not have many hopes for may get taken up or they may be able to secure a position by considering a different type of work and adapting their skills in some way. Determination will be required, but once in a new position, these Metal Monkeys will have the chance to prove themselves and gain the experience necessary for future progress. The long-term significance of the Snake year should *not* be underestimated. April, late May to July and September could see encouraging developments.

In view of some of the Metal Monkey's longer-term objectives, if he feels it would be helpful to obtain a further qualification or carry out more research and study, this would be an excellent year to do so. Snake years encourage personal development.

This emphasis need not just apply to career aspirations. Some Metal Monkeys may have a particular interest or recreational pursuit they would like to make more of, and their willingness to develop, whether through acquiring new skills, practising techniques or furthering ideas, can again benefit them and allow more to become possible.

The Metal Monkey could also find it helpful to give some consideration to his general level of exercise and quality of diet. If he feels either could be improved, he should seek advice on the best way to proceed. This is a year favouring constructive action.

The Metal Monkey can also enjoy a financial improvement this year. However, with his many commitments, he will need to remain disciplined and keep careful control of his budget. Early provision for large purchases and possible deposits could be helpful.

Once again the Metal Monkey will enjoy the opportunities he has for socializing this year. Late February to April, September and December could see the most social activity. Some friends will be grateful for the Metal Monkey's advice and he too could find it helpful to get their opinions on ideas he may be considering. As a Monkey, he does sometimes keep his thoughts to himself, but the input of others can be especially helpful this year. Metal Monkeys, do remember this and draw on the advice and expertise available to you, especially from those who have relevant experience.

For Metal Monkeys enjoying or hoping for romance, this is a year requiring care, time and attention. Romance needs careful nurturing. To rush, be preoccupied or take the feelings of another person for granted could risk undermining the relationship. To avoid possible heartbreak, the Metal Monkey needs to tread carefully.

This need for awareness also applies to his home life. Although the Metal Monkey will have a lot to do and think about, he still needs to set time aside to share with those around him. He usually does recognize the importance of this, however, and his input and thoughtfulness can once again make an important contribution to his home life.

Metal Monkeys who are parents or become parents in 2013 will find the pressures of babies and young children can be considerable, and the Metal Monkey does need to make allowance for this and draw on any help that may be offered. As with so many aspects of his life this year, he should remember that advice and support are available to him.

Overall, the Year of the Snake can be an interesting one for the Metal Monkey. Although his actual progress may be modest, what he does now can have great long-term value. It is by concentrating on those short-term tasks that the seeds of future success will be sown. The Metal Monkey's efforts now are very much an investment in his future. Also, throughout the year he should value and enjoy his relations with others, and draw on their help when needed. The benefits of the Snake year can be far-reaching and considerable.

TIP FOR THE YEAR

Focus on the things you can do rather than cannot. If you make the most of your situation and put in the effort, your commitment will bring results. Have self-belief and persist. This is an important stage on your journey towards the realization of your longer-term aspirations.

The Water Monkey

The Water Monkey has a keen and enquiring nature, and by using his strengths and seizing his opportunities, he can gain a lot from this year.

Water Monkeys in education can look forward to making important headway, either in securing a new qualification or moving on to more advanced work. This will require discipline and effort on their part, but they will often be inspired by what they have to do and motivated by the potential benefits their studying can bring. Also, many will find their studies can open up new possibilities. These could include the chance to specialize in a particular area or identify a new career possibility. With the Snake year having long-term implications, it would certainly reward all Water Monkeys to remain alert, put in the effort *and* be open to possibility.

This can also be a significant time for Water Monkeys in work. Over the year they will be encouraged to develop their skills and take on greater responsibilities. Admittedly, some of what is asked will bring increased pressures and the Water Monkey will sometimes have misgivings, but by rising to the challenge, he will acquire important new skills. For the keen and willing, the Snake year has great potential.

In view of the encouragement and training many Water Monkeys will receive this year, the majority will remain with their present employer. However, for those who feel unfulfilled or are seeking a position, the Snake year can offer important choices. These Water Monkeys should think seriously about what it is they actually want to do and seek advice from employment agencies. Some could be advised to consider further training or an apprenticeship scheme. Talking over the options and keeping alert for suitable vacancies can result in important decisions being made, and over the year many Water Monkeys will be offered a position they can subsequently build on. Admittedly, this may be in a slightly lesser capacity than the Water Monkey would have liked, but it will nevertheless be a valuable foothold on the employment ladder. Snake years may not be times of dynamic growth, but the potential the Water Monkey can show can be so important. April, June, July and September could see promising developments.

Financially, the Water Monkey may have limited resources, but by carefully controlling his spending and watching his budget, he can still go ahead with quite a few activities and purchases over the year. To help, he should try to plan ahead and be disciplined when shopping. He also needs to keep receipts and guarantees safe and be thorough when completing financially related forms. This is no time to be lax or careless.

However, the Water Monkey can get considerable pleasure from his interests this year. Whether he favours more physical and outdoor pursuits or something more creative, what he does can bring him satisfaction and sometimes open up new opportunities. If he is keen to make more of a particular interest or talent, it could be helpful to get further guidance and/or consider joining a group of enthusiasts. A lot can follow on from the positive actions he takes now.

With his lively and outgoing nature, the Water Monkey will also enjoy the many social opportunities of the year.

There will be parties and plenty of interesting things to do. At most times of the year the Water Monkey will have opportunities to go out, with March, April, September and December being particularly full and pleasurable months.

Where close friendships and romance are concerned, however, he will need to be careful. To make assumptions or ignore the views of another person could bring problems. For relationships to endure this year, great consideration will be needed. Water Monkeys, take note and give some time to those who are special to you.

In his home life, the Water Monkey can benefit from the assistance of family members during the year and will find it helpful to seek their advice when considering future possibilities. They speak with his best interests at heart and can make suggestions it would be worth bearing in mind. It would also be good for the Water Monkey to spend time with family members and join in with various activities and plans.

Overall, the Year of the Snake can be satisfying and constructive for the Water Monkey. It will give him the opportunity to gain new experience, add to his skills and grow in personal confidence. Effort will be required and some situations may not be easy or straightforward, but the Water Monkey knows he has many abilities, and by doing his best and making the most of his opportunities, he will be sowing important seeds for the future. He is at the start of what will be an interesting and fruitful period in his life.

TIP FOR THE YEAR

Be determined. With effort and the willingness to learn, you can make this a constructive time. Make the most of your opportunities, for they can often lead on to other possibilities. Also, be mindful of close friends and relations and be prepared to consult them. What you decide upon now can have long-term significance.

The Wood Monkey

The Snake year can bring the Wood Monkey considerable contentment. Although it may lack the activity of some years, it will give the Wood Monkey more chance to do some of the things he wants. These could include activities and plans he may have been thinking about for some time. In addition he will enjoy pursuing his own interests and will very much value having some 'me time'.

Throughout the year he will be well assisted by family members, and when he is considering ideas, it is important he talks these over with those around him and listens carefully to their views and suggestions. Original thoughts can often be improved upon. Similarly, when planning arrangements, the Wood Monkey will find that greater flexibility on his part can lead to more happening. In the Snake year he should be open-minded and adapt as opportunities arise – as they will.

One of the most rewarding aspects of the year concerns the Wood Monkey's personal interests. He will enjoy spending time on these and may be keen to attend special occasions. If a sport or music enthusiast in particular, he will delight in some of the events he goes to. With culture prominent in Snake years, some Wood Monkeys may also decide to visit places of interest in their area or while on holiday. The Wood Monkey's many interests will certainly ensure there is no shortage of things to do during the year.

For Wood Monkeys who enjoy creative pursuits, this can be a particularly inspiring time. By developing their ideas and skills, they can gain much pleasure from what they do. Some Wood Monkeys might also be tempted by new activities. Whatever the Wood Monkey does, a key factor of the year is that it will give him the time and opportunity to enjoy his pursuits in his own way, and he will greatly appreciate this.

The Snake year can also bring some good travel possibilities. If there is a destination the Wood Monkey is keen to visit, he should make enquiries. In addition to taking a holiday or short break, there could be chances for him to visit family and friends who live some distance away. As with quite a lot this year, it would be to his advantage to be fairly flexible, however, especially as some travel opportunities will arise at short notice.

In financial matters, the Wood Monkey can fare reasonably well and may benefit from an additional payment. While this will be welcome, he should keep a close watch on his outgoings. If involved in a large purchase, it would be to his benefit to compare costs and make ample allowance in his budget. He should also attend to paperwork carefully, otherwise issues could arise which could take some time to resolve.

The Snake year can provide some interesting social opportunities, and whether meeting his friends, joining others in interest-related pursuits or going to events, the Wood Monkey will enjoy much of his socializing. Some

Wood Monkeys may play a greater part in their community this year, perhaps helping in a local group, assisting a person in need or giving time to a charitable cause. This will be appreciated and the Wood Monkey will consider it time well spent.

However, while a lot can go well, the Snake year can have its problem areas. Some Wood Monkeys could find themselves onlookers in a dispute between friends or couples. At such times the Wood Monkey will need to tread carefully and not be too hasty in his response. In some cases it may be best to let the dust settle or the situation become clearer before coming to a conclusion or speaking out. Fortunately, not all Wood Monkeys will be affected by such difficulties, but if the Wood Monkey senses trouble brewing or is in an awkward situation, he will need to be guarded in his response.

In his home life he will be especially grateful for the support and encouragement he is given, and if he discusses his ideas with those around him, he will find some plans will be given added impetus. In addition to his own many and varied activities, he will take a caring interest in those of his family members, and the progress of a younger relation will be a source of particular delight. In some cases, the bond the Wood Monkey has with a grandchild or great-grandchild can mean a lot to both.

Overall, the Year of the Snake can be a satisfying one for the Wood Monkey and he will be pleased with the way many of his plans develop. To fully benefit, he does need to consult others and show some flexibility, but he has a keen and enquiring nature and the Snake year will be an encouraging and personally rewarding one for him.

Act on your ideas. With this year bringing some fine opportunities, you will find many of your activities developing well.

The Fire Monkey

The Fire Monkey will have seen a lot happen in recent years and there will have been times when he will have felt under pressure or not fully in control of his situation. For many Fire Monkeys, the Snake year will be a time of change and will offer the chance to get their lives back into balance. It is a time to take stock and to appreciate some of the pleasures that may have been missing in recent times.

To help get the Snake year off to an encouraging start, the Fire Monkey would do well to reflect on some of the improvements he would like to see happen. Having some ideas in mind will not only give him something to aim for but also give his plans added momentum. His thinking should involve some 'me time' and if there is an activity he has been considering taking up, now is the time for positive steps.

He would also find it helpful to talk his hopes and plans over with those close to him. If he explains what he wants to do, others can not only give useful support but also make some of his ideas happen. This is very much a year for action, with the Fire Monkey setting the agenda.

One particularly rewarding aspect of the year will be his personal interests. It is important he makes time for these, especially as they are so often a satisfying outlet for his talents, and the Snake year, with its emphasis on creativity, is an ideal one for developing his ideas and using the knowledge and skills he has built up. Any Fire Monkey who has let his interests lapse of late would find this an excellent year to rectify this. If his former interests no longer appeal, he should aim to start something new. Positive action on his part can help restore an important ingredient in his life and make a difference to his outlook. In addition, with this a year for giving attention to lifestyle, the Fire Monkey could benefit by thinking about the quality of his diet and general level of exercise and, if necessary, seeking advice on ways to improve. Used well, the Snake year can bring many personal benefits.

This can also be an interesting year for work matters. Many Fire Monkeys will have been subject to change and pressure in recent times and not always felt fulfilled or fully appreciated. However, Snake years are times of important developments. Many Fire Monkeys will now have the chance to focus on their duties and make better use of their skills and judgement. Some may also take on more specialist responsibilities. The Snake year will give many the opportunity to use their strengths to better advantage and make their work more rewarding.

Most Fire Monkeys will remain with their present employer, but for those who feel frustrated and desire change, as well as those seeking work, the Snake year can be significant. Although the job-seeking process will be difficult, these Fire Monkeys should give some serious thought to the sort of position they would like. By considering possibilities and making enquiries, many will find their initiative alerting them to opportunities and securing what will be an interesting new opening. This will take time and persistence, but the Fire Monkey's determination will help bring about the improvement he wants. April, June, July and September could be interesting months.

The Snake year is generally positive for financial matters, but to fully benefit the Fire Monkey does need to keep careful control of his budget and, where possible, set funds aside for specific plans. This will allow him to do more and often get better value as well.

The Fire Monkey will enjoy the social opportunities of the year and his interests will often bring him into contact with others. Some Fire Monkeys might join local groups during the year. March, April, September and December could see the most social activity.

Although a lot will go well for the Fire Monkey, the Snake year does require care. A lapse, disagreement or moment of indiscretion could cause problems and undermine the Fire Monkey's relationships with those around him. If he detects potential problems or places himself in an awkward situation, difficulties could follow. Fire Monkeys, be warned.

Domestically, a lot will be happening and quite a few Fire Monkeys will have an exciting occasion to arrange. Here the Fire Monkey's organizational talents will come into their own. However, while he will play a central role in his home life and do a lot for others, he does need to ensure that everyone plays their part and that he asks for help when needed as well as preserves time for his own activities. A good home, work and personal lifestyle balance will be a worthy aim for many Fire Monkeys this year. Also, if at any time the Fire Monkey is concerned about a certain matter, rather than bear this alone, he should seek advice.

Overall, the Year of the Snake can be a satisfying one for the Fire Monkey. It can be a time of positive change, although this does require the Fire Monkey to take the initiative. To realize his hopes, he needs to discuss them with others, explore his options *and* take action. In addition he should make the most of his experience and strengths. That way, he can benefit from a lot of his activities this year and make it both a pleasing and generally rewarding time.

TIP FOR THE YEAR

Devote time to yourself and your own aims. Develop your interests and ideas and rediscover and enjoy the real you. Positive action can benefit you in so many ways. Also, consult others and value your relationships with them. This can be a constructive and satisfying year. Use it well.

The Earth Monkey

The Earth element gives a sign a more pragmatic quality, and the Earth Monkey is often careful and thorough in his approach. He likes to plan ahead, yet still has the Monkey's drive and creative spark. In the Snake year he is set to do well.

One aspect of the year the Earth Monkey will particularly appreciate is its more settled nature. Unlike some years, which proceed at a frenetic pace, the Snake year is measured, and it will give the Earth Monkey the chance to concentrate on the things he wants to do rather than be drawn in many different directions.

In his work this can be a particularly constructive year. With the experience he has built up, the Earth Monkey may well feel ready to move ahead in his career, and when opportunities arise for a greater role or promotion, he will often be successful. The position he now takes on could be one he has been working towards for some considerable time and be a natural progression in his career.

The aspects are also encouraging for Earth Monkeys who decide to move on, perhaps feeling ready to build on their skills and do something else. These Earth Monkeys should make enquiries, talk to contacts and keep alert for vacancies. Diligence will reward many and give them the opportunity to further their career.

Earth Monkeys seeking work should also keep alert for openings. Even if they find themselves switching to a different type of work and adapting their skills, many will be able to secure a position which can help them develop in a new way. April, June, July and September could see important opportunities.

The Earth Monkey's progress at work will also help financially. Many Earth Monkeys will increase their income over the year and will sometimes benefit from something extra. Although this will be welcome, the Earth Monkey will have many expenses and will need to be disciplined in his spending. If wanting to buy something specific, he should investigate his options and wait for favourable buying opportunities. Snake years do not favour rush and the more consideration the Earth Monkey can give to more substantial purchases, the better his choice will be.

If possible, he should try to make allowance for a holiday or break this year, and if he is able to combine this with an interest or special attraction, this can make his time away all the more pleasurable.

The Earth Monkey uses his time well and enjoys a variety of interests. During the Snake year, some of these can develop in an encouraging way. Some Earth Monkeys may decide to enrol on courses or set themselves a new personal challenge. Whatever the Earth Monkey does, if he acts with purpose, he can find his interests bringing him considerable satisfaction. With this a year for giving thought to lifestyle, he may be attracted to a new fitness discipline or, if seeking to lose weight, follow a new diet. Some attention to his well-being can be highly beneficial.

His social life will be fairly active and the Snake year will contain a pleasing mix of things to do. The Earth Monkey could be particularly grateful for some advice and expert knowledge from his friends. This can be a positive and interesting year, although there is a 'but': when in company, the Earth Monkey does need to keep his wits about him. A *faux pas*, indiscretion or personal lapse could cause problems. Earth Monkeys, take note.

As far as the Earth Monkey's home life is concerned, this can be a full and interesting year. With his own work routine liable to change and those close to him often being affected by new commitments, there will need to be good co-operation, but the Earth Monkey's ability to organize and bring people together will be especially appreciated. During the year many Earth Monkeys can also look forward to some special family news.

Overall, the Year of the Snake is an encouraging one for the Earth Monkey and by taking action he can look forward to making useful headway. This is a time when determination and his personal strengths can lead to some good opportunities. In many ways a favourable year offering steady progress.

TIP FOR THE YEAR

You have great capabilities and now is the time to build on your situation and look to move ahead. To fully benefit, be adaptable in approach and remain open to possibility. Also, give time to those who are special to you. Your care and attention will be valued and important.

FAMOUS MONKEYS

Gillian Anderson, Jennifer Aniston, Christina Aguilera, Patricia Arquette, Lady Ashton, J. M. Barrie, José Manuel Barroso, Joe Cocker, Colette, John Constable, David Copperfield, Patricia Cornwell, Daniel Craig, Joan Crawford, Miley Cyrus, Leonardo da Vinci, Timothy Dalton, Bette Davis, Danny De Vito, Celine Dion, Michael Douglas, Mia Farrow, Carrie Fisher, F. Scott Fitzgerald, Ian Fleming, Paul Gauguin, Ryan Gosling, Jake Gyllenhaal, Jerry Hall, Tom Hanks, Harry Houdini, Hugh Jackman, P. D. James, Katherine Jenkins, Julius Caesar, Buster Keaton, Alicia Keys, Gladys Knight, Taylor Lautner, George Lucas, Bob Marley, Kylie Minogue, V. S. Naipaul, Lisa Marie Presley, Debbie Reynolds, Little Richard, Mickey Rooney, Diana Ross, Tom Selleck, Omar Sharif, Wilbur Smith, Rod Stewart, Jacques Tati, Elizabeth Taylor, Dame Kiri Te Kanawa, Justin Timberlake, Harry Truman, Michelle Williams, Venus Williams.

8 FEBRUARY 1921 ⁓ 27 JANUARY 1922   *Metal Rooster*

26 JANUARY 1933 ⁓ 13 FEBRUARY 1934   *Water Rooster*

13 FEBRUARY 1945 ⁓ 1 FEBRUARY 1946   *Wood Rooster*

31 JANUARY 1957 ⁓ 17 FEBRUARY 1958   *Fire Rooster*

17 FEBRUARY 1969 ⁓ 5 FEBRUARY 1970   *Earth Rooster*

5 FEBRUARY 1981 ⁓ 24 JANUARY 1982   *Metal Rooster*

23 JANUARY 1993 ⁓ 9 FEBRUARY 1994   *Water Rooster*

9 FEBRUARY 2005 ⁓ 28 JANUARY 2006   *Wood Rooster*

THE
ROOSTER

THE PERSONALITY OF
THE ROOSTER

With a clear destination
and firm will,
I raise my sails
to the winds of fortune.

The Rooster is born under the sign of candour. He has a flamboyant and colourful personality and is meticulous in all that he does. He is an excellent organizer and wherever possible likes to plan his various activities well in advance.

The Rooster is usually highly intelligent and very well read. He has a good sense of humour and is an effective and persuasive speaker. He loves discussion and enjoys taking part in any sort of debate. He has no hesitation in speaking his mind and is forthright in his views. He does, however, lack tact and can easily damage his reputation or cause offence by some thoughtless remark or action. He has a very volatile nature and should always try to avoid acting on the spur of the moment.

He is usually very dignified in his manner and conducts himself with an air of confidence and authority. He is adept at handling financial matters and organizes his financial affairs with considerable skill. He chooses his investments well and is capable of achieving great wealth. Most Roosters use their money wisely, but there are a few who are the reverse and are notorious spendthrifts. Fortunately, the Rooster has great earning capacity and is rarely without sufficient funds to tide himself over.

Another characteristic of the Rooster is that he invariably carries a notebook or scraps of paper around with him. He is constantly writing himself reminders or noting down important facts lest he forgets – the Rooster cannot abide inefficiency and conducts all his activities in an orderly, precise and methodical manner.

The Rooster is usually very ambitious, but can be unrealistic in some of what he hopes to achieve. He occasionally lets his imagination run away with him and while he does not like any interference from others, it would be in his own interests to listen to their views a little more often. He also does not like criticism, and if he feels anybody is doubting his judgement or prying too closely into his affairs, he is certain to let his feelings be known. He can also be rather self-centred and stubborn over relatively trivial matters, but to compensate for this he is reliable, honest and trustworthy, and this is appreciated by all who come into contact with him.

Roosters born between the hours of five and seven, both at dawn and sundown, tend to be the most extrovert of their sign, but all Roosters like to lead an active social life and enjoy attending parties and big functions. The Rooster usually has a wide circle of friends and is able to build up influential contacts with remarkable ease. He often belongs to several clubs and societies and involves himself in a variety of different activities. He is particularly interested in the environment, humanitarian affairs and anything affecting the welfare of others. He has a very caring nature and will do much to help those less fortunate than himself.

He also gets much pleasure from gardening, and while he may not spend as much time in the garden as he would like, his garden is invariably well kept and productive.

The Rooster is generally very distinguished in his appearance and if his job permits he will wear an official uniform with great pride and dignity. He is not averse to publicity and takes great delight in being the centre of attention. He often does well at PR work or any job which brings him into contact with the media. He also makes a very good teacher.

The female Rooster leads a varied and interesting life. She involves herself in many different activities and there are some who wonder how she can achieve so much. She often holds very strong views and, like her male counterpart, has no hesitation in speaking her mind or telling others how she thinks things should be done. She is supremely efficient and well organized and her home is usually very neat and tidy. She has good taste in clothes and usually wears smart but very practical outfits.

The Rooster usually has a large family and takes a particularly active interest in the education of his children. He is very loyal to his partner and will find that he is especially well suited to those born under the signs of the Snake, Horse, Ox and Dragon. Provided they do not interfere too much in his various activities, the Rat, Tiger, Goat and Pig can also establish a good relationship with him, but two Roosters together are likely to squabble and irritate each other. The rather sensitive Rabbit will find the Rooster a bit too blunt for his liking, and the Rooster will quickly become exasperated by the ever-inquisitive and artful Monkey. He will also find it difficult to get on with the anxious Dog.

If the Rooster can overcome his volatile nature and exercise tact, he will go far in life. He is capable and talented and will make a lasting – and usually favourable – impression almost everywhere he goes.

THE FIVE DIFFERENT TYPES OF ROOSTER

In addition to the 12 signs of the Chinese zodiac there are five elements and these have a strengthening or moderating influence on the signs. The effects of the five elements on the Rooster are described below, together with the years in which they were exercising their influence. Therefore Roosters born in 1921 and 1981 are Metal Roosters, Roosters born in 1933 and 1993 are Water Roosters, and so on.

Metal Rooster: 1921, 1981
The Metal Rooster is a hard and conscientious worker. He knows exactly what he wants in life and sets about everything in a positive and determined manner. He can at times appear abrasive and he would almost certainly do better if he were willing to reach a compromise with others rather than hold so rigidly to his beliefs. He is very articulate and most astute when dealing with financial matters. He is loyal to his friends and often devotes much energy to working for the common good.

Water Rooster: 1933, 1993

This Rooster has a very persuasive manner and can easily gain the co-operation of others. He is intelligent, well read and enjoys taking part in discussions and debates. He has a seemingly inexhaustible amount of energy and is prepared to work long hours in order to secure what he wants. He can, however, waste a lot of valuable time worrying over minor and inconsequential details. He is approachable, has a good sense of humour and is highly regarded by others.

Wood Rooster: 1945, 2005

The Wood Rooster is honest, reliable and often sets himself high standards. He is ambitious, but also more prepared to work in a team than some of the other types of Rooster. He usually succeeds in life but does have a tendency to get caught up in bureaucratic matters and attempt too many things at the same time. He has wide interests, likes to travel and is very caring and considerate towards his family and friends.

Fire Rooster: 1957

This Rooster is extremely strong-willed. He has many leadership qualities, is an excellent organizer and is most efficient in his work. Through sheer force of character he often secures his objectives, but he does have a tendency to be very forthright and not always consider the feelings of others. If he can learn to be more tactful he can often succeed beyond his wildest dreams.

Earth Rooster: 1969

This Rooster has a deep and penetrating mind. He is efficient, perceptive and particularly astute in business and financial matters. He is also persistent and once he has set himself an objective, he will rarely allow himself to be deflected from achieving his aim. He works hard and is held in great esteem by his friends and colleagues. He usually enjoys the arts and takes a keen interest in the activities of the various members of his family.

PROSPECTS FOR THE ROOSTER IN 2013

Many a Rooster will have found the Dragon year (23 January 2012–9 February 2013) an inspiring and energizing time and the closing months will often be special.

At work the Rooster could find his skills in demand and his organizational abilities and attention to detail leading to some fine results. Many Roosters will have a good chance to show their qualities and enhance their prospects, and for those looking to make headway or seeking work, November could contain interesting possibilities.

In money matters, the closing months of the Dragon year can see considerable outlay, especially as many Roosters will have the chance to travel at this time. As a result, spending does need to be watched and more expensive purchases carefully thought through.

The Rooster will enjoy an increasing number of social opportunities at the end of the year and may have the chance to spend time with friends he does not often see. For the unattached, romance could add excitement to this time.

In the Rooster's home life there will be a lot to do and his ability to plan and organize will be appreciated. However, while the Rooster does have his own ideas and ways of doing things, he does need to liaise with others and in some instances show greater flexibility about arrangements. His home life is, though, set to be full and interesting and the closing months of the Dragon year will bring some personally rewarding times.

The Year of the Snake starts on 10 February and will be a reasonably good one for the Rooster. During it he can make pleasing headway and see many of his ideas develop in an encouraging manner. However, throughout the year he will need to keep his wits about him. Although the Rooster may have considerable resolve, he will need to remain mindful of others and avoid jeopardizing his normally good relations through moments of outspokenness or candour. The Rooster speaks as he finds, but sometimes greater tact and discretion would be wise. Generally, however, he will have much in his favour in the Snake year.

At work many Roosters will be able to build on their present position and will have the chance to make more of their skills and specialisms. Those who have been involved in recent change or had the opportunity to take on new duties will find the Snake year will allow them to focus on what they have to do, and their judgement, efficiency and organizational talents will lead to some often impressive results. Snake years encourage creativity and many Roosters will welcome the chance to develop their ideas or use their creative talents to good effect. For those engaged in the arts, media, beauty, fashion or design industries, this can be an especially successful year.

To help, the Rooster should pay attention to his relations with colleagues and, if new to his position, make an effort to establish himself in his place of work. By liaising well with his colleagues, being an active team member and using any chances to network, he can impress others. However, should any volatile situation arise, he will need to tread carefully and think before he speaks out. Fortunately such situations will be few, but in the Snake year the Rooster does need to keep his candid nature in check.

For Roosters who decide to move on, as well as those seeking work, the Snake year can offer some interesting chances. To benefit, these Roosters will need to be flexible and adapt their skills where necessary, as well as be prepared to learn. What opens up can represent substantial change but nevertheless give the Rooster the chance to prove himself in another capacity. March, April, July and October could see important developments.

With the prospect of new responsibilities and pressures of work, quite a few Roosters will find some parts of the year demanding. Being conscientious, the Rooster does drive himself hard and in the Snake year it is important that he keeps his lifestyle in balance and gives himself time to relax and unwind. To push himself relentlessly could lead to stress and make him susceptible to minor ailments. To combat this, not only should the Rooster allow time for rest and recreation, but also give some consideration to his diet and level of exercise. He is set to accomplish a lot this year, but cannot ignore his own well-being.

One area which can bring the Rooster considerable pleasure is his social life. With his wide interests and fine conversational talents, he will once again make the most of his chances to spend time with other people. As always, there will be lots to discuss, and the Rooster will also do a great deal to help close friends. On a social level, he will find himself in demand, with April, June, August and the closing months of the Snake year seeing the most activity.

Affairs of the heart can also bring the Rooster considerable happiness over the year, although new relationships should be nurtured carefully and time should be allowed for each person to get to know the other better. That way romance can be built upon more solid foundations.

The Rooster can look forward to a rewarding home life and will do much to ensure the smooth running of his home, although he should make sure others do their fair share. Also, when considering plans for the home, it is important that everyone is involved and there is good discussion and agreement. With co-operation and combined effort, a lot can happen this year, including some home improvements that will be appreciated by all.

Loved ones will also be grateful for the Rooster's support, although if a delicate situation arises, he will need to pick his words carefully. The Rooster may like to be candid and upfront, but in 2013 it is important he remains aware of the sensitivities of others. This is a year for tact, mindfulness and thinking responses through.

The Rooster will fare reasonably well in financial matters, although in order to proceed with certain plans, he does need to make early provision for them. This is not a year to proceed on an ad hoc basis but to manage his budget carefully. Many Roosters will be keen to travel this year and by making allowance for this, they can look forward to some good times away.

Overall, the Rooster can derive much satisfaction from the Snake year. It may not have the dynamism he favours, but by adjusting to its more measured pace and concentrating on his objectives, he can make good headway, add to his experience and benefit from many of the year's developments. In particular, his ideas (and inventive streak) will often impress. He will also enjoy good relations with many people and see an increase in social activity, although it would be prudent for him to keep his candid nature in check. Nevertheless, a pleasing year with good possibilities.

The Metal Rooster

One of the Rooster's traits is that he likes to plan ahead and this is especially true of the Metal Rooster. Determined, ambitious and full of ideas, he is keen to put himself forward and make the most of his opportunities. The Snake year will offer him considerable scope, but the key will be flexibility. Although the Metal Rooster may have clear intentions, he should remember there are many ways forward and sometimes his plans may need to be altered as situations change and new opportunities arise.

This is especially the case at work. Metal Roosters who are established in a career could find events taking an interesting course. A senior colleague may suggest they broaden their experience by taking on new responsibilities or moving to a different role in their current organization. As many Metal Roosters will find, the Snake year is not one for standing still.

The Snake year also holds interesting prospects for Metal Roosters who are keen to move to a different type of work or are seeking a position. Their resourceful nature will help in their quest and while the job-seeking process can be wearying, by keeping alert, making enquiries and being flexible, many will obtain a new position that offers an interesting contrast to what they have done before. There will be adjustments to be made and much to learn, but the Snake year can provide good opportunities for many Metal Roosters and mark an important stage in their working lives, either in furthering their existing career or starting something new. March to mid-May, July and October could see promising developments.

The progress the Metal Rooster makes at work can also help financially, although in view of his many commitments and the accommodation and personal purchases he will be keen to make, he needs to manage his outgoings carefully. When he has particular plans in mind, he should keep alert, as he may benefit from attractive purchasing opportunities or see something suitable by chance. As many Metal Roosters will discover, Snake years can have their lucky moments.

For the many Metal Roosters who are interested in creative activities or work in creative environments, this is also an excellent year for developing and promoting their ideas. Quite a few could enjoy some deserved recognition of their talents. Any Metal Roosters who are feeling unfulfilled or have let their interests lapse recently will find this a good time to consider taking up something different.

Whether this is practical, physical (perhaps related to keep fit) or creative, by doing something positive these Metal Roosters can introduce a pleasurable new element into their lives. Again, it is a case of being open and receptive to the chances the Snake year presents.

Also, should the Metal Rooster see events advertised that appeal to him or have invitations to go out, he should do his best to go. The Snake year can provide a variety of things to do. Many activities can be enjoyed with family and friends too, and for the unattached Metal Rooster, this is a year of exciting romantic possibility. April, June, August, December and January could be especially active for socializing.

The Metal Rooster can also look forward to a full and rewarding home life. In view of some of the decisions and changes he will be involved with, he will be grateful for the support of his loved ones and should pay close attention to their advice. The words of more senior relations could be especially helpful.

The Metal Rooster himself will do a lot for his loved ones and will delight in some family news. If he is a parent, the progress of young children can bring him considerable pleasure and moments of pride, even if their demands and antics may occasionally exasperate him. He would also do well to try and arrange a family break or holiday during the year. Even if this does not involve travelling very far away, the change and rest can do everyone good.

Although the Metal Rooster will enjoy positive relations with many people this year, as a Rooster he is born under the sign of candour and should watch his forthright tendencies. If he finds himself in a volatile situation, feels under pressure or is in the company of those who may be sensitive, he should choose his words carefully. Metal Roosters, do take note and try not to jeopardize your relations with others with comments that may be regretted later. Snakes are masters of discretion and in the Snake year it is worth following their lead.

Overall, however, the Metal Rooster can fare well this year. He will not only have the opportunity to use his skills and ideas to advantage but also to extend them by taking on a new role or challenge. This is a time to move forward and seize the chances that will now become available. The Metal Rooster's relations with others can also be positive, although he would do well to watch his sometimes candid tongue. However, the ambitious Metal Rooster is always keen to make the most of himself and this is a year of important possibility.

TIP FOR THE YEAR

Be flexible. Make the most of situations, even if you sometimes have to modify your plans or adapt your skills. This is a time for moving forward, extending your capabilities and enjoying the possibilities that will open up for you.

The Water Rooster

This year marks the start of what will be an exciting new decade in the Water Rooster's life. As someone who looks ahead, he will already have thought about some of the things he hopes to achieve in the near future and the Snake year will help to pave the way. This will be a constructive time with some good opportunities.

One of the Water Rooster's strengths is his enquiring mind. He is not one who accepts things at face value, and whether through reading and questioning, thinking things through or taking practical action, he keeps himself well informed and is keen to build on his knowledge. This trait will serve him well both now and in following years.

For the many Water Roosters in education this can be an important year. Not only will they have exams to take and coursework to prepare, but also the chance to research certain topics in greater depth. This could alert them to aptitudes they could take further in the future.

While the Water Rooster will accomplish a lot this year, it will, however, require effort on his part. With his various interests and an often active social life, he does need to keep a sensible balance in all he does and use his time effectively. Also, while he likes to do a lot himself and make his own decisions, it is important he avails himself of the expertise of those around him. This includes seeking the advice of tutors on any aspect of his studies which may concern him as well as talking over future options. By being open and receptive, he will not only gain from the assistance given but also be advised of possibilities worth considering.

For Water Roosters in work, the Snake year can see important developments. These Water Roosters will have their sights set on the future and if opportunities arise in their place of work, they should be quick to put themselves forward. The effort they make and skills they learn this year can be instrumental in their future progress.

For Water Roosters who are feeling unfulfilled where they are or are seeking work, again the Snake year can be significant. Not only should these Water Roosters be active in their quest but also seek advice from experts and appropriate organizations. They could benefit from apprenticeship schemes or employment initiatives or find through their own efforts a position which gives them valuable working experience. March, April, July and October could prove important months.

The Water Rooster should also make the most of his interests this year. Not only can these give him the chance to unwind and have fun with his friends but also to use his ideas and skills. Whether he enjoys sporting pursuits or more creative activities, he should take advantage of the resources available to him. For Water Roosters who enjoy drama, dance and music in particular, this can be a time of exciting possibility.

The Snake year can also see interesting travel possibilities and some Water Roosters will decide to combine travelling with a personal interest or a visit to something specific. By carefully planning and costing their trip, they can make it one of the highlights of the year.

In view of the Water Rooster's often busy lifestyle, however, he should keep careful watch on his spending and be disciplined when shopping. Too many indulgences could mount up and lead to economies later. The Snake year requires good control over the purse-strings as well as care when conducting important transactions.

With his lively and outgoing personality, the Water Rooster can look forward to an interesting social life. Whether partying, sharing interests or enjoying a good chat, he will very much appreciate his circle of friends and the social opportunities the year opens up. This also applies to Water Roosters who may move over the year and have the opportunity to get to know a new group of people. Even Water Roosters who are shy and reserved (and there are some) will welcome the chance to meet like-minded people. April, June, August, December and January could see the most social activity. There can also be good romantic possibilities, although relationships should not be rushed but allowed to evolve in their own way and time.

The Water Rooster's family life will be important to him this year and those close to him will be keen to offer support. By being prepared to talk over decisions and future possibilities, the Water Rooster can benefit from some pertinent advice. He can reciprocate by assisting a relation under pressure or helping out with general household activities. What some Water Roosters do this year will mean more than they may realize.

Although the Water Rooster generally keeps himself active, with the late nights he sometimes keeps and all his various activities, it is important that he has a well-balanced diet and gives himself a chance to rest and catch up after strenuous activity. To make the most of the opportunities the year will bring, he cannot afford to neglect his own well-being. Water Roosters, take note.

Overall, the Snake year not only marks the start of a new decade in the Water Rooster's life, but will also be important in several other respects. Not only will the Water Rooster benefit from the knowledge and skills he now acquires but also from identifying strengths that he can build on in the future. The Snake year will give many Water Roosters a greater sense of direction. The Water Rooster's personal interests, social life and many activities can also bring him considerable pleasure this year. It *is* worth making the effort, as so much that he does now will prepare him for the exciting possibilities that lie ahead.

TIP FOR THE YEAR

Your twentieth year is a time of great possibility. Make the most of what arises. Skills and qualifications gained now can often be of benefit later. Enjoy this special and potentially valuable year.

The Wood Rooster

The Wood Rooster takes an interest in a great many things. Whether following the activities of his loved ones, pursuing his interests or keeping up to date with developments, he is both active and well informed. And in the Snake year he will continue to make full and satisfying use of his time.

As always, the Wood Rooster will value the special rapport he has with those close to him, and family activities are set to go well. In particular, the Wood Rooster will take great delight in sharing ideas and plans, and whether these concern home purchases or modifications, by tackling projects with those around him, he will find that more will happen and everyone will be better able to appreciate the results. This year favours joint undertakings.

The Wood Rooster's loved ones also have high regard for his judgement and will be glad of his views and advice several times during the year. In particular, younger relations could be especially grateful for his thoughts on changes they may be considering and his words will carry considerable weight. For a constructive assessment, few can better the Wood Rooster.

The Wood Rooster will also appreciate the travel opportunities the year brings, including the chance to visit family
who live some distance away. Some Wood Roosters may
take advantage of travel offers and go away almost on a
whim, with the spontaneity adding to the fun and excitement.

Many Wood Roosters will also delight in events held in
their area and will often find interesting things to do. In
addition, local facilities can be of benefit to the Wood
Rooster. If he wishes to give more attention to his well-
being, there may be keep-fit classes he could join or swim-
ming pools and recreational centres he could use. He may
also be tempted by courses available locally or online. By
following up things that interest him, whether out of
curiosity or to learn a new skill, he can benefit a lot this
year. It is important he remains open to opportunity.

Some of his interests can also have a good social
element. Wood Roosters who are members of a group or
class can look forward to playing an increasing part and
there will be meetings and other occasions they will enjoy
very much. For Wood Roosters who would welcome
company, it would be well worth considering joining a
community group. April, June, August, December and
January 2014 could be particularly pleasing and convivial
months.

Being an interesting speaker, the Wood Rooster will also
revel in the many conversations and discussions he has over
the year. His widespread knowledge and ability to relate to
other people will be once again very much to his advantage
and often endear him to others. However, a word of warning: Snake years can be times of intrigue and the Wood

Rooster should be wary of rumour and, if necessary, check and correct anything that may concern him. Fortunately these words only apply to a minority of Wood Roosters, but the mischief-making or possible jealousy of another person could cause problems if left unaddressed. Similarly, in potentially awkward situations, the Wood Rooster should think through the best approach to take rather than speak out or come to a conclusion too hurriedly.

In matters of finance, the Wood Rooster likes to keep a close watch on his situation and is thorough when dealing with important paperwork. His attentiveness will continue to serve him well this year. When considering large purchases, he should take the time to compare options. This way he will often find his original choices can be improved upon or obtained on more favourable terms. Also, if possible, he should try to make early provision for travel expenses or special purchases. With discipline and good housekeeping, he can fare well this year.

Overall, the Year of the Snake can be a satisfying one for the Wood Rooster. He will be able to carry out many activities and take pleasure in his family and social life, personal interests, travel and other opportunities. This is an encouraging year and the Wood Rooster's keen and personable nature will help to make it a rewarding time.

TIP FOR THE YEAR

Make the most of your ideas and opportunities. With a positive and willing attitude, you can make a lot happen. Also, share your thoughts with your loved ones and friends. The relationships you have with those around you can mean a great deal.

The Fire Rooster

The Fire Rooster has energy and panache. He also has ambition and is prepared to work hard for the things he wants. Often his efforts, commitment and compelling personality will prevail. In the Snake year he is set to do well, although certain plans may take an unexpected turn.

Many Fire Roosters will have seen changes in their work situation in recent years and the Snake year will give them more chance to concentrate on their role and immerse themselves in some interesting tasks. In addition they will have excellent opportunity to draw on their extensive knowledge, and whether advising and training others, putting forward ideas or initiating action, their skills will be appreciated. However, while the Fire Rooster can make satisfying progress, he should not be resistant to change. Sometimes he may be required to vary his role as new situations emerge or to learn new procedures and systems or to adapt as his employer makes changes. Overall, this can be a positive year, but the Fire Rooster will need to show some flexibility.

Fire Roosters who feel the time is right for change, as well as those seeking work, should not be too restrictive in the type of position they are considering. If they are flexible and prepared to adapt, there will not only be more possibilities available to them but they could be presented with an interesting career challenge. What opens up this year can give many Fire Roosters the sense of purpose they may have been lacking in recent times. March to mid-May, July and October could see interesting developments, but opportunities could arise at almost any time of the year and need to be seized quickly.

The progress the Fire Rooster makes at work can lead to an increase in income and he could also benefit from some moments of good fortune. These could include a gift or bonus as well as the acquisition of certain items on advantageous terms. Over the year, the Fire Rooster's astute and canny sense will serve him well. Where possible, he should also make provision for travel. It is favourably aspected in 2013 and some Fire Roosters could find offers or invitations arising suddenly and leading to some hurriedly arranged trips and visits.

Another encouragingly aspected area concerns the Fire Rooster's personal interests. These too can be subject to interesting developments. It could be the Fire Rooster becomes intrigued by a new subject, decides to set himself a new challenge or develops an existing interest in a new way. For any Fire Roosters who are feeling staid or unfulfilled, this is an ideal time for setting themselves a new aim or personal goal. As many will find, this can often have a positive impact on other areas of their life as well.

In general, the Fire Rooster will be encouraged in his activities by the support of those around him. At work certain colleagues and contacts could prove especially helpful, while in the Fire Rooster's personal interests, friends can be encouraging and shared activities prove a lot of fun. In his home life too, the Fire Rooster will value the interest and help of those close to him. By discussing his situation with them, particularly when affected by change or considering choices, he can not only benefit from their advice but, in the process, clarify his own preferences. In turn, he will have ample chance to advise and assist others. Younger relations in particular could be grateful for his help and there could be some splendid family achievements to celebrate as well.

With practical domestic projects, however, the Fire Rooster will need to show some flexibility. Situations may change, alternatives arise or projects develop in ways – and to timescales – that are different from those originally envisaged. Practical activities in the Snake year should not be set in stone and the Fire Rooster needs to remain open to possibility.

Socially, he will welcome the opportunities he has to go out. For Fire Roosters who are lonely and would welcome the chance to meet others and perhaps find romance, the Snake year holds bright prospects. Some will find a chance meeting (and chance does play a big part this year) becoming significant. April, June, August, December and January could be pleasing months. However, a word of warning: Snake years can be rife with rumour and speculation and should the Fire Rooster be concerned by anything he hears, he should check the facts for himself.

He would also do well to give some consideration to his well-being and aim to take regular and appropriate exercise as well as have a balanced diet. To neglect this could leave him prone to minor ailments or lacking his usual zest.

Overall, the Snake year is an encouraging one for the Fire Rooster. It will offer him the chance to use and extend his skills, to develop his interests and enjoy some rewarding times. He will need to adapt and make the best of situations as they arise, but he will often be able to turn events to his advantage in this year of interesting possibility.

TIP FOR THE YEAR

You already have a lot of experience behind you, but it is important that you keep learning. Your positive actions this year can give you the opportunity to prove yourself in new ways. As a Fire Rooster you thrive on challenge and the Snake year can be both inspiring and encouraging. Good luck, for this can be a successful and personally rewarding time.

The Earth Rooster

'A long journey will not deter one with high aspirations', as the Chinese proverb reminds us. The Earth Rooster certainly has his aspirations and he realizes that some of them will take time to achieve. However, one of his many qualities is that he *is* persistent. In the Snake year he will make excellent progress on his 'long journey' and this will be a significant time for him.

In his work the Earth Rooster will be able to use his skills to good effect. Not only will he set about his duties with his usual diligence but he may also take on new initiatives or become more involved in training and mentoring junior colleagues. There may be promotion opportunities too and the Earth Rooster should rise to the challenge. The Snake year can often mark an important stage in his career.

Throughout the year the Earth Rooster should also work closely with his colleagues and, if relevant, use any chances to network or join a professional organization. This is an excellent year for raising his profile.

For Earth Roosters who feel there are limited opportunities in their current place of work, as well as those seeking a position, the year can hold interesting developments. The opportunities that arise may not always be those the Earth Rooster had envisaged, but by being prepared to make the most of them, he can not only add to his experience but also often secure a position that has the potential for future development. March, April, July and October to mid-November could see encouraging prospects.

Snake years favour creativity and the Earth Rooster should also aim to make the most of his talents. In particular, Earth Roosters who enjoy writing or take pleasure in some aspect of the arts should develop their skills and interests. Should these Earth Roosters see events, exhibitions or shows that appeal to them, they should try to go. Snake years can be personally enriching and during this one the Earth Rooster should award himself some 'me time' to appreciate the things he enjoys.

With travel favourably aspected, he should also try to take a holiday during the year or, if this is not possible, consider a short break away. A change of scene can do him good.

In addition he should give some consideration to his well-being, including his diet and level of exercise. To be neglectful could leave him under par and prone to minor ailments. Some attention would be wise if he is to remain on top form this year.

Socially, the Earth Rooster will appreciate the opportunities that come his way. The Snake year can bring some interesting occasions and there will be ample chance for the lively Earth Rooster to once again delight in conversation. April, June, August and December could see the most social activity. For the unattached, the Snake year holds good romantic possibilities and someone met in fortuitous circumstances could become special. However, the year could see some awkward moments too, and in common with all Roosters, the Earth Rooster needs to be wary of rumour and possible mischief-making or jealousy. Should anything trouble him, he should check the facts himself rather than believe all he hears.

The Earth Rooster is both conscientious and attentive and this will be to his advantage where finance is concerned this year. He needs to keep a careful watch on spending and make advance provision for more expensive plans. His discipline will ultimately give him more chance to proceed with certain undertakings as well as make some useful purchases.

His home life can bring him considerable pleasure, although with the Earth Rooster and other household members likely to be leading busy lifestyles, there will need to be good consultation and, where domestic plans are concerned, joint decision-making. The better the liaison, the better – and more appreciated – the results will be. During the year the Earth Rooster will also do much to support close relations and his encouragement and understanding will be valued and in some cases mean more than he may realize. The Snake year can also give rise to some memorable family moments and, as travel is favourably aspected, a holiday, reunion or visit to a special attraction could be especially enjoyable.

Overall, the Year of the Snake can be a pleasing one for the Earth Rooster. However, to benefit fully, he does need to be open to possibility and make the most of situations. As he acknowledges, there are many ways forward. If he is able to make the most of the opportunities that arise this year, his actions can have far-reaching significance. The Snake year will also encourage him to use his personal qualities, ideas and creativity to good effect, and positive action now can lead to further opportunities in the future.

TIP FOR THE YEAR
Value the good relations you have with those around you and set quality time aside for your loved ones. You have a lot of support this year.

FAMOUS ROOSTERS

Fernando Alonso, Beyoncé, Cate Blanchett, Barbara Taylor Bradford, Gerard Butler, Sir Michael Caine, the Duchess of Cambridge, Enrico Caruso, Eric Clapton, Joan Collins, Rita Coolidge, Daniel Day Lewis, Minnie Driver, the Duke of Edinburgh, Gloria Estefan, Roger Federer, Errol Flynn, Benjamin Franklin, Dawn French, Stephen Fry, Melanie Griffith, Josh Groban, Goldie Hawn, Katharine Hepburn, Paris Hilton, Jay-Z, Catherine Zeta Jones, Quincy Jones, Diane Keaton, Søren Kierkegaard, D. H. Lawrence, David Livingstone, Jayne Mansfield, Steve Martin, James Mason, W. Somerset Maugham, Paul Merton, Bette Midler, Ed Miliband, Van Morrison, Willie Nelson, Kim Novak, Yoko Ono, Dolly Parton, Matthew Perry, Michelle Pfeiffer, Natalie Portman, Priscilla Presley, Joan Rivers, Kelly Rowland, Jenny Seagrove, George Segal, Carly Simon, Britney Spears, Johann Strauss, Verdi, Richard Wagner, Serena Williams, Neil Young, Renée Zellweger.

28 JANUARY 1922 ～ 15 FEBRUARY 1923   *Water Dog*

14 FEBRUARY 1934 ～ 3 FEBRUARY 1935   *Wood Dog*

2 FEBRUARY 1946 ～ 21 JANUARY 1947   *Fire Dog*

18 FEBRUARY 1958 ～ 7 FEBRUARY 1959   *Earth Dog*

6 FEBRUARY 1970 ～ 26 JANUARY 1971   *Metal Dog*

25 JANUARY 1982 ～ 12 FEBRUARY 1983   *Water Dog*

10 FEBRUARY 1994 ～ 30 JANUARY 1995   *Wood Dog*

29 JANUARY 2006 ～ 17 FEBRUARY 2007   *Fire Dog*

THE
DOG

THE PERSONALITY OF THE DOG

I have my values
and beliefs.
These are my beacon
in an ever-changing world.

The Dog is born under the signs of loyalty and anxiety. He usually holds very firm views and beliefs and is the champion of good causes. He hates any sort of injustice or unfair treatment and will do all in his power to help those less fortunate than himself. He has a strong sense of fair play and will be honourable and open in all his dealings.

The Dog is very direct and straightforward. He is never one to skirt round issues and speaks frankly and to the point. He can be stubborn, but he is prepared to listen to the views of others and will try to be as fair as possible in coming to his decisions. He will readily give advice where it is needed and will be the first to offer assistance when things go wrong.

The Dog instils confidence wherever he goes and there are many who admire him for his integrity and resolute manner. He is a very good judge of character and can often form an accurate impression of someone very shortly after meeting them. He is also very intuitive and can frequently sense how things are going to work out long in advance.

Despite his friendly and amiable manner, the Dog is not a big socializer. He dislikes having to attend large functions or parties and much prefers a quiet meal with friends or a chat by the fire. He is an excellent conversationalist and is

often a marvellous raconteur of amusing stories and anec-
dotes.

The Dog is also quick-witted and his mind is always
alert. He can keep calm in a crisis and although he does
have a temper, his outbursts tend to be short-lived. He is
loyal and trustworthy, but if he ever feels badly let down
or rejected by someone, he will rarely forgive or forget.

The Dog usually has very set interests. He prefers to
specialize and become an expert in a chosen area rather
than dabble in a variety of different activities. He usually
does well in jobs where he feels that he is being of service
to others and is often suited to careers in the social services,
the medical and legal professions and teaching. He does,
however, need to feel motivated in his work. He has to have
a sense of purpose and if ever this is lacking he can quite
often drift through life without ever achieving very much.
Once he has the motivation, however, very little can
prevent him from securing his objective.

Another characteristic of the Dog is his tendency to
worry and to view things rather pessimistically. Quite
often his worries are totally unnecessary and are of his
own making. Although it may be difficult, worrying is a
habit that all Dogs should try to overcome.

The Dog is not materialistic or particularly bothered about
accumulating great wealth. As long as he has the money
necessary to support his family and to spend on the occasional luxury, he is more than happy. However, when he does
have any spare money he tends to be rather a spendthrift and
does not always put it to its best use. He is also not a very
good speculator and would be advised to get professional
advice before entering into any major long-term investment.

The Dog will rarely be short of admirers, but he is not an easy person to live with. His moods are changeable and his standards high, but he will be loyal and protective to his partner and will do all in his power to provide a comfortable home. He can get on extremely well with those born under the signs of the Horse, Pig, Tiger and Monkey, and can also establish a sound and stable relationship with the Rat, Ox, Rabbit, Snake and another Dog, but will find the Dragon a bit too flamboyant for his liking. He will also find it difficult to understand the imaginative Goat and is likely to be highly irritated by the candid Rooster.

The female Dog is renowned for her beauty. She has a warm and caring nature, although until she knows someone well she can be both secretive and very guarded. She is highly intelligent and despite her calm and tranquil appearance can be extremely ambitious. She enjoys sport and other outdoor activities and has a happy knack of finding bargains in the most unlikely of places. She can also get rather impatient when things do not work out as she would like.

The Dog usually has a very good way with children and can be a doting parent. He will rarely be happier than when he is helping someone or doing something that will benefit others. Providing he can cure himself of his tendency to worry, he will lead a very full and active life, and in that life he will make many friends and do a tremendous amount of good.

THE FIVE DIFFERENT TYPES OF DOG

In addition to the 12 signs of the Chinese zodiac there are five elements and these have a strengthening or moderating influence on the signs. The effects of the five elements on the Dog are described below, together with the years in which they were exercising their influence. Therefore Dogs born in 1970 are Metal Dogs, Dogs born in 1922 and 1982 are Water Dogs, and so on.

Metal Dog: 1970

The Metal Dog is bold, confident and forthright and sets about everything he does in a resolute and determined manner. He has a great belief in his abilities and no hesitation about speaking his mind or devoting himself to some just cause. He can be rather serious at times and can become anxious and irritable when things are not going according to plan. He tends to have very specific interests and it would certainly help him if he were to broaden his outlook and become more involved in group activities. He is loyal and faithful to his friends.

Water Dog: 1922, 1982

The Water Dog has a very direct and outgoing personality. He is an excellent communicator and has little trouble in persuading others to fall in with his plans. He does, however, have a somewhat carefree nature and is not as disciplined or as thorough as he should be in certain matters. Neither does he keep as much control over his finances as he should, but he can be most generous to his family and friends and will make sure that they want for nothing. He is usually very good with children and has a wide circle of friends.

Wood Dog: 1934, 1994

This Dog is a hard and conscientious worker and will usually make a favourable impression wherever he goes. He is less independent than some of the other types of Dog and prefers to work in a group rather than on his own. He is popular, has a good sense of humour and takes a keen interest in the activities of the various members of his family. He is often attracted to the finer things in life and can obtain much pleasure from collecting items of interest, beauty or antiquity. He prefers to live in the country rather than the town.

Fire Dog: 1946, 2006

This Dog has a lively, outgoing personality and is able to establish friendships with remarkable ease. He is an honest and conscientious worker and likes to take an active part in all that is going on around him. He also likes to explore new ideas and providing he can get the necessary support and advice, he can often succeed where others have failed. He does, however, have a tendency to be stubborn. Providing he can overcome this, he can often achieve considerable fame and fortune.

Earth Dog: 1958

The Earth Dog is very talented and astute. He is methodical and efficient and is capable of going far in his chosen profession. He tends to be rather quiet and reserved, but has a very persuasive manner and usually secures his objectives without too much opposition. He is generous and kind and always ready to lend a helping hand when it is needed. He is also held in very high esteem by his friends and colleagues and is usually most dignified in his appearance.

PROSPECTS FOR THE DOG IN 2013

The Dog may not have felt at ease in the fast-moving and disruptive Dragon year (23 January 2012–9 February 2013). Faced with many pressures, he could have found himself worrying about his situation. Progress may have been difficult, but as the Dragon year draws to a close, there is excellent reason for the Dog to take heart: the approaching Snake year heralds an improvement.

In what is left of the Dragon year the Dog can do himself a lot of good. In his work he should concentrate on his specific responsibilities but also take advantage of any opportunity to add to his role. What he accomplishes at this time can help his prospects next year. Similarly, for Dogs who are seeking work, a position they obtain now can often give them an introduction to a new company or type of work and be something they can build on in the future. Work-wise, this may not be an easy or smooth year, but it can be instructive.

In money matters, the Dog will need to be vigilant and should try to make early provision for any increased spending towards the year's end. He also needs to be thorough and check the terms and conditions should he enter into any new agreement. This is no time for risk.

Although the Dog has a tendency to keep his thoughts to himself, it would be beneficial to him to share any concerns at this time with those close to him. 'A worry shared is a worry halved', as the saying goes, and this can hold true for many Dogs in the Dragon year.

Overall, this may not have been the easiest of years, but in the closing months there will be quite a few occasions the Dog can look forward to, including parties and social events. He will also have the chance to spend quality time with his family, including some relations he does not often see. Some plans made towards the end of the year could be both helpful and significant.

The Year of the Snake starts on 10 February and will be a pleasing one for the Dog. Rather than be buffeted by events, he will feel able to reassert himself and use his strengths to better effect. For many Dogs, especially those who have felt bruised by recent developments, this is a time to draw a line under what has gone before and concentrate on the present and near future. With resolve, purpose and a certain amount of luck, the Dog will find his prospects are on the up!

An encouraging aspect will be the way the Dog is able to plan ahead. Snake years favour careful thought and consideration rather than rush, and this suits the Dog personality well. Accordingly, as the Snake year starts, the Dog would do well to set himself some goals. These could be personal, home or career related, but with something to aim for the Dog will not only be able to direct his energies more purposefully but also to benefit from moments of serendipity. As Goethe observed, 'Whatever you can do or dream you can, begin it./Boldness has genius, power and magic in it./Begin it now.' In so many respects this year, once the Dog starts to take action, things *will* start to happen.

This is especially the case at work. Dogs who start the year feeling held back and unfulfilled would do well to look at ways of moving their career forward. This could be at their current place of work or elsewhere, but by keeping alert, making enquiries and putting themselves forward, these Dogs will find their initiative resulting in opportunities being found. For some, there could be the chance to secure the promotion they have been working towards for some time.

The prospects are also encouraging for Dogs seeking work. Although the job-seeking process can be difficult, the Dog is tenacious, and by persisting and having faith in his abilities he can secure what can be a significant new opening. This could be in a new type of work and require some adjustment, but nevertheless it could offer the Dog the chance to extend his skills in often satisfying ways. March, May, June and September could see interesting opportunities, but throughout the year the Dog's actions can be far-reaching, and tentative or chance enquiries could result in possibilities opening up.

The progress the Dog makes in his work can also benefit his financial position. Many Dogs will enjoy an increase in earnings over the year and some may also receive something extra, perhaps an overdue payment or a gift, or be able to put a personal interest to profitable use. Moneywise, the Snake year can definitely bring an improvement, although the Dog still needs to budget carefully. Without care, anything extra he has received could be quickly spent, and not always in the best way. Large purchases or expensive plans do need to be thought through and should not be rushed. Everyday spending should also be watched. Snake years favour a cautious and conservative approach.

One area in which the Dog is usually cautious is his relations with others. He prefers to build up trust and friendship over time, and can also be fairly selective in his socializing, often preferring a quiet lifestyle. However, while the aspects indicate limited social activity this year, the Dog should not be too reclusive. Socializing can bring an important balance to his lifestyle as well as give him the chance to relax, enjoy himself and do something different. March, May, July and November could see interesting social opportunities and chances to meet new people. Dogs who are seeking new friends or romance will take their time to get to know any new acquaintance, but some of the people the Dog meets this year could, in time, become very significant.

The Dog's personal interests are favourably aspected and during the year he should not only set aside time to enjoy these but also consider ways he could take them further, perhaps through setting himself a project, learning new techniques or trying out a new recreational activity. Dogs who would welcome a new challenge should delay no longer in starting something new. In the process these

Dogs could reignite a spark which has been missing in recent years. For Dogs who are interested in their well-being, a local fitness class may be worth considering.

The Dog always attaches particular importance to his home life and this year can enjoy some special times. Not only will his loved ones be keen to share in his progress, but there could also be a family or personal milestone to mark, perhaps a special birthday, anniversary, birth or marriage. Over the year there may well be events that will make the Dog especially proud. As always, he will give advice and encouragement, and may instigate some ambitious home projects. A lot is set to happen in Dog households this year, but plans should not be rushed and ample time should be allowed for discussion. However, the more measured nature of the Snake year suits the Dog's temperament and his home life can be especially rewarding.

Overall, the Dog is set to do well this year. By being determined and seizing his opportunities, he can make good progress and enjoy some well-deserved (and sometimes overdue) success. He will value the love and support of those close to him and will have the chance to use his strengths to good effect.

The Metal Dog

The Metal Dog will have seen a lot happen in recent years and there will have been occasions when he will have felt disillusioned, been thrown off-course and found his objectives difficult to realize. However, he will have gained both useful insights about his capabilities and experience he can build on. As the Snake year starts, he can look forward to a more settled and productive time. Some of the things he has been working towards will now become possible. Snake years support the Metal Dog and the tide is turning in his favour.

Work prospects are particularly encouraging. In recent times many Metal Dogs will have been involved in change that they will not have been entirely comfortable with. However, early on in the Snake year, new possibilities can arise. The Metal Dog may become involved in new projects, transfer to other duties or benefit from promotion opportunities. His experience, reputation and loyalty can be important factors now. Metal Dogs who have felt staid recently and just want to move forward can find the Snake year offering that chance. March, May, June and September could see encouraging developments.

This also applies to Metal Dogs desiring more substantial change or seeking work. If they actively explore possibilities, their drive and diligence can lead to openings being found. As these Metal Dogs recognize, considerable effort will be required, but persistence will prevail. Importantly, the positions that many Metal Dogs secure now will not only allow them to use their skills in new ways but often open up other possibilities in the near future.

There will also be some Metal Dogs who will be tempted to become self-employed this year. These Metal Dogs should seek advice and backing. The more solid their preparation, the better their chance of success.

The progress the Metal Dog makes at work can also help financially. However, with his many commitments, he will need to keep careful control of his budget and plan his spending accordingly. This is not a year for proceeding on an ad hoc basis, particularly if he is to go ahead with some of the plans he has in mind. Similarly, when involved in large transactions, the Metal Dog needs to allow time to make comparisons and check the implications. To fare well in money matters this year, he should remain thorough and disciplined.

His personal interests are encouragingly aspected, however, and the Metal Dog should aim to set time aside for them. Not only can they give him the chance to relax but also the opportunity to do something different from his more usual activities. Metal Dogs who have let their interests lapse recently will find it worth rectifying this. And with the year's emphasis on culture and the arts, if the Metal Dog has the chance to visit museums, exhibitions or special events, he should try to go. The Snake year can broaden his perspective.

This also applies to his travelling over the year. Whether taking a holiday, enjoying a short break or visiting friends and relations, the Metal Dog will often welcome the chance to go away and in many cases will see some fascinating sights. There could be additional travel opportunities towards the end of the year.

With his various commitments, the Metal Dog will be selective in his socializing. However, he should make sure he does not lose contact with his friends. Metal Dogs, do take note – even if meeting up is not always possible, a phone call or e-mail can still be appreciated. Also going out – even if just occasionally – can do the Metal Dog good and bring balance to his lifestyle. In the Snake year it is important that he does not become too reclusive.

Any Metal Dogs who have recently experienced personal difficulty and would welcome company and perhaps romance will find this is a year when positive action can make a difference. If they go out and make the most of their chances to meet others, perhaps by joining an interest group, they can forge new friendships and perhaps find romance too. The Snake year can make many of the Metal Dog's hopes come true, but he does need to take action. March, May, June and November could be good months for meeting others.

In his home life, while the Metal Dog and those close to him will all be busy with various commitments, the Metal Dog can be particularly good at bringing everyone together and making sure time is set aside for sharing. He will offer advice when needed and play a much appreciated role this year. He may also be keen to carry out home improvements. However, while he may be eager to get these underway, Snake years do not favour rush, and allowing time for discussion will bring about much better results.

Overall, the Snake year can be an encouraging one for the Metal Dog. His determination and skills can lead to good headway being made. This is very much a time for moving forward and building on strengths. The Metal Dog can also derive considerable pleasure from his home life and personal interests, with various undertakings proceeding well. He does need to keep his lifestyle in balance and should not neglect his social life, but he will have much in his favour this year and can make this a successful and personally rewarding time.

Look to build on your skills and ideas. You know you have much to offer and now is your chance. Determined action and effort can lead to a lot opening up for you.

The Water Dog

The element of Water can add awareness to a sign as well as strengthen its communication skills. And this holds true for the Water Dog. He is perceptive and also expresses himself well. In this promising year he can enjoy considerable good fortune.

At work the aspects are especially encouraging and the Water Dog will have the chance to make greater use of his strengths. In some cases promotion opportunities will open up which will allow him to further his career and change the nature of his duties. Opportunities can occur quite early on in the Snake year and by embracing them the Water Dog can look forward to making good headway. Quite a few Water Dogs could find one opportunity leading on to others. For those who change jobs early on in 2013, further possibilities could arise later in the year.

For Water Dogs who start the year unhappy in their current position, as well as those seeking work, the Snake year can be significant. Although securing a new position will be difficult, by being flexible and considering a wide range of options, the Water Dog could be offered a position that will be something to build on. Admittedly, this could involve considerable adjustment, but by rising to the challenge, the Water Dog will have the opportunity to prove himself in new ways. As he will have found many times before, life can be a series of twists and turns, and what happens this year can be one of those curious twists which sets him off on a new and rewarding career path. Late February, March, May, June and September could see interesting developments.

Another important aspect of the year will be the chance the Water Dog will have to expand his working knowledge. Often this will come through training and a change of duties, but if the Water Dog feels another qualification could be helpful or he wants to develop himself in some way, he should investigate possibilities. Sometimes an online or locally run course might be suitable. Snake years favour personal and career development.

This emphasis on progress also applies to the Water Dog's personal interests. Again, if there is a skill, subject or project that interests him, now is the time to follow it up. In addition some Water Dogs could be attracted by a new recreational activity, possibly one which can help them make more of their potential.

The progress many Water Dogs make at work this year can also lead to an increase in earnings. Quite a few could benefit from some money luck too, possibly a gift, bonus or even a competition win. However, while the Water Dog's financial prospects are promising, he has many obligations and may be hoping to carry out expensive plans as well. As a result, he will need to manage his money carefully. With good control he will fare well, but any laxity on his part, including overreaching his budget, could mean certain plans or purchases have to be put back. While an improved year financially, it still calls for discipline.

However, if possible, the Water Dog should try to make provision for travel this year. Not only will a change of scene do him good, but by choosing his destination well, and possibly linking his trip with an event or interest, he will find his travels taking on greater meaning. This is a year which rewards careful planning.

In view of his various commitments, the Water Dog may cut back on his socializing this year. However, he should still keep in regular contact with his friends and do his best to accept invitations to events that appeal to him. Some Water Dogs could find their interests leading to significant new friendships or romance. Snake years have a capacity to delight and surprise. March, May, July and November could be interesting and personally rewarding months.

The Water Dog's home life will also be a source of considerable pleasure and he will often share his hopes and plans with those close to him. If a parent, he will do much to support his children, and time spent together can provide some wonderful and proud moments. One of the Water Dog's strengths is his ability to relate to others and this is something that many people will appreciate during the year.

However, while a lot will go well domestically, there will still be pressures and moments of concern. Willing though he may be, the Water Dog should not assume responsibility for everything and should consult others and obtain further help if necessary. This may be a good year, but there is a limit to what the Water Dog can do. Water Dogs, take note and do draw on the readiness of others to assist.

Overall, the Year of the Snake can offer the Water Dog considerable opportunity. In both his work and personal interests he will have more chance to develop his skills and use his natural talents. This is a year of personal growth, and important possibilities can follow on. Although it is a quiet year socially, the Water Dog will value his relations with those close to him and many shared plans will proceed well. A year of pleasing possibility.

TIP FOR THE YEAR
Make the most of your opportunities, even if some adjustment is required. What occurs this year can often give you the chance to prove yourself in a new way. This is a time to learn, move forward and enjoy.

The Wood Dog

This is an encouraging year for the Wood Dog and he can add considerably to his skills as well as enjoy some fine personal developments.

The many Wood Dogs in education will now have more opportunity to select and focus on subjects that interest them. As a result, not only can their studying become more satisfying but they can also form a clearer idea of future career paths. The Snake year can do a lot to widen the perspective of these Wood Dogs as well as give them skills and knowledge they can take further in the future. Many Wood Dogs will be inspired by the work they do during the year and could also have the chance to take an additional (possibly optional) course or decide to pursue a new activity. The Snake year very much favours personal development.

Also, as the Chinese proverb reminds us, 'You won't get lost if you frequently ask for directions.' For Wood Dogs in education, if there are areas of study they find difficult or if they have to make decisions about topics for study, it is important they seek advice. With proper guidance, better decisions can be made.

This is equally true for Wood Dogs in work. If a problem occurs or the Wood Dog is uncertain how best to proceed, he should ask. By getting directions, he will not only find out what to do but also indicate his willingness to learn. He is, after all, at the start of his working life and by proving himself now he will be placing himself in a good position for the future. Wood Dogs who are already established in a position will often have a chance to take on greater responsibilities as the year progresses.

Wood Dogs seeking work can also help their situation by getting advice, including on ways to improve their applications and interview technique. If they actively pursue possible vacancies, the time and effort they put in will eventually pay off. Their quest may not be easy, but they may be rewarded with an opportunity that can be the foundation of future success. If they are able to take advantage of an apprenticeship scheme and continue their learning while they work, this too can be an effective way to establish themselves in a particular line of work. Late February to early April, May, June and September could see some encouraging developments.

In financial matters, the Wood Dog will fare reasonably well. However, he will need to watch his spending and make allowance for his regular commitments. Also, if he enters into any important agreement or is considering a major purchase, it would be worth him seeking advice and checking the terms before proceeding. Many Wood Dogs will be tempted to travel over the year and early provision for this would also be helpful.

The Wood Dog will be pleased with the way he is able to pursue his interests and develop his ideas over the year. Many Wood Dogs will enjoy going to concerts, festivals, sporting events or exhibitions that are related to their interests. The Snake year will certainly contain an interesting mix of things to do. Often the Wood Dog will be able to share his activities with his close friends and there will be chances for him to meet new people during the year. A few Wood Dogs will also find romance, with someone they meet during the Snake year becoming special over time. Late February, March, May, July and November could see the most social activity.

Although the Wood Dog will often be immersed in his own activities, he should also contribute to his home life. Helping with tasks and taking an informed interest in what is going on will help understanding and rapport. The Wood Dog also needs to be communicative. If he talks about what he is doing, runs over his ideas with others and asks for advice, he can find more senior relations in particular offering greater assistance.

Overall, this can be a positive year for the Wood Dog. Whether studying or developing his skills in another way, by building on his knowledge and capabilities, he will be investing in his future. He will also find this a more satisfying year, as he will be able to concentrate on the things he wants to do. This is a time of opportunity and by making the most of it, the Wood Dog can do well.

Be forthcoming. If a situation concerns you or you would welcome advice on any matter, do ask. Those around you are keen to see you make the most of your potential. Also, if new subjects or interests appeal to you, find out more. Some of what you start now can have long-term value. This is a year of opportunity and its benefits can be significant. Use it well.

The Fire Dog

This will be a pleasing year for the Fire Dog. However, as he will quickly discover, Snake years move at a measured pace. While the Fire Dog may be keen to get certain plans underway, they will often take longer than anticipated. Ample time should be allowed and the best results will be obtained by proceeding steadily.

Also, throughout the year it is important that the Fire Dog draws on the support of others. Although he may have his own ideas, if he discusses them with those around him and considers their viewpoints, he will find his plans can often be improved upon.

During the year many Fire Dogs will spend time on their home, either adding comforts or setting themselves projects, including, for some, cleaning and tidying storage areas. What the Fire Dog undertakes can prove very satisfying. Some projects can also bring surprises. Fire Dogs who embark on sorting through belongings could find possessions they had forgotten about which could be of sentimental, personal or even monetary value. Some Fire Dogs may also be reminded of former interests or find fascinating books or photo collections which they decide to look through and sort in greater detail.

Those who buy new equipment this year, whether a computer, camera, smart phone or entertainment system, will also spend time exploring its potential. The Fire Dog has a practical and enquiring mind and is frequently inspired by new technology.

As well as some of the year's more practical undertakings, he can look forward to some special family moments. There could be good news to celebrate concerning a younger relation, and with some family members likely to be involved in important decision-making this year, the Fire Dog will be glad to advise. His ability to understand and empathize will be especially valued.

There also will be quite a few social occasions which the Fire Dog will enjoy. He will particularly appreciate the variety of things he gets to do during the Snake year. In particular it would be worth keeping informed about what is going on locally.

This also applies to his personal interests. The Fire Dog may find there is a local group he could become involved with to develop an existing interest, and if he is tempted by a new pursuit, he may discover there are classes he could join or facilities he could use. Very often joining a group can give impetus to an activity as well as be a good way to meet new people. Particularly for Fire Dogs who are alone and would welcome new friends, this can be a valuable aspect of the year. March, May, July and November could see some fine occasions.

The Fire Dog will also appreciate the travel opportunities that arise over the year. Whether going away for a short or long break, he will delight in some of the (sometimes quite unusual) places he visits and things he gets to do.

He can fare well in financial matters, although when considering large purchases, he should take the time to check details, compare options and ensure that his needs are fully met by the item he is considering. The more thorough he is, the better. The Snake year can also spring some pleasant surprises and some Fire Dogs will enjoy some money luck this year, perhaps an unexpected gift or a competition win.

Overall, the Fire Dog will be reasonably content with how the Snake year turns out. He will derive particular satisfaction from some of the domestic projects and home improvements he carries out and the way he is able to enjoy his various interests. This can be an interesting and frequently fulfilling time, and with the support of those around him, the Fire Dog can see his plans develop in a pleasing way.

TIP FOR THE YEAR
Share your hopes and ideas. That way you can benefit from support and synergy as well as from some interesting opportunities. Your personal interests can also bring you considerable pleasure and give rise to possibilities worth developing.

The Earth Dog
In recent years many an Earth Dog will have faced considerable pressure, had misgivings about certain developments and found himself buffeted by change. The Snake year will

usher in a much more settled time and give him the chance to concentrate on his priorities. Admittedly, effort will be required in order to make progress, but the benefits of the year can be considerable.

As the Snake year starts the Earth Dog could find it helpful to give some thought to what he would like to see happen over the next 12 months. He should also talk his ideas over with his loved ones. As many Earth Dogs will find, once plans have been formed, serendipity will kick in and fortunate developments take place. Snake years are encouraging for the Earth Dog and can bring a few pleasant surprises.

One important area will be the Earth Dog's work. Earth Dogs who are established in a career will have an excellent chance to make greater use of their experience. This is a year offering progress and many Earth Dogs will feel more inspired than they have for a long time. Another factor in the Earth Dog's favour will be the reputation he has built up and the good working relations he has with many of his colleagues. Not only will his colleagues be supportive but the Earth Dog could take on a mentoring role and have the chance to share his knowledge. Throughout the year he should keep alert for chances to make use of his skills, expertise and ideas. Professionally, this can be a satisfying and encouraging time.

The majority of Earth Dogs will remain with their present employer over the year, but for those who would welcome change or are seeking work, the Snake year can have interesting developments in store. With the current economic climate, obtaining a new position will not be easy. However, by keeping alert and informed, the Earth Dog could identify some possibilities worth following up. If he learns more about the responsibilities involved in a particular position and emphasizes his experience, he may well be successful in his quest. It will take determination, persistence and self-belief, but important doors will open for many Earth Dogs this year. Late February, March, May, June and September could see interesting developments.

The Earth Dog should also allow himself time to enjoy his personal interests. If he has ideas for projects, he should take these further. Similarly, if there is an interest-related skill he would like to learn or a new pursuit that appeals to him, he should follow it up. His interests can not only bring him pleasure but also help balance his often busy lifestyle.

In addition, the Earth Dog could find it beneficial to give some consideration to his well-being over the year and if he is lacking regular exercise or does not have a particularly balanced diet, he should seek medical advice on the best action to take.

Although the Earth Dog likes to keep his social circle relatively small, he should also take up any invitations he receives as well as go to events that appeal to him. With the cultural emphasis of the Snake year, there could be a lot happening and it would be a shame for the Earth Dog, with his wide interests, to miss out or deny himself the pleasure some special occasions could bring. March, May, July and November could see the most social activity.

There can also be interesting developments in the Earth Dog's home life this year. Many Earth Dogs will have plans they are keen to pursue, possibly including carrying out alterations to their home and replacing old or uneconomical equipment as well as improving their living areas. By discussing their ideas and considering their choices carefully, these Earth Dogs will take great satisfaction in what is undertaken over the year and the benefits that follow on. However, all Earth Dogs should remember that Snake years do not favour rush and some activities are likely to take longer than anticipated.

As well as home improvements, in many an Earth Dog household there could be personal or family news to celebrate and a special occasion to mark. The Earth Dog may not only have reason to feel proud of certain family achievements but also be instrumental in planning domestic activities, making arrangements and dispensing advice. His skills, care and empathy will be very much in evidence this year and appreciated by many people.

Overall, the Year of the Snake can be a rewarding one for the Earth Dog. He will have the chance to use his skills and strengths to good effect and in both his work and his personal interests this is a time of interesting possibility and growth. In addition, he may benefit from some moments of good fortune. Encouraging (and sometimes surprising) developments can often help his plans along. His family life can also be a source of much contentment and many Earth Dogs will have some special occasions to enjoy. A pleasing year with many positive developments.

TIP FOR THE YEAR
This can be a special year, but to get the most from it, do be active, alert and involved. Follow up your ideas, use your strengths and seize your opportunities. Then enjoy the benefits that follow on.

FAMOUS DOGS

King Albert II of Belgium, Brigitte Bardot, Gary Barlow, Candice Bergen, Andrea Bocelli, David Bowie, George W. Bush, Naomi Campbell, Fabio Capello, Mariah Carey, King Carl Gustaf XVI of Sweden, José Carreras, Paul Cézanne, Cher, Sir Winston Churchill, Bill Clinton, Leonard Cohen, Matt Damon, Charles Dance, Claude Debussy, Dame Judi Dench, Kirsten Dunst, Dakota Fanning, Joseph Fiennes, Robert Frost, Ava Gardner, Judy Garland, George Gershwin, Anne Hathaway, O. Henry, Victor Hugo, Barry Humphries, Holly Hunter, Michael Jackson, Al Jolson, Jennifer Lopez, Sophia Loren, Joanna Lumley, Andie MacDowell, Shirley MacLaine, Madonna, Norman Mailer, Barry Manilow, Freddie Mercury, Liza Minelli, Gary Oldman, Simon Pegg, Sydney Pollack, Elvis Presley, Tim Robbins, Paul Robeson, Andy Roddick, Susan Sarandon, Claudia Schiffer, Dr Albert Schweitzer, Matt Smith, Sylvester Stallone, Robert Louis Stevenson, Sharon Stone, Donald Sutherland, Chris Tarrant, Mother Teresa, Uma Thurman, Donald Trump, Voltaire, Prince William, Shelley Winters.

16 FEBRUARY 1923 〜 4 FEBRUARY 1924   *Water Pig*

4 FEBRUARY 1935 〜 23 JANUARY 1936   *Wood Pig*

22 JANUARY 1947 〜 9 FEBRUARY 1948   *Fire Pig*

8 FEBRUARY 1959 〜 27 JANUARY 1960   *Earth Pig*

27 JANUARY 1971 〜 14 FEBRUARY 1972   *Metal Pig*

13 FEBRUARY 1983 〜 1 FEBRUARY 1984   *Water Pig*

31 JANUARY 1995 〜 18 FEBRUARY 1996   *Wood Pig*

18 FEBRUARY 2007 〜 6 FEBRUARY 2008   *Fire Pig*

THE
PIG

THE PERSONALITY OF THE PIG

It's the doing,
the giving,
the playing the part,
that makes life what it is.
And what it can be.

The Pig is born under the sign of honesty. He has a kind and understanding nature and is well known for his abilities as a peacemaker. He hates any sort of discord or unpleasantness and will do everything in his power to sort out differences of opinion or bring opposing factions together.

He is also an excellent conversationalist and speaks truthfully and to the point. He dislikes any form of falsehood or hypocrisy and is a firm believer in justice and the maintenance of law and order. In spite of these beliefs, however, he is reasonably tolerant and often prepared to forgive others for their wrongdoings. He rarely harbours grudges and is never vindictive.

The Pig is usually very popular. He enjoys other people's company and likes to be involved in joint or group activities. He will be a loyal member of any club or society and can be relied upon to lend a helping hand at functions. He is also an excellent fundraiser for charities and is often a great supporter of humanitarian causes.

The Pig is a hard and conscientious worker and is particularly respected for his reliability and integrity. In his early years he will try his hand at several different jobs, but he is usually happiest where he feels that he is being of service to others. He will unselfishly give up his time for the common good and is highly valued by his colleagues and employers.

The Pig has a good sense of humour and invariably has a smile, joke or some whimsical remark at the ready. He loves to entertain and to please others, and there are many Pigs who have been attracted to careers in show business or who enjoy following the careers of famous stars and personalities.

There are, unfortunately, some who take advantage of the Pig's good nature and impose upon his generosity. The Pig has great difficulty in saying 'no', and although he may dislike being firm, it would be in his own interests to say occasionally, 'Enough is enough.' He can also be rather naïve and gullible; however, if at any stage in his life he feels that he has been badly let down, he will try to become self-reliant. There are many Pigs who have become entrepreneurs or forged a successful career on their own after some early disappointment in life. Although the Pig tends to spend his money quite freely, he is usually very astute in financial matters and there are many Pigs who have become wealthy.

Another characteristic of the Pig is his ability to recover from setbacks reasonably quickly. His faith and his strength of character keep him going. If he thinks that there is a job he can do or there is something that he wants to achieve, he will pursue it with dogged determination. He can also be stubborn and no matter how many may plead with him, once he has made his mind up he will rarely change his views.

Although the Pig may work hard, he also knows how to enjoy himself. He is a great pleasure-seeker and will quite happily spend his hard-earned money on a lavish holiday or an expensive meal – for the Pig is a connoisseur of good food and wine – or a variety of recreational activities. He also enjoys small social gatherings and if he is in company he likes he can very easily become the life and soul of the party. He does, however, tend to become rather withdrawn at larger functions or when among strangers.

The Pig is a creature of comfort and his home will usually be fitted with the latest in luxury appliances. Where possible, he will prefer to live in the country rather than the town and will opt to have a big garden, for the Pig is usually a keen and successful gardener.

The Pig is very popular with others and will often have numerous romances before he settles down. Once settled, however, he will be loyal to his partner and he will find that he is especially well suited to those born under the signs of the Goat, Rabbit, Dog and Tiger and also to another Pig. Due to his affable and easy-going nature he can also establish a satisfactory relationship with all the remaining signs of the Chinese zodiac, with the exception of the Snake. The Snake tends to be wily, secretive and very guarded, and this can be intensely irritating to the honest and open-hearted Pig.

The female Pig will devote all her energies to the needs of her children and her partner. She will try to ensure that they want for nothing and their pleasure is very much her pleasure. She can be a caring and conscientious parent and has very good taste in clothes. Her home will either be very clean and orderly or hopelessly untidy. Strangely, there seems to be no in between with Pigs – they either love housework or detest it! The female Pig does, however, have considerable talents as an organizer and this, combined with her friendly and open manner, enables her to secure many of her objectives.

The Pig is usually lucky in life and will rarely want for anything. Provided he does not let others take advantage of his good nature and is not afraid of asserting himself, he will go through life making friends, helping others and winning the admiration of many.

THE FIVE DIFFERENT TYPES OF PIG

In addition to the 12 signs of the Chinese zodiac there are five elements and these have a strengthening or moderating influence on the signs. The effects of the five elements on the Pig are described below, together with the years in which they were exercising their influence. Therefore Pigs born in 1971 are Metal Pigs, Pigs born in 1923 and 1983 are Water Pigs, and so on.

Metal Pig: 1971

The Metal Pig is more ambitious and determined than some of the other types of Pig. He is strong, energetic and likes to be involved in a wide variety of different activities. He is very open and forthright in his views, although he can be a little too trusting at times and has a tendency to accept things at face value. He has a good sense of humour and loves to attend parties and other social gatherings. He has a warm, outgoing nature and usually has a large circle of friends.

Water Pig: 1923, 1983

The Water Pig has a heart of gold. He is generous and loyal and tries to remain on good terms with everyone. He will do his utmost to help others, but sadly there are some who will take advantage of his kind nature and he should, in his own interests, be a little more discriminating and be prepared to stand firm against anything that he does not like. Although he prefers the quieter things in life, he has a wide range of interests. He particularly enjoys outdoor pursuits and attending parties and social occasions. He is a hard and conscientious worker and invariably does well in his chosen profession. He is also gifted in the art of communication.

Wood Pig: 1935, 1995

This Pig has a friendly, persuasive manner and is easily able to gain the confidence of others. He likes to be involved in all that is going on around him but can sometimes take on more responsibility than he can properly handle. He is loyal to his family and friends and derives much pleasure from helping those less fortunate than himself. He is usually an optimist and leads a very full, enjoyable and satisfying life. He also has a good sense of humour.

Fire Pig: 1947

The Fire Pig is both energetic and adventurous and sets about everything he does in a confident and resolute manner. He is very forthright in his views and does not mind taking risks in order to achieve his objectives. He can, however, get carried away by the excitement of the moment and ought to exercise more caution in some of the enterprises in which he gets involved. He is usually lucky in money matters and is well known for his generosity. He is also very caring towards the members of his family.

Earth Pig: 1959

This Pig has a kindly nature. He is sensible and realistic and will go to great lengths in order to please his employers and to secure his aims and ambitions. He is an excellent organizer and is particularly astute in business and financial matters. He has a good sense of humour and a wide circle of friends. He also likes to lead an active social life, although he does sometimes have a tendency to eat and drink more than is good for him.

PROSPECTS FOR THE PIG IN 2013

Dragon years (23 January 2012–9 February 2013) are times of great activity and during this one the Pig will have had a lot to do. As it draws to a close, there will be no let-up in the pace.

On a personal level the Pig will find himself in demand and, being the keen socializer that he is, will appreciate his chances to go out. With his genial manner, he will enjoy the company of many people and find his circle of acquaintances increasing. December and January will be especially active months. For unattached Pigs, there could be good romantic possibilities, while those enjoying romance can look forward to some often exciting times as the year draws to an end.

The Pig's home life is also set to be busy, and plans need to be talked through, arranged carefully and spaced out if possible, otherwise some weeks could become pressured and rushed.

Many Pigs will also see an increase in their workload at this time and will need to be focused and well organized. However, one benefit is that many will have the chance to get to know other colleagues and make new contacts. November and early December could see encouraging developments and possible openings.

With much financial outlay likely in the closing months of the year, the Pig could also find it helpful to spread out certain purchases and avoid buying too much in rush.

In general, the Year of the Dragon will have been a busy one for the Pig. He may have been concerned about some of its developments, but there will also have been personal achievements which will have meant a great deal to him.

The Year of the Snake begins on 10 February and will not be the easiest for the Pig. Being open and upfront, he could be bemused by the not always straightforward workings of the Snake year and will need to keep his wits firmly about him.

One of the year's trickier aspects concerns the Pig's relations with others. Although he is normally adept in handling personal relationships, the Snake year can bring its problems. Disagreements may take place and some Pigs may also be concerned by the pettiness or jealousy of another person. Also, where affairs of the heart are concerned, any lapses could result in problems and heartache. In Snake years, Pigs need to be their honourable selves and be wary of intrigue and sometimes the mischief-making of other people. Fortunately the Pig has an excellent understanding of human nature and its foibles and the majority of Pigs will steer their way successfully through the complexities of the year, but the more care the Pig gives to his relations with others, the better.

In his home life in particular it is important that he preserves some quality time for those around him. Here his empathy and genuine interest in the activities and well-being of his loved ones will be especially valued. Also, when differences of opinion arise (as they do in any year), it is best for the Pig to talk these through before they have the chance to escalate.

Snake years proceed at a measured pace and if the Pig is considering any domestic undertakings, he needs to allow ample time to carry these out. Although he may be eager to get certain plans underway, delays and hidden problems could occur. Snake years can have their annoyances, but by showing patience and dealing with situations as they arise, the Pig will be able to carry out many of his plans, even if not to his timescale. However, despite the variable aspects, there will still be many domestic occasions to enjoy.

In addition the Snake year can bring some good travel opportunities and if possible the Pig should aim to take a holiday or short break with his loved ones. A change of scene can do everyone good.

The outgoing Pig attaches a lot of importance to his social life and March, April and the closing months of the year could be especially active. However, while he will often enjoy himself, the Pig does need to bear in mind the year's more cautionary aspects. Any personal lapse or *faux pas* could rebound on him. This is a year requiring care and awareness.

Any new romance will also need careful nurturing and time should be allowed for each person to get to know the other better. Rush, haste or building high expectations early on can lead to heartache. Snake years favour patience and proceeding with care.

Although the Pig will often be kept busy, it is important that he also allows time for his own interests. Snake years encourage learning and personal growth and it may be of benefit to the Pig to acquire new skills.

He would also do well to give some consideration to his own well-being over the year, including the quality of his diet and his level of exercise, and should he have any concerns, he should get these checked out.

At work, the Snake year can prove significant. Many Pigs will have large workloads to deal with and new challenges to meet. It will be a case of knuckling down and showing commitment, but by giving his best and rising to the challenge, the Pig will not only have the chance to demonstrate his skills but also, through his fortitude, impress others. Results do not come easily for Pigs in Snake years, but the Pig is resilient, enterprising and above all determined, and this will serve him well.

Most Pigs will remain with their present employer over the year, but for those who decide to move on or are seeking work, there can be important developments in store. To benefit, these Pigs should consider a wide range of possibilities and take advantage of the advice and other resources available to them. These could include retraining or refresher courses or possibilities offered through employment initiatives. By investigating what is available and keeping alert for vacancies, the Pig will demonstrate his redoubtable nature and often secure a new position that offers him the chance to prove himself in a different capacity. April, May, July and October could see important work developments.

In matters of finance the Snake year will require care. Home purchases, repairs and some maintenance could involve additional outlay, and throughout the year the Pig should keep a close watch on spending and, where possible, set funds aside for specific requirements. Also, when entering into agreements he should check the details and obligations and be vigilant when dealing with tax and other financial paperwork. This is a year to avoid risk and rush.

It has often been said that difficulties can help bring out the qualities and strengths of a person and this will be the case for many a Pig this year. The situations he will have to deal with will require effort on his part, and in his relations with others, lapses and preoccupation could bring problems. Throughout the year the Pig will need to remain attentive and aware. However, while the aspects may be mixed, provided the Pig proceeds with care, he can do much to avoid the problems and pressures the Snake year can bring and can emerge from it with experience and achievements he can build on in the future, particularly in the following, more favourable Horse year.

The Metal Pig

The element of Metal can strengthen a sign's qualities and will often make it more determined and resilient. Determination and resilience are not only an essential part of the Metal Pig's make-up but can prove especially important this year. The Snake year may not be the smoothest for the Metal Pig, but with care and persistence he can emerge with some important gains to his credit.

As with all Pigs, the Metal Pig will need to be mindful of those around him. Although he has his own views, he will need to listen to those of others and very often show some flexibility too. This is no year for obstinacy or intransigence.

In addition, when in company the Metal Pig needs to keep his wits about him and avoid acting in ways which could lead to problems. Lapses, indiscretions or misunderstandings could all embarrass him and undermine his position. Metal Pigs, do take careful note. Snake years are not ones for risk, especially where personal relations are concerned.

However, provided the Metal Pig remains his careful self, he can look forward to many positive developments over the year. In his home life, both younger and more senior relations could be especially grateful for his support, especially at busy times. Throughout the year, however, it is important that everyone does their fair share in the home and that time is set aside for spending together and sharing various activities. Home life should not always be conducted at such a pace that its pleasures are missed.

Also, as travel is favourably aspected, if possible the Metal Pig should take a holiday with his loved ones at some time over the year, or at least enjoy a short break.

THE PIG

Going somewhere new and doing something different can do everyone good.

The Metal Pig will appreciate the social opportunities the year will bring, but here again he needs to remain attentive and mindful. Indeed, he would do well to remember the Chinese proverb, 'Walls have ears.' If tempted to speak too freely, he could find his words rebounding on him. Snake years can punish lapses and Metal Pigs need to be on their guard. March, April and November to early January could see the most social activity.

For the unattached, affairs of the heart could feature prominently, and some Metal Pigs are set for a rollercoaster year. For some, love may arise suddenly and throw their emotional world into turmoil, while others may find an existing friendship becoming much more significant. Romance will not necessarily be straightforward this year, and in keeping with the Snake year's more measured pace, the Metal Pig should not act too hurriedly. It is better to allow time for a relationship to develop than to rush into things.

With his busy lifestyle, the Metal Pig should also give some consideration to his well-being. This includes allowing time for rest and suitable exercise and making sure his diet is balanced. Should he have any concerns, he should get these checked out. Also, to help keep his lifestyle in balance, he should allow time for activities he enjoys. The Snake year can open up some pleasing possibilities, and with its emphasis on the arts, some cultural visits or shows could delight the Metal Pig.

In work matters, this can be a time of interesting opportunity. Although many Metal Pigs will be grappling with a heavy workload, they may be able to turn events to their advantage. If new projects or initiatives are introduced, the Metal Pig could have the chance to become involved, and if colleagues are absent, there could be the opportunity for him to do more. By showing willing, the Metal Pig can gain skills that can be to his advantage.

Metal Pigs seeking work or hoping to make a change in their working life will find their resilient and determined nature helping in their quest. Although the employment situation may be difficult, by being prepared to consider a wide range of possibilities, they may be able to secure a position which can introduce them to a new type of work and be a platform they can subsequently build on. It *will* require effort to make that breakthrough, but once focused on an objective, the Metal Pig usually gets results in the end. April, May, July and October could see some interesting work developments.

Although the Metal Pig's progress at work can also lead to an increase in income, he will have a great many outgoings and will need to budget accordingly. Finance requires careful attention this year.

Overall, the Snake year may test the character and capabilities of the Metal Pig in many ways. However, provided he takes the time to think things through, avoids unnecessary risk and seizes his opportunities, he can make headway and gain important new skills. This may not be an easy or straightforward year, but the Metal Pig's determination will enable him to emerge from it with gains to his credit.

Give time and attention to those who are important to you. They are treasures in your life and need to be treasured. Also, avoid acting hastily. This is a year for proceeding with care.

The Water Pig

This year marks a new decade in the Water Pig's life and ushers in a busy and fulfilling time. In his thirties, his unique talents can lead to some important achievements, both personal and professional. However, there will be inevitable bumps along the way, with 2013 containing its fair share. This year the Water Pig will need to proceed with caution.

At work many Water Pigs will face disruption, pressure and some volatile situations. The conscientious Water Pig will often be worried and sometimes in a dilemma about the best approach to take. However, while parts of the year will be demanding, it can still be an instructive and potentially important time. Not only will it give the Water Pig a chance to demonstrate and extend his skills, but also deal with an increased range of responsibilities. Some of the developments of 2013 will highlight his potential and this can be to his future benefit.

The majority of Water Pigs will remain with their present employer over the year, but for Water Pigs who feel the time is right for a new career challenge, as well as those seeking work, this can be a significant time. Suitable positions may be few and far between, but by making enquiries, talking to experts and, in some cases, taking advantage of employment initiatives, the Water Pig may gain the chance to prove himself in another capacity. April, May, July and October could see encouraging developments.

A further benefit of the year will be the way the Water Pig is able to develop his own skills. If he feels an additional skill or qualification could help his prospects, he should look at ways he could obtain this, including courses he could take in his own time. By investing in himself he will also be investing in his future.

This also applies to his personal interests. If there is an activity he wants to master or interest he is keen to take further, he should explore possibilities. Snake years encourage study and personal development.

All Water Pigs should also give some consideration to their well-being this year and, if they are leading stressful lives, make sure they allow time to rest and unwind. Should they have any concerns, they should get these checked out.

The progress many Water Pigs will make at work can also lead to an increase in income, but the Snake year can be an expensive one. Quite a few Water Pigs will decide to mark their thirtieth year with a special holiday, and with careful planning this could be one of the highlights of the year, but throughout the year the Water Pig will need to keep careful control of his budget. With discipline he will be able to proceed with his plans and purchases, but should he be lax then some may have to be delayed.

With his enquiring and genial nature, the Water Pig sets great store by his relations with others and over the year he will continue to enjoy the friendship and support of many, but should he detect that something is wrong at any time, he should see if he can find the cause and talk the matter through. With care and dialogue, problems can often be diffused and this is not a year to ignore them or risk them escalating. The Water Pig should also be careful not to place himself in a position which could lead to difficulties. Snake years have the potential to undermine relationships. Water Pigs, take note.

However, with care, a lot can still go well for the Water Pig. For the unattached, the Snake year can suddenly unleash exciting romantic prospects. Any relationship will still require careful nurturing, however. March, April and November to early January could be the busiest months for socializing and meeting others.

The Water Pig's domestic life can also see much activity. For Water Pigs who are or become parents, the needs of babies and young children will add to the joy but also pressure of the year. Co-operation and flexibility will be required, but amid all the activity there will be many special times. The Water Pig may also be touched by the affection shown him in the celebrations held for his thirtieth birthday.

Overall, the Year of the Snake can be significant for the Water Pig. While it will have its challenges, it will give him a chance to draw on his strengths and add to his skills. This new decade in his life promises a great deal and what he accomplishes now will be excellent preparation for the promising times that lie ahead.

Avoid unnecessary risk. Ignoring warning signals can lead to problems. Be sure to value your relations with others and seize any chances to extend your skills and experience. You may need to tread carefully, but this can be a year with long-term significance.

The Wood Pig

There is a Chinese proverb which advises, 'Walk slowly and you won't fall down; act carefully and you won't make mistakes.' This is good advice for the Wood Pig in 2013. By focusing on his priorities and putting in the effort, he can fare well. However, should he sit back or take risks, problems and disappointments could loom. Snake years require Wood Pigs to be on their mettle.

While the aspects may be mixed, the main feature of the Snake year is that it favours learning and personal development, and the many Wood Pigs in education can benefit from this. By making good use of the facilities in their place of learning and possibly also focusing on particular areas of study, they can not only make important advances but also gain wide-ranging skills. These opportunities should not be missed or frittered away.

Many Wood Pigs will also be preparing for exams this year and will need to be disciplined and allow sufficient time for revision. The more solid their preparation, the better their results. Snake years reward effort and commitment.

Throughout the year the young Wood Pig should also draw on the help of those around him. If any educational matter concerns him, it is important he seeks guidance rather than struggles on alone. Similarly, if thinking about future choices, he should talk to those who are able to advise. He could learn of educational courses or job areas worth considering. The Snake year can indicate interesting ways forward.

In addition to his studying, the Wood Pig can get much pleasure from his personal interests this year and may be encouraged to make more of his ideas and individual talents. For Wood Pigs who are creatively inclined, this can be an inspiring time. Also, should the Wood Pig be intrigued by a new activity, he should find out more.

The Snake year will also bring some good travel opportunities. However, to make the most of his time away, the Wood Pig should go well prepared as well as find out about his destination beforehand.

He can look forward to a lively social life this year and will enjoy many fine times with his friends. Romance can also add sparkle to the year, although, as many Wood Pigs will discover, the ways of love can be mysterious and sometimes hurtful. Snake years can have their pitfalls and the Wood Pig does need to keep his wits about him in his dealings with others and to be especially careful in volatile or potentially awkward situations. Also, when in company, he should not go against his instincts. If risks are taken, repercussions can follow. The Wood Pig can enjoy himself this year, but he does need to take note of the more cautionary aspects.

This also applies to money matters. The Wood Pig will need to be disciplined and consider purchases and other outgoings carefully. Prioritizing and taking his time making choices will be of benefit. Snake years do not favour rush or risk.

Although the Wood Pig will often be occupied with his studying and other activities, he should also help out at home when he can. By being involved, he will be better able to enjoy some of the domestic activities that take place. Many Wood Pigs can look forward to special celebrations as they mark their eighteenth birthday, and the Snake year is capable of springing some surprises.

For Wood Pigs in work, the Snake year can be volatile but constructive. These Wood Pigs could find themselves affected by change, possibly working with new colleagues and facing alterations to their duties and routine. Some of the year can be difficult, but all the time the Wood Pig will be adding to his working knowledge and this will be useful when he looks to move on.

Wood Pigs seeking work should not only keep alert for vacancies but also stay informed about training schemes and employment initiatives that could help their situation. Although their quest will be difficult, opportunities can be found and valuable working experience gained.

Overall, the Year of the Snake can be a demanding but instructive one. The Wood Pig will need to be disciplined and committed as he sets about his studies and various activities. It is also important he takes advantage of the resources and advice available to him, as his decisions now can have an important bearing on the next few years. He will need to proceed carefully this year and be aware of the potential hazards that rush or risk can bring. However, with effort and good support, many Wood Pigs will be able to obtain skills, qualifications and practical experience that they can build on in the future.

TIP FOR THE YEAR

Avoid rush. Be thorough and persevere. With care and vigilance, you can gain a lot from the year, but it *will* require a disciplined approach. The future is bright, however, and your current efforts will help prepare the way forward.

The Fire Pig

After all the activity of recent years, the Fire Pig will be glad to know that the Snake year will bring a respite. This will be a time when he will be able to pursue his plans and concentrate on his priorities. Snake years also allow time for thought and contemplation and this will suit the Fire Pig.

Fire Pigs who continue to work this year should take careful note of developments around them and be prepared to adapt as required. Snake years require care and some flexibility.

For Fire Pigs who retire, there will be considerable adjustments to be made. However, many will have already given careful thought to how they want to fill their time. They may have decided to move, carry out home improvements and/or spend more time on their interests, but whatever their choice, these Fire Pigs will often relish the chance to put their ideas into practice.

One area which is particularly favourably aspected is personal development and if the Fire Pig hears of a course that interests him or a skill that could be useful, he should find out more. Many Fire Pigs will also get considerable pleasure from creative activities. For those who enjoy photography, art, writing or working with their hands, this can be a satisfying time. Gardening, whether outdoor or indoor, can also be a source of great delight.

In addition the Fire Pig will enjoy his travelling this year, possibly including a holiday which allows him to attend a special event or visit a place he has long wanted to see. With careful planning, this could be a highlight of the year. Many Fire Pigs will also take pleasure in visiting family and friends living some distance away, possibly whom they have not seen for some time.

With travelling and all the other activities the Fire Pig has in mind for the year (possibly including a move), he will need to keep a close watch on his financial situation, however, and budget in advance for more expensive undertakings. He should also check the terms and obligations of any major transaction as well as be vigilant when dealing with forms relating to finance, tax or benefits. Financially, this is not a time for risk or haste.

With his many interests and sociable nature, the Fire Pig will once again welcome his chances to go out and socialize. Those who move will enjoy immersing themselves in their new area, including finding out about local amenities and getting to meet new people. Social groups and interest-related activities could be a source of particular pleasure. For Fire Pigs who would welcome more company, there will be a chance to make some important new friendships. Late February to April and November to early January could see the greatest social activity.

However, while the Fire Pig's relations with others can go well, a warning does need to be sounded: Snake years can have their difficult moments, and lapses and indiscretions can cause problems. Disagreements can arise and, if unaddressed, escalate. And if the Fire Pig finds himself in an awkward situation, he should tread carefully. Fire Pigs, do take note.

This need for awareness also applies to the Fire Pig's home life. Rather than rush into making plans, he needs to allow time to talk over his ideas with those around him. That way, disagreements and misunderstandings can be avoided. Should family arrangements clash or alternative ideas be put forward in response to some of the Fire Pig's suggestions, he would also do well to show some flexibility. This is no year to risk inflaming others by being obtuse. However, with good co-operation, many ideas can be implemented and good times enjoyed. The Fire Pig will also have the opportunity to give assistance to younger relations, and his support and generosity will be appreciated.

He would do well to give some consideration to his own well-being too, including ensuring he has a balanced diet and takes appropriate exercise. If he feels modifications are needed or has any concerns, he should seek advice.

Overall, the Year of the Snake can be a reasonable one for the Fire Pig. It is a time of possibility and will give him greater opportunity to proceed with his ideas and enjoy his interests. However, throughout the year he does need to be mindful of others. Any lapses have the potential to undermine the good relationships he enjoys. Fire Pigs, take note, but remember that with care you can make this an interesting year and accomplish a great deal.

TIP FOR THE YEAR

Do not be tempted to ignore problems. If anything concerns you, talk to others and seek advice. More positively, develop your personal interests and be receptive to new possibilities.

The Earth Pig

The Earth element can give a sign additional foresight, planning ability and effectiveness. This certainly holds true for the Earth Pig. He often secures his aims by thinking ahead and working steadily towards particular objectives. He is also realistic in his undertakings and prepared to hold back when necessary. He reads situations accurately and this year his instincts will serve him well.

In view of the many changes the Earth Pig will have seen in his work over the last few years, he may welcome the opportunity to consolidate his position and focus on specific responsibilities. As a result, this can often be a more satisfying year, with the Earth Pig having the chance to make greater use of his experience and be an integral part of a team. The majority of Earth Pigs will remain in their existing role this year, but there will be scope to make headway. Certain initiatives may require specialist staff or changes in personnel may open up promotion prospects, and if tempted, the Earth Pig should put himself forward.

For Earth Pigs who are unfulfilled and longing for change, as well as those seeking work, the Snake year can have interesting developments in store. By showing initiative and keeping alert for vacancies, the Earth Pig may well find an opening which brings a welcome challenge and has potential for the future. He could also benefit from government employment schemes and retraining opportunities. April, May, July and October could see important developments.

With personal, family and accommodation expenses, he will, however, need to remain disciplined in financial matters. With good control of his budget, he will be able to proceed with many of his plans, but this is no year for risk or proceeding on an ad hoc basis. Snake years reward careful planning.

Travel could do the Earth Pig considerable good, though, and he should aim to go away for a holiday if possible. Even if he is not able to travel too far, there could be interesting places to visit within easy reach.

His personal interests can also be a good way for him to unwind as well as allow him to explore ideas. With his enquiring nature, he may well be attracted by a new recreational pursuit (sometimes with a keep fit or outdoor element) and take pleasure in how this develops over the year.

He will also enjoy his socializing, and while he may not go out as frequently as in some years, if he sees events that appeal to him, he should do his best to attend. His work and personal interests can also give him chances to meet others and, for the unattached, there will be romantic possibilities too. March, April and November to early January could see the most social activity.

However, while the Earth Pig will enjoy positive relations with many people, in the Snake year he will need to keep alert. Petty disagreements, jealousies, rumours or someone letting him down could upset him. At such times, he would find it helpful to talk matters through rather than keep his anxieties to himself. Fortunately not all Earth Pigs will be affected by the year's more difficult aspects, but problems do need to be addressed early. Earth Pigs, take note and at the first sign of any potential difficulty, do act in a careful and mindful way.

The Earth Pig sets great store by his home life and his organizational skills will be particularly valued this year. With the busy lifestyles of many in his household, there will need to be good communication and co-operation. Home projects should be tackled jointly and decisions carefully considered. The Earth Pig will be able to advance many domestic plans this year and also give what will be important assistance to a close relation, and his support, advice and understanding will be valued.

Overall, although the Snake year does call for care, it can be an encouraging one. At work, many Earth Pigs will have the chance to use their skills to good effect and take greater satisfaction in what they do. Personal interests can also develop well and during the year many Earth Pigs will extend these or try something new. The Earth Pig's home life will also see much activity. In his relations with others he will need to be his mindful self, but he is blessed with great personal skills and may well be able to steer his way round the Snake year's more difficult aspects and take genuine pleasure in what his efforts now make possible.

TIP FOR THE YEAR

Be alert for opportunities. Whether these involve developing your working skills and knowledge or furthering your personal interests, they can bring important benefits. These are times of interesting possibility. Also, value your relationships and spend time with your loved ones. Increased care and attention can make an important difference this year.

FAMOUS PIGS

Bryan Adams, Woody Allen, Julie Andrews, Marie Antoinette, Fred Astaire, Pam Ayres, Emily Blunt, Humphrey Bogart, James Cagney, Maria Callas, Samantha Cameron, Hillary Rodham Clinton, Glenn Close, Sacha Baron Cohen, Cheryl Cole, Alice Cooper, the Duchess of Cornwall, Noël Coward, Simon Cowell, Oliver Cromwell, Billy Crystal, the Dalai Lama, Ted Danson, Richard Dreyfuss, Ben Elton, Ralph Waldo Emerson, Henry Ford, Jonathan Franzen, Stephen Harper, Emmylou Harris, Ernest Hemingway, Chris Hemsworth, Henry VIII, Conrad Hilton, Alfred Hitchcock, Sir Elton John, Tommy Lee Jones, Carl Gustav Jung, Stephen King, Kevin Kline, Hugh Laurie, David Letterman, Jerry Lee Lewis, Meat Loaf, Ewan McGregor, Ricky Martin, Johnny Mathis, Pippa Middleton, Dannii Minogue, Morrissey, Wolfgang Amadeus Mozart, George Osborne, Sir Michael Parkinson, James Patterson, Luciano Pavarotti, Iggy Pop, Maurice Ravel, Ronald Reagan, Harry Redknapp, Ginger Rogers, Mitt Romney, Winona Ryder, Françoise Sagan, Carlos Santana, Arnold Schwarzenegger, Kevin Spacey, Steven Spielberg, Lord Sugar, David Tennant, Emma Thompson, Herman Van Rompuy, Jules Verne, David Walliams, Michael Winner, the Duchess of York.

APPENDIX

The relationships between the 12 animal signs, both on a personal level and business level, are an important aspect of Chinese horoscopes and in this appendix the compatibility between the signs is shown in the two tables that follow.

Also included are the names of the signs ruling the hours of the day and from this it is possible to find your ascendant and discover yet another aspect of your personality.

Finally, to supplement the earlier chapters on the personality and horoscope of the signs, I have included a guide on how you can get the best out of your sign and the year.

RELATIONSHIPS BETWEEN THE SIGNS

Personal Relationships

KEY

1 Excellent. Great rapport.
2 A successful relationship. Many interests in common.
3 Mutual respect and understanding. A good relationship.
4 Fair. Needs care and some willingness to compromise in order for the relationship to work.
5 Awkward. Possible difficulties in communication with few interests in common.
6 A clash of personalities. Very difficult.

	Rat	Ox	Tiger	Rabbit	Dragon	Snake	Horse	Goat	Monkey	Rooster	Dog	Pig
Rat	1											
Ox	1	3										
Tiger	4	6	5									
Rabbit	5	2	3	2								
Dragon	1	5	4	3	2							
Snake	3	1	6	2	1	5						
Horse	6	5	1	5	3	4	2					
Goat	5	5	3	1	4	3	2	2				
Monkey	1	3	6	3	1	3	5	3	1			
Rooster	5	1	5	6	2	1	2	5	5	5		
Dog	3	4	1	2	6	3	1	5	3	5	2	
Pig	2	3	2	2	2	6	3	2	2	3	1	2

Business Relationships

KEY

1 Excellent. Marvellous understanding and rapport.
2 Very good. Complement each other well.
3 A good working relationship and understanding can be developed.
4 Fair, but compromise and a common objective are often needed to make this relationship work.
5 Awkward. Unlikely to work, either through lack of trust, understanding or the competitiveness of the signs.
6 Mistrust. Difficult. To be avoided.

	Rat	Ox	Tiger	Rabbit	Dragon	Snake	Horse	Goat	Monkey	Rooster	Dog	Pig
Rat	2											
Ox	1	3										
Tiger	3	6	5									
Rabbit	4	3	3	3								
Dragon	1	4	3	3	3							
Snake	3	2	6	4	1	5						
Horse	6	5	1	5	3	4	4					
Goat	5	5	3	1	4	3	3	2				
Monkey	2	3	4	5	1	5	4	4	3			
Rooster	5	1	5	5	2	1	2	5	5	6		
Dog	4	5	2	3	6	4	2	5	3	5	4	
Pig	3	3	3	2	3	5	4	2	3	4	3	1

YOUR ASCENDANT

The ascendant has a very strong influence on your personality and will help you gain an even greater insight into
your true personality according to Chinese horoscopes.

The hours of the day are named after the 12 animal
signs and the sign governing the time you were born is
your ascendant. To find your ascendant, look up the time
of your birth in the table below, bearing in mind any local
time differences in the place you were born.

11 p.m.	to	1 a.m.	The hours of the Rat
1 a.m.	to	3 a.m.	The hours of the Ox
3 a.m.	to	5 a.m.	The hours of the Tiger
5 a.m.	to	7 a.m.	The hours of the Rabbit
7 a.m.	to	9 a.m.	The hours of the Dragon
9 a.m.	to	11 a.m.	The hours of the Snake
11 a.m.	to	1 p.m.	The hours of the Horse
1 p.m.	to	3 p.m.	The hours of the Goat
3 p.m.	to	5 p.m.	The hours of the Monkey
5 p.m.	to	7 p.m.	The hours of the Rooster
7 p.m.	to	9 p.m.	The hours of the Dog
9 p.m.	to	11 p.m.	The hours of the Pig

RAT

The Rat ascendant is likely to make the sign more outgoing, sociable and careful with money. A particularly beneficial influence for those born under the signs of the
Rabbit, Horse, Monkey and Pig.

OX

The Ox ascendant has a restraining, cautionary and steadying influence that many signs will benefit from. This ascendant also promotes self-confidence and willpower and is especially good for those born under the signs of the Tiger, Rabbit and Goat.

TIGER

The Tiger ascendant is a dynamic and stirring influence that makes the sign more outgoing, action-orientated and impulsive. A generally favourable ascendant for the Ox, Tiger, Snake and Horse.

RABBIT

The Rabbit ascendant has a moderating influence, making the sign more reflective, serene and discreet. A particularly beneficial influence for the Rat, Dragon, Monkey and Rooster.

DRAGON

The Dragon ascendant gives strength, determination and ambition to the sign. A favourable influence for those born under the signs of the Rabbit, Goat, Monkey and Dog.

SNAKE

The Snake ascendant can make the sign more reflective, intuitive and self-reliant. A good influence for the Tiger, Goat and Pig.

HORSE

The Horse ascendant will make the sign more adventurous, daring and on some occasions fickle. Generally a beneficial influence for the Rabbit, Snake, Dog and Pig.

GOAT

The Goat ascendant will make the sign more tolerant, easy-going and receptive. It could also impart some creative and artistic qualities. An especially good influence for the Ox, Dragon, Snake and Rooster.

MONKEY

The Monkey ascendant is likely to impart a delicious sense of humour and fun to the sign. It will make the sign more enterprising and outgoing – a particularly good influence for the Rat, Ox, Snake and Goat.

ROOSTER

The Rooster ascendant helps to give the sign a lively, outgoing and very methodical manner. Its influence will increase efficiency and is good for the Ox, Tiger, Rabbit and Horse.

DOG

The Dog ascendant makes the sign more reasonable and fair-minded and gives an added sense of loyalty. A very good ascendant for the Tiger, Dragon and Goat.

PIG

The Pig ascendant can make the sign more sociable and self-indulgent. It is also a caring influence and one that can make the sign want to help others. A good ascendant for the Dragon and Monkey.

HOW TO GET THE BEST FROM YOUR CHINESE SIGN AND THE YEAR

Each of the 12 Chinese signs possesses its own unique strengths and by identifying them you can use them to your advantage. Similarly, by becoming aware of possible weaknesses you can do much to rectify them and in this respect I hope the following sections will be useful. Also included are some tips on how you can get the best from the Year of the Snake.

The Rat

The Rat is blessed with many fine talents, but his undoubted strength lies in his ability to get on with people. He is sociable, charming and a good judge of character. He also possesses a shrewd mind and is good at spotting opportunities.

However, to make the most of his abilities, he does need to impose some discipline upon himself. He should resist the (sometimes very great) temptation of getting involved in too many activities all at the same time and should decide upon his priorities and objectives. By concentrating his energies on specific matters he will fare much better. Also, given his personable manner, he should seek out positions where he can use his personal relations skills to good effect. For a career, sales and marketing could prove ideal.

The Rat is astute in dealing with finance, but while often thrifty, he can sometimes give way to moments of indulgence. Although he deserves to enjoy the money he has so carefully earned, it would sometimes be in his interests to exercise restraint when tempted to satisfy too many expensive whims!

The Rat's family and friends are important to him and while he is loyal and protective towards them, he does tend to keep his worries and concerns to himself and would be helped if he were more willing to discuss his anxieties. Others think highly of him and are prepared to do a lot to help him, but for them to do so the Rat does need to be less guarded.

With his sharp mind, keen imagination and sociable manner, he does, however, have much in his favour. When he has commitment, he can be irrepressible and, given his considerable charm, often irresistible as well! Provided he channels his energies wisely, he can make much of his life.

Advice for the Rat's Year Ahead

GENERAL PROSPECTS

Although the Rat likes quick results, this is a year for patience and steady effort. The Rat can develop his skills and move his plans forward, but he must avoid rush. This is a time for planning, careful thought and waiting for chances and results to filter through.

CAREER PROSPECTS

This will be an often satisfying year with the Rat having a good chance to build on his skills. For those wanting change or seeking a position, it is a case of being flexible and open-minded. But experience gained now can lead to other possibilities later.

FINANCE

With commitments and some expensive plans, the Rat will need to manage his budget carefully and check the details and implications of any major transaction. Not a year for risk or rush.

RELATIONS WITH OTHERS

Born under the sign of charm, the Rat will have the chance to extend his social circle and impress others, but he does need to remain aware and be forthcoming. This is no year to keep his thoughts to himself and deny himself the support that others can give. A year for openness *and* sharing.

The Ox

Strong-willed and resolute, the Ox certainly has a mind of his own! He is persistent and sets about achieving his objectives with dogged determination. In addition he is reliable and tenacious and is often a source of inspiration to others. He is an achiever, and he often achieves a great deal. However, to really excel, he would do well to try and correct some of his weaknesses.

Being so resolute and having such a strong sense of purpose, the Ox can be inflexible and narrow-minded. He can be resistant to change and prefers to set about his activities in his own way rather than be dependent on others. His dislike of change can sometimes be to his detriment and if he were prepared to be more adaptable and adventurous he would find his progress easier.

The Ox would also be helped if he were to broaden his range of interests and become more relaxed in his approach. At times he can be so preoccupied with his own activities that he is not always as mindful of others as he should be, and his demeanour can sometimes be studious and serious. There are times when he would benefit from a lighter touch.

However, the Ox is true to his word and loyal to his family and friends. He is admired and respected by others and his tremendous willpower usually enables him to achieve a great deal in life.

Advice for the Ox's Year Ahead

GENERAL PROSPECTS
The Ox is careful and cautious and set to do well this year. However, while he may be keen to implement certain plans, he does need to show some flexibility as new possibilities arise. This can be a year of progress, but the Ox should not be too narrow in his approach. His personal interests can develop particularly well.

CAREER PROSPECTS
Determined and conscientious, the Ox can make his skills count this year. His experience will often help him move ahead and he should remain alert to opportunity.

Additional skills and training can help his situation both now and in the near future.

FINANCE

A much improved year, with the Ox often enjoying an increase in income. However, with ambitious and sometimes costly plans in mind, he does need to keep good control of his budget. Early provision for future expenses could be helpful.

RELATIONS WITH OTHERS

The Ox will enjoy a lot of support this year. However, to benefit fully he does need to be open and forthcoming rather than keep his thoughts to himself. Domestically, there will be special family times, while socially there will be good opportunities to meet new people, some of whom could potentially be important. Romantic prospects are good.

The Tiger

Lively, innovative and enterprising, the Tiger enjoys an active lifestyle. He has a wide range of interests, an alert mind and a genuine liking of other people. He loves to live life to the full. However, despite his enthusiastic and well-meaning ways, he does not always make the most of his considerable potential.

Being so versatile, the Tiger does have a tendency to jump from one activity to another or dissipate his energies by trying to do too much at the same time. To make the most of himself he should try to exercise a certain amount of self-discipline. Ideally, he should decide how best he can use his abilities, give himself some objectives and then stick to them. If he can overcome his restless tendencies, he will find he will accomplish far more as a result.

Also, in spite of his sociable manner, the Tiger likes to retain a certain independence in his actions, and while few begrudge him this, he would sometimes find life easier if he were more prepared to work in conjunction with others. His reliance on his own judgement does sometimes mean that he excludes the views and advice of those around him, and this can be to his detriment. He may possess an independent spirit, but he must not let it go too far!

The Tiger does, however, have much in his favour. He is bold, original and quick-witted. If he can keep his restless nature in check, he can enjoy considerable success. In addition, with his engaging personality, he is well liked and much admired.

Advice for the Tiger's Year Ahead

GENERAL PROSPECTS

The Tiger may have his ideas, aims and wants, but rather than rush ahead, he should take his time. This is a year that requires careful planning. If the Tiger works steadily towards his objectives, his results will not only be more satisfying but often of lasting value.

CAREER PROSPECTS

Although overall progress may be modest this year, there will be an excellent chance for the Tiger to use his skills and demonstrate his capabilities. What is achieved now can give him additional experience and pave the way for future success. This is an important and instructive year.

FINANCE
The Tiger can benefit from an increase in earnings, but will need to keep careful control of his budget. By keeping alert and taking his time over more major transactions, he could often be fortunate in his acquisitions.

RELATIONS WITH OTHERS
The Tiger will enjoy many of the social occasions of the year as well as play a full and valued role in his home life. However, he will need to remain aware of potential problems, be mindful of others and handle tricky situations with care and consideration.

The Rabbit
The Rabbit is certainly one who appreciates the finer things in life. With his good taste, companionable nature and wide range of interests, he knows how to live well – and usually does!

However, for all his finesse and style, the Rabbit does possess traits he would do well to watch. His desire for a settled lifestyle makes him err on the side of caution. He dislikes change and as a consequence can miss out on opportunities. Also, there are many Rabbits who will go to great lengths to avoid difficult and fraught situations, and again, while few may relish these, sometimes in life it is necessary to take risks or stand your ground. At times it would certainly be in the Rabbit's interests to be bolder and more assertive in going after what he desires.

The Rabbit also attaches great importance to his relations with others and while he has a happy knack of getting on with most people, he can be sensitive to criticism. Difficult though it may be, he should really try to develop a thicker skin and recognize that criticism can provide valuable learning opportunities, as can some of the problems he strives so hard to avoid.

However, with his agreeable manner, keen intellect and shrewd judgement, the Rabbit does have a lot in his favour and invariably makes much of his life – and enjoys it too!

Advice for the Rabbit's Year Ahead

GENERAL PROSPECTS

The Rabbit should look ahead. By having ideas in mind and seizing his opportunities, he can benefit from what opens up for him. This is a good year for him and with a willing attitude, he can achieve – and enjoy – a great deal.

CAREER PROSPECTS

This is a year for progress, but to benefit, the Rabbit needs to be active and make the most of any chances to develop his skills as well as network. He can make his strengths count this year but he *will* need to put himself forward.

FINANCE

Although income may increase, some Rabbits will move and many will travel, as well as spend money on their family and interests. Outgoings need to be watched and early provision made for more expensive plans and undertakings.

RELATIONS WITH OTHERS

Special and rewarding times are ahead for the Rabbit, particularly in his home life. Romance is favourably aspected and new friends and contacts can be important, but the Rabbit may be faced with gossip or a difficult friendship issue and may need to proceed carefully and possibly seek appropriate advice. With this proviso, a pleasing year.

The Dragon

Enthusiastic, enterprising and honourable, the Dragon possesses many admirable qualities and his life is often full and varied. He always gives his best and even though not all his endeavours meet with success, he is nonetheless resilient and hardy, and is much admired and respected.

However, for all his qualities, the Dragon can be blunt and forthright and, through sheer strength of character, sometimes domineering. It would certainly be in his interests to listen more closely to others rather than be so self-reliant. Also, his enthusiasm can sometimes get the better of him and he can be impulsive. To make the most of his abilities, he should give himself priorities and set about his activities in a disciplined and systematic way. More tact and diplomacy might not come amiss either!

However, with his lively and outgoing manner, the Dragon is popular and well liked. With good fortune on his side (and the Dragon is often lucky), his life is almost certain to be eventful and fulfilling. He has many talents, and if he uses them wisely he will enjoy much success.

Advice for the Dragon's Year Ahead

GENERAL PROSPECTS

This is a year of possibility and by using his skills and seizing his opportunities, the Dragon can benefit from it. He can also enjoy an element of good fortune. However, he does need to balance his activities and give time to others. Without care, lifestyle imbalance can lead to problems. Dragons, this can be a successful year, but *keep things in balance*.

CAREER PROSPECTS

With his drive, skills and resourcefulness, the Dragon can make good headway this year, often building on his present position and benefiting from new openings. He should make the most of chances to expand his knowledge and skills. This can help both his current situation and his future prospects.

FINANCE

The Dragon's progress at work can lead to an increase in income, but to benefit he needs to be disciplined in spending and take time when considering more major purchases.

RELATIONS WITH OTHERS

The Dragon's various activities can bring him into contact with many people this year. At work, colleagues can be helpful, but in his personal life, he does need to devote time to his loved ones. New romances need particularly careful nurturing. Generally the Snake year can be a good one for the Dragon, but it does require mindfulness.

The Snake

The Snake is blessed with a keen intellect. He has wide interests, an enquiring mind and good judgement. He tends to be quiet and thoughtful and plan his activities with considerable care. With his fine abilities he often does well in life, but he does possess traits which can undermine his progress.

The Snake is often guarded in his actions and sometimes loses out to those who are more action-oriented and assertive. He also likes to retain a certain independence in his actions and this too can hamper his progress. It would be in his interests to be more forthcoming and involve others more readily in his plans. The Snake has many talents and possesses a warm and rich personality, but there is a danger that this can remain concealed behind his often quiet and reserved manner. He would fare better if he were more outgoing and showed others his true worth.

However, the Snake is very much his own master. He invariably knows what he wants in life and is often prepared to journey long and hard to achieve his objectives. He does, though, have it in his power to make that journey easier. Lose some of that reticence, Snake, be more open and assertive, and do not be afraid of the occasional risk!

Advice for the Snake's Year Ahead

GENERAL PROSPECTS

Snakes are patient and watchful and choose their moments well. And in their own year, there will be many moments they can turn to their advantage. This is a time to act with determination and make those dreams come true. It is a good year for the Snake, but he *will* need to act, otherwise chances could slip by.

CAREER PROSPECTS

This is a year of exciting possibility, but to benefit the Snake needs to pursue openings and follow through ideas. Snakes who are creatively inclined can fare particularly well and should make the most of their talents. New skills can also open up interesting possibilities.

FINANCE

Income can improve over the year and many Snakes will benefit from some fortunate purchases or lucky moments. But where important transactions and long-term decisions are concerned, the Snake needs to be vigilant and thorough. This may be his own year, but it is still one for care.

RELATIONS WITH OTHERS

Some wonderful times are possible and the Snake will be in demand. To benefit fully in this auspicious year, however, he needs to be active and forthcoming. Some Snakes may need to overcome their slightly reserved nature, but the effort will be well worth their while.

The Horse

Versatile, hardworking and sociable, the Horse makes his mark wherever he goes. He has an eloquent and engaging manner and makes friends with ease. He is quick-witted, has an alert mind and is certainly not averse to taking risks or experimenting with new ideas.

He possesses a strong and likeable personality, but he does also have his weaknesses. With his wide interests he does not always finish everything he starts and he would do well to be more persevering. He has it within him to achieve considerable success, but to make the most of his talents he does need to overcome his restless tendencies. When he has made plans, he should stick with them.

The Horse loves company and values both his family and friends. However, there will have been many a time when he will have lost his temper or spoken in haste and regretted his words later. Throughout his life he needs to keep his temper in check and be diplomatic in tense situations, otherwise he could jeopardize the respect and good relations he so values.

However, the Horse has a multitude of talents and a lively and outgoing personality. If he can overcome his restless and volatile nature, he can lead a rich and highly fulfilling life.

Advice for the Horse's Year Ahead

GENERAL PROSPECTS

The Horse may be action-oriented, but this year favours a steadier approach. Rather than rush ahead, it is a time to appreciate the present. It is a good time for the Horse to get his lifestyle into balance. He will benefit from spending time on personal development and this can pave the way for the exciting times that await in 2014, the Year of the Horse.

CAREER PROSPECTS

A year to be involved and aware and gain experience. What the Horse can accomplish now can often have an important bearing on his future, especially with the exciting possibilities that await in 2014.

FINANCE

Financially, the Horse should be wary about making assumptions. If entering into an agreement or conducting an important transaction, he needs to check the terms and conditions and ensure that his requirements are being met. With some large outgoings likely, this is a year to be vigilant.

RELATIONS WITH OTHERS

Although relations with many people will be positive this year, the Horse does need to keep his wits about him and watch his independent tendencies. By involving others, he will achieve more. Where romance is concerned, care is needed. Lapses and indiscretions risk undermining a great deal. Horses, take note.

The Goat

The Goat has a warm, friendly and understanding manner and gets on well with most people. He is generally easygoing, has a fond appreciation of the finer things in life and possesses a rich imagination. He is often artistic and enjoys the creative arts and outdoor activities.

However, despite his engaging manner, there lurks beneath his skin a sometimes tense and pessimistic nature.

The Goat can be a worrier and without the support and encouragement of others can feel insecure and be hesitant in his actions.

To make the most of himself he should aim to become more assertive and decisive as well as more at ease with himself. He has much in his favour, but he really does need to promote himself more and be bolder. He would also be helped if he were to sort out his priorities and set about his activities in an organized and disciplined manner. There are some Goats who tend to be haphazard in the way they go about things and this can hamper their progress.

Although the Goat will always value the support of others, it would also be in his interests to become more independent and not be so reticent about striking out on his own. He does, after all, possess many talents, as well as a sincere and likeable personality, and by always giving his best he can make his life rich, rewarding and enjoyable.

Advice for the Goat's Year Ahead

GENERAL PROSPECTS

The Goat can do well in the Snake year, although how well is very much down to him. By making the most of his ideas, opportunities and strengths, he can enjoy some very encouraging results, but he does need to take action and demonstrate his capabilities. Fortune will favour the bold and enterprising.

CAREER PROSPECTS

Snake years encourage creativity and the artistic Goat's prospects are particularly promising. However, this is a time for all Goats to develop their skills. The year offers growth and considerable possibility, and with involvement and willingness, all Goats can benefit.

FINANCE

The Goat's progress at work can lead to an increase in income, but with travel favourably aspected, plus his other plans and requirements, he does need to keep a watchful eye on his financial situation.

RELATIONS WITH OTHERS

The Goat values his relations with others and will enjoy many good times with family and friends this year. Work and personal interests will often help him add to his social circle, and for the unattached, romance can also bring excitement. The Goat does need to draw on the willingness of others to help and advise, but with this additional support, he can make this year even more successful.

The Monkey

Lively, enterprising and innovative, the Monkey certainly knows how to impress. He has wide interests, a good sense of fun and relates well to others. He also possesses a shrewd mind and often has a happy knack of turning events to his advantage.

However, despite his versatility and considerable gifts, he does have his weaknesses. He often lacks persistence, can get distracted easily and also places tremendous reliance upon his own judgement. While his belief in himself is a commendable asset, it would certainly be in his interests to be more mindful of the views of others. Also, while he likes to keep tabs on all that is going on around him, he can be evasive and secretive with regard to his own feelings and activities, and again a more forthcoming attitude would be to his advantage.

In his desire to succeed, the Monkey can also be tempted to cut corners or be crafty and he should recognize that such actions can rebound on him!

However, he is resourceful and his sheer strength of character will ensure that he has an interesting and varied life. If he can channel his considerable energies wisely and overcome his sometimes restless tendencies, his life can be crowned with success. And with his amiable personality, he will have many friends.

Advice for the Monkey's Year Ahead

GENERAL PROSPECTS
Rather than viewing this as a progressive, action-packed year, the Monkey should give some thought to his personal development. This is a good time to take stock and get his lifestyle into better balance. By using his ideas to good effect, he can benefit from his actions as well as appreciate some deserved 'me time'.

CAREER PROSPECTS
The Monkey can make useful headway and, importantly, prepare for future success. Creative Monkeys in particular should make the most of their talents. For all Monkeys, this is a year to be focused and disciplined and use skills and strengths to advantage.

FINANCE

The Monkey may well increase his income this year, but does need to manage his budget well, take the time to consider his purchases and be thorough with important paperwork.

RELATIONS WITH OTHERS

The Monkey sometimes has a tendency to keep his thoughts to himself, but in the Snake year he will need to be communicative as well as attentive when in company. A *faux pas* or personal lapse could cause problems. While this is a generally good year, care is advised.

The Rooster

With his considerable bearing and incisive and resolute manner, the Rooster cuts an impressive figure. He has a sharp mind, is well informed on many matters and expresses himself clearly and convincingly. He is meticulous and efficient in his undertakings and commands a great deal of respect. He also has a genuine and caring interest in others.

The Rooster has much in his favour, but there are some aspects of his character that can tell against him. He can be candid in his views and over-zealous in his actions, and sometimes he can say or do things he later regrets. His high standards also make him fussy, even pedantic, and he can get diverted into relatively minor matters when in truth he could be occupying his time more profitably. This is something all Roosters would do well to watch. Also, while the Rooster is a great planner, he can sometimes be unrealistic in his expectations. In making plans – indeed, in most of his activities – he would do well to consult others. He would benefit greatly from their input.

The Rooster has many talents as well as commendable drive and commitment, but to make the most of himself he does need to channel his energies wisely and watch his candid and sometimes volatile nature. With care, however, he can make a success of his life, and with his wide interests and outgoing personality, he will enjoy the friendship and respect of many.

Advice for the Rooster's Year Ahead

GENERAL PROSPECTS

A favourable year with many fine possibilities to pursue. The Rooster's inventiveness and ability to put himself across effectively will serve him well. He can enjoy pleasing results, but will need to adapt to situations rather than stick firmly to existing plans. He should also keep his candid nature in check and, despite an often busy lifestyle, preserve some time for himself.

CAREER PROSPECTS

The Rooster's skills, experience and creativity can enable him to make good progress. He should also be prepared to consider new possibilities. The Snake year can open up interesting opportunities, although the Rooster will be required to adapt and learn. Work-wise, a promising and significant year.

FINANCE

The Rooster's efforts at work can lead to a rise in income, but with travel, family and home expenses, spending does need to be watched and advance provision made for more expensive plans.

RELATIONS WITH OTHERS

The Rooster will welcome the many social opportunities of the year. For the unattached, this is a good time for romance. Family members will be especially grateful for advice and support. However, in all his relations with others the Rooster needs to be attentive and watch his candid tongue. Roosters, take note.

The Dog

Loyal, dependable and with a good understanding of human nature, the Dog is well placed to win respect and admiration. He is a no-nonsense sort of person and hates any sort of hypocrisy and falsehood. With the Dog you know where you stand and, given his direct manner, where he stands on any issue. He also has a strong humanitarian nature and often champions good causes.

The Dog has many fine attributes, although there are certain traits that can prevent him from either enjoying or making the most of his life. He is a great worrier and can get anxious over all manner of things. Although it may not always be easy, he should try to rid himself of the 'worry habit'. Whenever he is tense or concerned, he should be prepared to speak to others rather than shoulder his worries all by himself. In some cases, they could even be of his own making! Also, he has a tendency to look on the pessimistic side and he would certainly be helped if he were to view his undertakings more optimistically. He does, after all, possess many skills and should have faith in his abilities. Another weakness is his tendency to be stubborn over certain issues. If he is not careful, at times this could undermine his position.

If the Dog can reduce the pessimistic side of his nature, he will not only enjoy life more but also find he is achieving more. He possesses a truly admirable character and his loyalty, reliability and sincerity are appreciated by all he meets. In his life he will do much good and befriend many people – and he owes it to himself to enjoy life too. Sometimes it might help him to recall the words of another Dog, Sir Winston Churchill: 'When I look back on all these worries, I remember the story of the old man who said on his deathbed that he had had a lot of trouble in his life, most of which never happened.'

Advice for the Dog's Year Ahead

GENERAL PROSPECTS

Sam Goldwyn observed, 'The harder I work, the luckier I get.' This will hold good for the Dog this year. If he puts in the effort and uses his skills to advantage, benefits will often follow. This is a greatly improved year for the Dog and an excellent time to make more of his strengths and personal qualities.

CAREER PROSPECTS

This is a year of considerable opportunity and the Dog should keep alert for chances to pursue. With determination and a willingness to learn, he can both enjoy the benefits now and, significantly, pave the way to future opportunities.

FINANCE

The Dog can not only look forward to a rise in income but may also enjoy some financial luck this year. However, to fully benefit, he would do well to watch his everyday spending and take his time when considering major purchases.

RELATIONS WITH OTHERS

Socially, this may be a quieter year than some, but the Dog should not deny himself the pleasure certain occasions can bring. This is an excellent year for personal interests and if the Dog is able to share these with others, this can add meaning to what he does. His home life, too, can bring much contentment, with family activities going well.

The Pig

Genial, sincere and trusting, the Pig gets on well with most people. He has a kind and caring nature, a dislike of discord and often a good sense of humour. In addition, he has a fondness for socializing and enjoying the good life!

The Pig possesses a shrewd mind, is particularly adept at dealing with business and financial matters and has a robust and resilient nature. Although not all his plans may work out as he would like, he is tenacious and will often rise up and succeed after experiencing setbacks and difficulties. In his often active and varied life he can accomplish a great deal, although there are certain aspects of his character that can tell against him. If he can modify these or keep them in check then his life will certainly be easier and possibly even more successful.

In his activities the Pig can sometimes over-commit himself and while he does not want to disappoint, he would certainly be helped if he were to set about his activities in an organized and systematic manner and give himself priorities at busy times. He should also not allow others to take advantage of his good nature and it would be in his interests to be more discerning. There will have been times when he has been gullible and naïve; fortunately, though, he quickly learns from his mistakes. However, he possesses a stubborn streak and if new situations do not fit in with his line of thinking, he can be inflexible. Such an attitude may not always be to his advantage.

The Pig is a great pleasure-seeker and while he should enjoy the fruits of his labours, he can sometimes be self-indulgent and extravagant. This is also something he would do well to watch.

However, though the Pig may possess some faults, those who come into contact with him are invariably impressed by his integrity, amiable manner and intelligence. If he uses his talents wisely, his life can be crowned with considerable achievement and he will also be loved and respected by many.

Advice for the Pig's Year Ahead

GENERAL PROSPECTS

A year of mixed fortunes. Although there will be excellent chances to develop his skills and interests, the Pig will need to proceed carefully. Risks and personal lapses have the potential to undermine a great deal. The Pig will need to be on his mettle this year.

CAREER PROSPECTS

This can be a demanding year with many Pigs facing increased pressure. However, this will give the Pig a good chance to demonstrate his capabilities and learn more. It is an instructive time and what is achieved now can be successfully built on in the future.

FINANCE

With many expenses likely, the Pig will need to manage his budget well and ideally make early provision for more expensive outgoings. Good planning and control will help.

RELATIONS WITH OTHERS

The Pig attaches much importance to his relations with others, but these could prove problematic this year. The Pig needs to be aware and attentive; lapses could cause difficulty. Disagreements should be addressed rather than left to linger. Fortunately the Pig has a great understanding of human nature and, with care and consideration, can successfully overcome many of the year's difficulties.